Adaptation of the Jarawa to Andaman Islands

UMESH KUMAR

ANTHROPOLOGICAL SURVEY OF INDIA
Kolkata

MANOHAR
2025

First published 2023

Reprinted 2024, 2025

ISBN 978-93-94262-30-0

Published by
Ajay Kumar Jain *for*
Manohar Publishers & Distributors
4753/23 Ansari Road, Daryaganj
New Delhi 110 002

Typeset by
Kohli Print
Delhi 110 051

Printed at
Replika Press Pvt. Ltd.

Contents

Illustrations

FIGURES

PLATES

Tables

Foreword

On 17 November 2018, American missionary John Allen Chau was killed on Sentinel Island of Andaman and Nicobar. Chau died (murdered) while he was trying to contact the Sentinelese in spite of the fact that this Island was out of bound for outsiders and the Sentinelese were known to be hostile to outside contacts. In 2006, the Sentinelese had killed two fishermen and confiscated their boat. Much before, in 1896 also, a convict escaping from Cellular Jail was speared to death by them. The death of American missionary became a matter of discussion worldwide and global media learnt about the indigenous people of Andaman and Nicobar Islands. International agencies like the Christian Missionary Organizations and Survival International started making it a sensitive issue and put pressure on Indian Government to not retrieve the body of Chau as it may lead to spread of disease creating germs on the Sentinelese. The Sentinelese are the last of the indigenous communities to be brought into the fold of modern civilization. The other indigenous people of Andaman and Nicobar Islanders have been in variable contact and the outcome of human contact has not been very beneficial for them.

The approach of colonial administration towards them was termed 'carrot and stick' policy which ultimately resulted in near obliteration of the many indigenous groups now labeled as the Great Andamanese. The Great Andamanese, the Onges and the Jarawas have faced the brutalities in post-mutiny penal settlement of Mr. Walker, then reconciliatory policy of Portman changing again to aggressive overtone post 1905 Bush Police Force phase. Even the three years of second World War occupation of the Japanese were full of murderous aggression. It was only in the post-independence that a policy of non-interference with 'wait and watch' was adopted but still the forests were cleared, Andaman Trunk Road was constructed and other activities were undertaken disturbing the indigenous people of the smooth utilization of their natural resources. The fate of the Great Andamanese and Onges was already decided; the population of the Onges dropped from 700 in 1858 to 150 in 1951 and of the Great Andamanese from 3,500 to 50.

It has been quite adequately demonstrated that the strategy of haphazard and hasty contact, even if the intensions are noble will not bring any good to the indigenous communities of Andaman and Nicobar Islands. We have the case of the Jarawas, who have been maintaining hot-cold relations with the outside world in past and finally, thanks to the medical intervention, we are in a position to establish good contacts with them. However, the vices of modern society have started showing their ill-effects on the Jarawas already, and the government policy has been fluctuating from no contact to variable contact. It calls for an urgent and in-depth study of the social, cultural, ecological and impact of already established contact of the Jarawas. It is also important for the simple reason that our earlier experience of contact with the Great Andamanese and Onges have been disastrous and annihilating.

In the present book, the first ever comprehensive anthropologically informed account of the Jarawas, showing interrelationship between human, society, culture, forest, land and physical contiguity with outsiders, the holistic understanding of the complexities of this highly fragile human group has been delineated. A deeper understanding of the book will bring to light factors that are going to be crucial in the survival of this, and the so far pristine, Sentinelese of these Islands. In a country like India, which clearly lacks any worthwhile tribal policy, it is important that these fragile and highly vulnerable indigenous populations are protected from ill-effects of globalizing world and at the same time, given an opportunity to live a life of freedom, dignity, self-respect and informed choice to decide about their future course of life. We will have to think beyond 'isolationism' and 'integration' with out of box, innovative and protective policy for the negrito population of Andaman Islands. We must treat the Andaman Negrito indigenous groups distinct from the other scheduled tribes and even the Particularly Vulnerable Tribal Groups, primarily because these indigenous population have passed through a very cataclysmic and exterminating experience like the Tasmanians of Australia or the Yaghans of Tierra del Fuego. A little mistake, even if the intensions are noble, may eliminate these vulnerable communities for ever from the face of the earth. Although, the culturecide of the Great Andamanese has already taken placed and it has partially affected the Onges, the fate of the Jarawas and the Sentinelese is yet to be decided before it is too late. The Anthropological Survey of India has come up with a policy document published in its journal and the present author is one of the co-authors of this policy. This policy needs to be given due consideration as in matters concerning tribal and indi-genous people, anthropologists are in the best positioned to advise than others.

The indigenous people of the Andaman and Nicobar Islands need not simply be treated as parasitical beneficiary needed government support for sustaining themselves but as original owners of these natural wonders, inhabiting these groups of Islands for thousands of years. These communities are also custodians of precious indigenous knowledge, a sample of which was revealed during Asian Tsunami of 2004. Besides the unique indigenous culture and language, they also possess ancient DNA which is also of great use to the humanity at large. Their survival is not only crucial for their sake but also for the world community as they cut across boundaries of any one state or nation. The outcry of the world community in the episode of Allen Chau was precisely for this reason.

India has the track record of being one of those countries where the indigenous people are given the best possible treatment and institutions like the Anthropological Survey of India and nearly fifty University Departments of Anthropology make sure that the ethnographically informed data is provided to polity and bureaucracy so that the tribal development takes place without much damage. In instance of clash between development needs and interests of the indigenous communities, the critical analysis by anthropologists and timely intervention of the judiciary makes sure that the indigenous communities are not harmed beyond limits. The Andaman Trunk Road is a very good case study in this sense. It is heartening to note that India is continuing with the policy of least interference and guided development with respect to the indigenous people of Andaman and Nicobar Islands. Adoption of a flexible but firm policy for these groups will go a long way for their bright future. With reference to the Jarawas in particular, the present book contains valuable insight for moving in the right direction.

PROF. P. C. JOSHI
Former, Vice Chancellor (I/C)
University of Delhi

Preface

This book is based on the author's PhD thesis titled, 'Ecology, Conflict and Adaptation of the Jarawa in the Andaman Islands', submitted to the North-Eastern Hill University, Shillong in 2008. The original content has been re-arranged, condensed, modified and updated. The present work is the outcome of seven years of rigorous field investigation from 1998 to 2005. Thereafter, short trips were made to the field to update the information.

The genesis of the present work goes back to 1997, when the author, as a member of the 'contact team for the Jarawa', visited the Jarawa territory and had the opportunity to meet a group of Jarawas at a place called 'Lakara Lunta' in the Kadamtala area. During this period, the Jarawa were still hostile to outsiders. In the following years, they gradually became friendly with the outsiders. While the pre-1997 period, also known as the 'hostility phase', provided only glimpses of the economy and lifeway of the Jarawa, the post-1997 period gave the opportunity to study the Jarawa at close quarters.

The cultural landscape of the Andaman Islands is a mirrored ecosystem consisting of great complexity, formed by the interaction of man and nature, coupled with a host of ecological processes. It assumes greater significance against the backdrop that only a few contemporary societies are classified as hunter-gatherers, and the Jarawa are one among them. More importantly, like the Sentinelese, they still subsist through the hunting of wild animals, fishing and gathering of wild plants.

Human societies have adapted to various environments. However, the adaptation of hunting and gathering groups, like the Jarawas, to an island ecosystem has specific patterns and processes. The present work assesses the relationships among the resource base, work and population dynamics and examines in detail how the Jarawa have adapted to the requirements of the island ecosystem. It is also of great significance to understand the interaction of the Jarawa with the outsiders in the pre and post-hostility phase, and how they have adopted to the changed situation.

There are six chapters in the present study. The first chapter discusses the background of the current study, its relevance and research issues. Chapter 2 elucidates the natural endowment of the Andaman Islands. It gives a detailed geographic account of the Andaman Islands in general and the 'Jarawa Reserve', in particular. In addition, it provides information about the antiquity of the Andaman islanders and their population over decades. Chapter 3 provides a detailed account of the resource inventory, both edible and non-edible. It also illustrates the seasonality of resources. Chapter 4 deals with the adaptation of the Jarawa to the island ecology. The discussion centres on technology and strategy employed by the Jarawa for the collection and utilization of resources. The foraging strategy of the Jarawa has been discussed in detail with reference to the location of camps, movement patterns, selections of resources, foraging methods, search image, role specialization and pattern of sharing of resources. The ecological context of the subsistence activity of the Jarawa has been explained with the help of 'input-output analysis'. It is followed by an analysis of the foraging behaviour of the Jarawa in relation to 'optimal foraging theory'. Chapter 5 examines the impact of contact between the Jarawa and the non-Jarawa. It discusses the history of contacts and conflicts. Both the positive and negative aspects of the contact in the post-hostility phase have been discussed in relation to resources and how the Jarawa have adapted themselves to the changed situation. Finally, Chapter 6 provides the summary and conclusion of the major findings derived from the study. It also provides recommendations based on the understanding of the present research problem. The scope of further research on the related topics has also been discussed.

First and foremost, I express my heartfelt gratitude to my supervisor, Late Prof. Zahid Husain Qureshi, Department of Geography, North-Eastern Hill University, Shillong, whose excellent supervision, invaluable advice, suggestions and constant encouragement enabled me to complete the PhD thesis. I would remain indebted to him forever.

I am extremely grateful to Dr. R.K Bhattacharya, the then Director of the Anthropological Survey of India, for giving me the opportunity to work among the Jarawa. I am also obliged to Shri Deepak Tyagi, the then Director-in-Charge, Anthropological Survey of India, for granting permission to use the field data for my doctoral thesis. I would remain deeply grateful to Late Prof. Vinay Kumar Srivastava, Former Director, Anthropological Survey of India, who not only encouraged me to publish the PhD work, but also took pains to go through the manuscript and gave valuable suggestions for updating it. I also express my sincere thanks to Dr M. Sasikumar, Joint Director, Anthropological Survey of India for his insightful comments and suggestions.

I sincerely thank my office colleagues, Dr Kanchan Mukhopadhyay, Dr Ramesh Sahani, Shri S.S. Barik, Shri Samir Biswas, Dr Amitava Dinda and Dr Sumitabha Chakravorty, for helping me in many ways throughout the study. I extend my sincere thanks to Dr Amit Kumar Ghosh, Dr Venugopal P.N., Dr Shiv Kumar Patel and Dr Priyanka Airi Goyal for helping me update the information.

I offer my special thanks to the Andaman Administration, particularly Shri S.A. Awardi, the then Director, Tribal Welfare, Executive Secretary, Andaman Adim Janjati Vikas Samiti and their staff for extending all possible help and logistic support during the fieldwork.

I am very grateful to Prof. P.C. Joshi, Former Vice Chancellor, University of Delhi, for writing the Foreword.

Finally, I owe heartfelt gratitude to my wife and my daughter, who have been there with me through thick and thin. Without their tremendous understanding and encouragement, it would not have been possible to complete the present study.

Umesh Kumar
Senior Ecologist
Anthropological Survey of India
Kolkata

CHAPTER 1

Background and Research Issues

INTRODUCTION

Modern humans, *Homo sapiens*, have inhabited the earth for more than 300,000 years. For at least 97 per cent of this time, they lived as hunter-gatherers in small groups within the confines of local ecosystems (Stringer & Galway-Witham 2017, Gowdy 1998). Until approximately 12,000 years ago, all humans practised hunting and gathering. It has been observed that the hunting and gathering way of life has been the most successful and persistent adaptation man has ever achieved. Today, most of the hunter-gatherers live in environments, like frozen arctic, tundra, desert, islands and inaccessible forests. It shows that they have adapted to a wide range of environments. The form and process of adaptation vary with space and time. It, therefore, becomes all the more important that human adaptation in each of these environments should be understood in relation to its ecology.

Islands are one of the unique ecosystems of the world owing to their location amidst the sea and a well defined boundary. The 'island ecology' is characterised by an interface between land (terrestrial) and sea (aquatic) resources. The land-sea interface in the island habitat represents a distinct boundary for most of its inhabitants, where readily defined area of the island and the functional niches of the inhabitants correspond in many respects. Mueller-Dombois and Bridge (1981) have identified a few essential features of island ecosystems, viz., isolation/insularity and size of the islands, low diversity of the island biota, high endemicity, poor representation of certain organisms, like large predators and ecological release, i.e. expansion of the ecological niche by occupation of more area of the habitat and use of many types of resources. Of these, the insularity of the island ecosystem and typical resource base make islands interesting for geographical and ecological studies.

The human groups inhabiting the island ecosystems have the advantage of utilising resources of the islands as well as that of the adjoining sea. They develop different means and ways to harness terrestrial and aquatic resources. As a result, human adaptation to the island environment has a peculiar form and process, hence worth studying from an anthropological and geographical angle.

The Jarawa, a hunting and gathering community of the Andaman Islands, is one of the four simplest Negrito human groups. They are confined along the western parts of South and Middle Andaman. They derive their sustenance from terrestrial and marine ecosystems through hunting, fishing and gathering. Their adaptation to the island environment has a distinct form and process. The Jarawa had been living in the Andaman Islands in almost isolated conditions till the British occupied these islands in the eighteenth and nineteenth centuries and established penal settlement. The Jarawa, along with the other Negrito groups, resented the establishment of settlements for the convicts and exploitation of the resources. The hostility between the Jarawa and the non-Jarawa continued till the end of 1997. Consequently, the post-1997 period has witnessed frequent and free interaction between the Jarawa and the non-Jarawa which, in turn, has ushered in many changes. Many of these changes are detrimental to the survival of the Jarawa as a hunting and gathering community. It is, therefore, important to understand how the Jarawa are coping with the changing situation and why they are finding it difficult to adapt to the changing situation.

EARLIER WORKS

There are many studies available on the human adaptation to a particular environment but only a few on the human adaptation to islands, particularly that of the classical foraging groups, which have also been mentioned here.

Ecology

Ernst Haeckel (1866) made the first use of the term 'ecology' in its modern sense. He described the meaning of ecology 'as the body of knowledge concerning the economy of nature- the investigation of the total relations of animal to its organic and inorganic environment. . . .' In simple words, ecology is the study of the interrelationship between organism and environment. However, during the last 150 years, meaning and scope of the term ecology have broadened considerably. Today it is viewed as the study of ecosystem, flow of energy and matter and ecological balance. Castri (1981) opined that it is a science of converging disciplines to form a common trunk of ecology.

The adaptation of an organism to its biophysical environment is the subject matter of ecology. Adaptation is a response of an organism to its environment. Husain (2002, 12-13) has considered human adaptation to the environment as a process involving technology and strategy employed by man harness biophysical resources of an ecosystem for his subsistence and future growth. Actually, human adaptation in its totality includes cultural, behavioural, biological and physical adaptation, whereas in geography, it is primarily the behavioural and, to some extent, technological responses that are taken into account while dealing with human adaptation.

Many scholars have explored the role of 'ecological edges' in human adaptation to a particular ecosystem. Odum (1971) describes the edges of the ecosystem as high in productivity and species richness or biodiversity. Berks and Folk (1994) explain that the benefit of the ecological edge can be created across cultural edges through the development of institutions that allow people from different ecological areas to share knowledge and goods. Similarly, the 'resilience' concept, originally developed for the study of ecosystem dynamics (Holling 1973) has been applied to the study of socio-ecological system by Gunderson et al., (1995), Berkes and Folk (1998), Adger (2000), Davidson-Hunt and Berkes (2003) as well as others. McCay (2000) has described how the integration of ecological edges and cultural knowledge system and practices of the human group living there enhances the resilience of local communities. The studies by Anderson (1996) and Peacock and Turner (2000) on the aboriginal people show that the beneficial effect of the ecological edges is also created spatially and temporally through purposive human activity. Another example of intentional maintenance and development of ecological edges is provided by Deur (2000) in his research on tidal marsh garden of Kwakwaka'wakw and Nuu-Chah-Nulth people of the northwest coast of North America.

HUMAN ECOLOGY AND ISLAND ECOSYSTEM

The term 'human ecology' (like the term 'island') means different things to different people. Human ecology in simple words is a study of the totality of dynamic interrelationship between man and environment, particularly focussing on means and ways of human adaptation to the environment. The Chicago School of Urban Sociology brought it to prominence in the 1920s (Park and Burgess 1921), while Barrows (1923) made an early attempt to define the discipline of geography as the study of human ecology. By the early twentieth century, human ecology was taken by other social sciences to deal with man, society and their environment (Mckenzie 1926, Park 1936, Quinn 1939). For example, Mukerjee (1926) defined social or human ecology as a 'synoptic study of the balance of plant, animal and human activities, which are systems of correlated working parts in the organisation of the regions (ecosystems)'. Mukerjee (1938) said that from Frederick La Play to Patric Geddes has come the valuable insight that the organism (man, folk), functions (work, occupation) and environment (place, region and nature) cannot be treated separately.

More recently, researchers approaching the man's ecology from two rather different standpoints have revived the term. A group of social scientists in geography, anthropology, physiology and nutrition have attempted to broaden their explanations of human function and variation by considering man as an organism in relation to his environment (Sargent 1974). This approach of study is known as 'organism-ecology' approach. At the same time, the researchers in social sciences have also found it extremely useful to study the economic, social and geographical aspects of human populations in relation to their environment and this is known as 'population-ecology' approach. Of these approaches, the present work has mostly adopted the latter approach to study the Jarawa in the Andaman islands ecosystem.

Two main trends within human ecology can be distinguished. The first is the adoption of an explicitly holistic viewpoint on man-environment interactions; the second is a move towards quantification. Both developments are to some extent general within the human sciences, but in studies of human ecology, they have resulted in part from the stimulus provided by biological concepts, particularly the concept of 'ecosystem' (Ackerman 1963, Stoddart 1965, Watt 1968, Binford and Binford 1968, Buckley 1969, Chorley 1971, Chapman 1970). Arthur Tansley (1935) coined the term 'ecosystem' for both the biome and its habitat. Stoddart (1965) recommended the adoption of ecosystem concept in the geographical investigation.

Though the system analysis appears to offer much to the investigator of a human adaptation to the environment, it can be criticised on two grounds. The first concerns the capacity of the investigator to cope with the daunting complexity of the natural world, in particular the interaction between man and his biophysical environment. It is usually not possible to define a system, to identify its components and to specify its linkages within it, without first making subjective decisions about the critical processes in operation. When direct measurement and observation are not possible, for example in a historical context, the problem of defining the system is even greater. Quantification of an incorrectly constructed or partially defined system suggests merely a spurious precision. A second and perhaps more important problem is the difficulty of analysing the change in a system which is inhabited by man, whereas, in a natural system, this problem does not arise. Ecological succession and perhaps evolutionary changes, can be envisaged as being essential processes of self-organisation in which successive states that are more probable follow less probable patterns (Margalef 1968).

Much socio-economic change, although having its ultimate origin in purposive behaviour, does not itself have adaptive value for any particular system (e.g., an island ecosystem) within which it occurs. This contrasts with the change in natural systems, which operates in many ways to achieve greater stability for the ecosystem through greater species diversity (Odum 1971). Ecosystems are dominated by negative feedback loops and homeostatic tendencies, whereas, all present day systems involving man have, in contrast, much stronger inbuilt feedbacks (increasing populations, rising material expectations, the impact of innovation diffusion, etc.) and the factor of active control (Chorley 1973). The nature and effectiveness of control and the purpose of a particular system can perhaps be specified in terms of the aspirations of groups and individuals and the various constraints that make it unlikely that these goals will be achieved. Nevertheless, there remains the problem of continual and essentially unpredictable change in the inputs to the system (Brookfield 1975). Far from being equilibrium-bound, most of the real world's systems that human ecologists study are increasingly dynamic, '. . . lurching from one state of disequilibrium to another in response to changing impulses . . .' (Brookfield 1975). From this viewpoint, systems analysis appears far from a panacea, but concomitantly the simplicity, manageable scale and insularity of island ecosystems make it worth studying.

For the small islands, insularity, whether actual or conceptual, has particular value for ecological studies. At the 1961 symposium on 'Man's Place in the Island Ecosystem' Fosberg (1963: 5) identified two essential features of real islands that made them attractive for study, i.e. isolation and limited size. The limited and well-defined size of the islands makes it easier to have an in-depth study and generalisation because of the greater ecological and cultural unity of small human groups of the islands. It also becomes easier to analyse in detail, because the studied sample inevitably represents a large percentage of the total population. Any isolation of society, even if relative, also presents the practical advantage of boundedness or togetherness that facilitates the operational definition of a population/group, and simplifies the measurement of the flow of energy and matter. In addition to these methodological considerations, insularity also provides circumstances particularly suitable for the study of human ecology, since in the case of islands the spatial definition of man's ecosystem is relatively unambiguous. The land-sea interface represents a distinct boundary for most organisms so that a readily defined area of the island and the functional interactions of inhabitants within the ecosystem correspond in many respects.

HUMAN HABITATS IN ISLAND ECOSYSTEM

Many of the island ecosystems have become the interesting and unique habitats of man (and of plants and animals too) where distinct cultures have flourished. Changes have been noticed in the human groups and the island ecosystems owing to the interaction between the two. The importance of change is, of course, recognised by researchers into the human ecology of island populations, but within the explicit ecosystem framework. Among those who have used the ecosystem model more effectively is Rappaport, whose work is discussed by several authors (McArthur 1977, Morren 1977 and Bayliss-Smith 1977). Rappaport's writings (1968, 1971a) about the Tsembaga Maring, a small and essentially insular community in the Bismarck Mountains of New Guinea Island, illustrate well the conceptual problem that is posed by ecosystem change. Rappaport was concerned with two types of systems: firstly, the actual mountain forest ecosystem controlled and inhabited by the Maring, which he termed the 'operational model' of the system; secondly, knowledge and beliefs concerning the environment that the people themselves possess, which he termed the 'cognised model'. The Maring's cognised model is dominated by the pig cycle, which is associated with religious and political rituals (Wagner 1977), but it also has important environmental implications through changing land-use pressure.

Inherent in the ecosystem approach is the study of the management of ecosystem. Chorley (1973: 160) views the management of the ecosystem as '. . . the manipulation of the equilibrating operations of the ecosystem to achieve the higher levels of production, generally within the existing structure of the system. . . .'

Management of the ecosystem appears to be difficult when it is being transformed in an irreversible way either due to government intervention or other reasons. In studying such changes, and in predicting the future of small insular groups, a steady-state ecosystem approach tends to offer limited insights. Even more, the majority of the problems of island population today concern change and response to innovation, rather than to the dynamics of internal stability. Besides environmental alteration, this transformation involves an increase in the dependency of the community upon external inputs. It may pose an ultimate threat to the once isolated populations of the interiors, such as the Jarawa. As elsewhere in the tropics, the traditional culture of foraging populations maintained an ecological balance through sustainable use of resources. The effects of interaction with external systems generally result in lowered subsistence diversity as new food items replace traditional ones and a reduced capacity to respond to signs of degradation within the ecosystem as people's dependence upon external inputs increases. In the long run, such changes have a negative impact as they lead to social and ecological instability, and ultimately threaten people's own welfare (Rappaport 1971b, Howlett 1973, Waddel 1974, Lee 1984, Ndagala 1988).

HUNTER-GATHERERS OR FORAGERS

The Cambridge Encyclopedia of Hunter-Gatherers (Lee and Daly 1999: 3) defines 'foraging' as subsistence based on hunting of wild animals, gathering of wild plant foods, and fishing, with no domestication of plants and no domesticated animals except the dog. The people who practise such subsistence activities are known as hunter-gatherers or foragers. In contemporary theory, this minimal definition is only the starting point in defining hunter-gatherers. Recent research has brought a more nuanced understanding of the issue. In defining foragers, it must be recognised that many of the contemporary foragers practise a mixed subsistence: gardening in tropical South America, reindeer herding in northern Asia, trading in South/Southeast Asia and parts of Africa. Given this diversity, Lee and Daly (1999, 3) proposed that modern hunter-gatherers are typically characterised by a cluster of traits, '. . . subsistence is one part of a multi-faceted definition of hunter-gatherers, social organisation forms a second major area of convergence, and cosmology and world-view a third. All three sets of criteria have to be taken into account in defining and understanding hunting and gathering communities today. . . .'

The basic unit of social organisation of most hunting and gathering communities is the 'band', a small scale nomadic group of fifteen to fifty people related by kinship. Band societies are found throughout the Old and New Worlds and share a number of common features. First, they are relatively egalitarian. Leadership is less formal. Mobility is another characteristic of band societies. People tend to move their settlements frequently, several times a year or more, in search of food. A third characteristic is that all band-organised people exhibit a pattern of concentration and dispersion. Rather than living in uniformly sized groupings throughout the year, band societies tend to spend part of the year dispersed into small foraging units and another part of the year aggregate into much larger units. A fourth characteristic common to almost all band societies is common access to resources of a particular territory. It is further characterised by rules of reciprocity. Another broad area of commonalities lies in the domains of the quality of interpersonal relations and forms of consciousness. Sharing is recognised as a common trait and the central rule of social interaction among hunters and gatherers (Kent 1993). The most prized resources are shared among the constituent families of a band. However, the easily available resources are not shared normally; instead, these are shared within a family. The hunter-gatherers' perception of the environment is as the 'giving environment'. It is found among many hunter-gatherers who perceive the environment around them as their home and the source of all good things (Bird-David 1990, Turnbull 1968). Invariably, the terms hunter-gatherers and foragers have been interchangeably used but it has the same meaning.

The human groups who were much later to be called 'hunters and gatherers' or 'foragers' have been central in the debates of European social and political thought from the sixteenth century onwards. Philosophers from Hobbes, Locke, and Rousseau onwards have drawn upon contemporary accounts of 'savages' as a starting point for speculations about life in the state of nature (Meek 1976, Barnes 1937, Barnes and Becker 1938). These constructions became more detailed as more information accumulated from travellers' accounts, resulting in elaborate schemes for human adaptation in the works of the eighteenth century scholars like Smith, Millar, Ferguson, etc. (Barnes 1937, Harris 1968).

With the rise of European imperialism and the conquest of new lands, some detailed studies were made on hunter-gatherers. William Sollas (1911) was one of the first to define hunting and gathering as a specific way of life. The study of the Central Eskimo by Boas (1888), a physical geographer, is one of the earliest seminal works on hunter-gatherers where the man-environment relationship has been seen from an ecological point of view.

Modern studies of hunting and gathering people can be traced to two landmark works of the 1930s. The first is an essay by Julian Steward (1936) on 'the social and economic basis of primitive bands' in which he argued that resource exploitation determines to a significant extent the shape and dynamics of band organisation. It was followed by another seminal work by him on the Great Basin Shoshone, Ute and Paiute (Steward 1938), where he analysed the functional relationship among the different aspects of their cultures, and of their cultures to the local environment. In doing so, he shed light on the patterns and processes of cultural change, especially among hunter-gatherers, that could be understood in terms of adaptation to a specific environment and human ecology and represents the pivotal bridge between culture and natural environment. In his later work, Steward (1955, 32) shifted focus from 'human community' as a strictly biological construct to 'human community' as a cultural construct. In this study, he focussed on analysing the relationship between technology and the environment along with behaviour employed in the exploitation of a particular environment by means of a particular technology. The second seminal work was the classic essay by Radcliffe-Brown (1930-1) on Australian aboriginal social organisation. However, unlike Steward, for whom ecological factors were paramount,

Radcliff-Brown saw structural factors of kinship as primary to the man-environment relationship.

The publication of the edited book *Man the Hunter* by Lee and DeVore (1968) is considered the first detailed collection of works on hunting and gathering human groups. In yet another work on the Bushmen of Kalahari, Lee (1969) examined the foraging pursuits of the Bushman through the application of 'input-output analysis' and came to the conclusion that the ratio of labour expenditure to food collection in such society is generally low. The 'input-output analysis' has been done while examining the foraging activities of the Jarawa in the present work.

A burst of research activities followed the publication of *Man the Hunter* (Lee and DeVore 1968) resulting in the publication of a number of monographs and edited volumes. Those worth mentioning among them are by Damas (1969), Balikci (1970), Bicchieri (1972) on the Netsilik Eskimo, Sahlins (1972) on stone age economics of the Kung, Watanbe (1973) on the Ainu ecosystem, Marshall (1976) on the Kung of Nyae Nyae, Binford (1978) on the Nuniamiut ethnoarchaeology, Lee (1979) on the !Kung San: Men, Women and Work in a foraging society, Suttle (1990) edited handbook on North American Indian, etc. While studying the adaptation of the Kung to their habitat in Kalahari, Sahlins (1972, 1-39) called them 'original affluent society'. He argued that except in times of scarcity, hunter-gatherer populations have to spend only a few hours per day in subsistence-related activities. He further articulated his theoretical position by stating that the work input in terms of time is an indicator of the state of the resources in the habitat. It means the higher the resource density, the less time a hunting and gathering community spends searching for food and vice versa.

Based on his extensive work on the Hadza of Africa, Woodburn (1988) introduced the concept of the two types of economic systems in foraging groups, i.e. 'immediate return' and 'delayed return'. He put the economies of the classical or full time foragers in the category of 'immediate return', because of the absence of accumulation or surplus. In this type of economy, consumption and sharing of resources are immediate in time and space. Those based on a 'delayed-return principle' allow for planning and investment of time in keeping of bees, rearing of horses or planting of some trees and making of traps.

Villoro (1982) and Deloria (1995) have studied the system of knowing and explaining the universe among the hunter-gatherers and concluded that it is the result of the collective wisdom and experience of generations in local or regional settings and history. The indigenous knowledge system puts the focus on many things: the nature and functioning of the physical world; the supernatural realm and human interaction therewith. Bird-David (1990) has described that most of the foraging groups consider the environment rich and kind to them that she termed as 'giving environment'. Further, she explains that since the environment is considered the repository as well as a provider of all resources, the interaction between man and environment in such a society is organic.

A major development in hunter-gatherers research involves the study of foraging strategies. Winterhalder and Smith (1981) provide a detailed account of the application of the 'optimal foraging theory' to the hunter-gatherer subsistence behaviour. Based on the theoretical model, they conclude that the hunter-gatherers seek to maximise their chances of finding food with the least effort. The hunter-gatherers exhibit a kind of economic 'rationality' in their subsistence strategies, and that 'rationality' is a product of their adaptation to a particular ecosystem. Bettinger (1991, 106), while taking cognisance of the fact that rationality is culturally conditioned, puts stress on the fact that analysis of the human foraging behaviour is grounded in concepts of objective rationality and it remains the desired objective in hunting-gathering studies. The versatility of 'optimal foraging theory' is reflected in the way it has been adopted in a wide range of studies. Analyses of hunter-gatherers occupying the South American rainforest (Kaplan and Hills 1992), Central Australia (O'Connel and Hawkes 1981, 1984), Arctic region (Smith 1991) and numerous regions in between, have all relied heavily on the insight provided by 'optimal foraging theory'. In an interesting application, some scholars have also employed foraging theory to illustrate the ways in which hunter-gatherers design their subsistence activities to minimise risk (Yellen 1986, Winterhalder 1986, 1990).

Human adaptation to the rainforest ecosystem, particularly of hunting and gathering groups, has always been of much interest to the researchers as the resources have typical diversification and dispersal. Hart and Hart (1986) have examined the ecological basis of subsistence in the African rainforest. Hoffman (1986) in his study on Punan and other Borneo foragers, contends that the foragers cannot live on the forest resources alone. Similar views have been aired by Headland (1986 and 1987) while discussing the adaptation and subsistence strategies employed by the Negrito hunter-gatherers in the Philippines. Bailey and Peacock (1988) analysed the foraging pattern of the Efe Pygmies in the Ituri rainforest of northeast Zaire. Bailey et al. (1989) have studied the possibility of independent foraging in the rainforest in the face of ecological constraints in detail. They conclude that energy-rich wild plant foods are too scarce in the rain forest to allow independent subsistence by foraging peoples. But the study by Stearman (1991) on the Yuqui foragers in the Bolvian Amazon and by Bahuchet (1988) on the pygmy foraging peoples of the Congo basin, like the Aka, suggest that there are significant variations in the tropical forest ecosystems on a worldwide as well as a regional scale. Hence, the sustainability of the subsistence system of these foraging groups depends on a refined knowledge of their environment and the freedom of movement over a large territory to access the resources. In their study on the Batek of Peninsular Malaysia, Endicott and Bellwood (1991) have concluded that small nomadic groups of foragers can live off wild resources alone as their foraging strategy takes into account the availability, seasonality and density of wild food resources in the rainforest ecosystem.

Like the human adaptation to rainforest ecology in a continental situation, the island ecology and human adaptation therein have also been an area of major interest for researchers. Among the earlier works, the study by Fosberg (1963) discusses in detail the mechanics and behaviour of ecosystems in general and certain peculiarities of island ecosystem in particular with respect to the insularity and size of the island. Simmons (1966) explains the functionality of the ecological approach when applied to land use and the balance between man and environment. Rappaport (1968) discusses the critical role of pigs in the Melanesian ecosystem, and traces the evolution of pristine ecosystems and human alterations in it. He finds that the extent of human impact varies; the high islands are most susceptible to human alteration, the coral atolls less, and the reef-lagoon systems the least. Watanbe (1973) analyses in detail the changing man-environment relationship in an island ecosystem with respect to the Ainu, a hunting and gathering tribe of Japan, and how the changes brought about by the introduction of new technology have proved detrimental to them. While drawing a comparison between two human groups regarding the utilisation of forest resources and its consequences in Malaysia, Dunn (1975) explains the sustainable harvesting of forest resources by the Jahai, a foraging community of northern Malaysia during ancient time, and ecologically unsustainable commercial extraction of forest resources by the traders in modern times.

The impacts of contacts and resultant conflict of foraging groups with non-foraging groups have been studied by many scholars. Among the earlier works, the study by Cooper (1946: 131, 138) describes the complete disappearance of the Tehuelche and the Puelche peoples by 1885 from the Pampas of Argentina because of war and diseases. The study by Bodley (1999) describes how the European settlers and venture capitalists, during the 150 years of colonial period from approximately 1795 to 1945, took half of the globe from small scale cultures to feed the suddenly expanded appetite of the market economy for natural resources and in the process killed more than 50 million tribal people.

Lee (1984) has discussed the survival challenges of the Bushmen in the modern world after their being partly adopting the sedentary agriculture in the late 1970s due to thinning as well as receding of the resource base, introduction of new tools and techniques and competition from the other human groups having a superior technology. Ndagala (1988) has pointed out major threats to the Hadza due to land loss and breach of land rights because of granting of the hunting licences to commercial companies, and how these companies are jeopardising the very survival of the Hadza.

Apart from the aforementioned studies, there are some classical studies on hunter-gatherers in which attempts have been made to bring together much of the rich geographical, historical and ethnographic material that had accumulates since the 1940s. *The Handbook of North American Indians* (1978), under the general editorship of William Sturtevant, chronicles the 500 nations of the continent in a series of landmark regional volumes. Six of these volumes deal largely, if not exclusively, with hunting and gathering peoples, e.g., *Northwest Coast,* edited by Wayne Suttles (1990); *Subarctic,* edited by June Helm (1981); *The Great Basin,* edited by Warren D' Azevedo (1986); *California,* edited by Robert Heizer (1978); *Arctic,* edited by David Damas (1984); and *Northeast,* edited by Bruce Trigger (1978). On other continents, Barnard (1992) and Edwards (1987) produced overview volumes on the Khoisan people and the aboriginal Australians, respectively.

INDIAN PERSPECTIVE

About 75 communities in India have been put in the category of Particularly Vulnerable Tribal Groups (PVTGs). However, very few of them are full time hunter-gatherers. In the present literature review, only those communities have been considered who derive much of their subsistence from hunting and gathering pursuits.

The subsistence pattern of the Birhor has been analysed by Sinha (1958) from the cultural ecology point of view. Adhikari (1984) adopted a structural approach in the study of the Birhor. The hunting-gathering mode of subsistence of the Nayaka of Karnataka has been discussed and analysed in detail by Bird-David (1992). She has also analysed the process of change in the Nayaka economy in the wake of their contact with outsiders. Gardner (1993) has discussed the adaptation of the Paliyan of Tamil Nadu to the forest ecosystem.

Models drawn from ecology as well as from studies of modern and Pleistocene geographical and environmental changes have been applied in some of the studies of Indian hunter-gatherers. Murty (1985), while examining the cultures of hunter-gatherers of Eastern Ghat, argues that the tremendous indigenous knowledge of plant species results from ecological adaptation and exploitation over a long period, and thus justifies the use of analogies drawn from the recent tribal subsistence pattern along the south-east coast to predict past subsistence strategies. Dutta (1974) and Cooper (1990, 1992, 1994) have tried to determine the antiquity of the Andaman Islanders based on the study of kitchen midden found on the old encampment sites.

Among the earliest studies on the foraging communities of the Andaman Islands, the studies by Man (1883) and Portman (1899) are important. Man (1883) has described the life and economy of the Great Andamanese. Portman (1899) has discussed the subsistence activities of the Negrito communities of the Andaman Islands, except the Sentinelese. More importantly, it records the process of contact and conflict between the Negrito communities and others and their impact on society and the environment. Social organisations and economic activities of the Onge and the Great Andamanese have been described by Radcliff Brown (1922). Bose (1964), in his study on the Onge, has analysed their foraging pursuits. Cipriani (1966) has discussed in detail the culture and economy of the Onge and the Great Andamanese. Among the recent studies on the Negrito communities of the Andaman Islands, the studies on the Great Andamanese by Chakravarty (1990), on the Sentinelese by Pandit (1990), on the Onge by Basu (1990) and on the Jarawa by Sarkar (1990) are worth mentioning. These studies have been able to reveal human response to island ecosystem through the material culture and social organisations of the communities and the changes that are taking place due to contact with other non-Negrito human groups. Pandya (1993), in his study on the Onge of Little Andaman Island, has given a detailed account of ethnography, cosmology and rite and rituals of the Onge. Mukhopadhyay (2002) has elucidated the history of contacts and conflicts of the Negrito population, particularly of the Jarawa with non-Negrito population. Kumar and Biswas (2002) have analysed the man-environment relationship of the Jarawa. The book edited by Sekhsaria and Pandya (2010) has a number of articles which deal with the issues of contact and conflict in the post-hostility phase (post-1997), impact on the Jarawa and policy suggestions.

As regards the antiquity of the Negrito population of the Andaman Islands, the genomic study by Thangraj et al. (2005) suggests that they arrived at these islands much earlier, about ~60,000 years ago. The later studies (Palanichamy et al. 2006, Barik et al. 2008 and DNA Polymorphism Consortium 2018) arrived on the conclusion that once the Jarawa, the Great Andamanese and the Onge along with the Rajbanshi, the Paudi Bhuyan, the Munda, the Bhoi Khasi and the Savara belonged to the same stock around ~45,000 years ago. Thereafter, the Andaman communities moved to the Andaman Islands.

Although several studies have been conducted on the hunting and gathering communities, there are only a few on the hunting and gathering communities of the Andaman and Nicobar Islands and a very few on the Jarawa.

ISSUES AND OBJECTIVES

The study of adaptation of a foraging community to the environment (like that of the island ecosystem) has been of special interest in ecology because the relationship between man and environment is organic and most direct. The Andaman and Nicobar Islands, which abound in tropical rainforests, are home to four Negrito foraging groups including the Jarawa. They have been living there for thousands of years and have adapted to the environment of the Andaman Islands. Besides the Sentinelese, the Jarawa are perhaps one of the best examples of full time hunter-gatherers anywhere in the world today. For long, they avoided friendly relations with the non-Jarawa. However, since late-1997, friendly contacts have been established with the Jarawa and that has ushered changes in the resource base and the adaptation pattern of the Jarawa. Now, there is a conflict between the Jarawa and the non-Jarawa in sharing the resources of their area. In fact, it is a competition between two sets of technology; a simple one used by the Jarawa and a developed one used by the non-Jarawa. Like their counterparts in the Andaman Islands, namely the Great Andamanese and the Onge who have not only been reduced in number from about 5000 to 40 and 600 to 95 respectively but also have almost abandoned the hunting and gathering practices, the Jarawa may also give up the foraging activities someday under the changed situation. It means it is a race against time for the social scientists to collect information on the pattern and process of adaptation of a hunting and gathering community to an island ecosystem.

The form and process of adaptation of a community is a function of the availability and density of resources in the environment and the tools, techniques and strategies used to harness the resources. The Jarawa's adaption to the island ecosystem has been studied taking into account the traditional technology and strategy employed by them for harnessing the resources for their sustenance. Emphasis has also been given to understand the changes in the technology and strategy under the influence of new challenges and sharing of resources of their territory with the non-Jarawa. The issues investigated in the present work can easily be understood with the help of the flow diagram shown in Figure 1.1.

Traditional hunting and gathering practices	**Changes**
↓	↓
Natural resource endowment	Contact
↓	↓
Resource perception	Change in resource base and environment
↓	
Physiographic zones	
↓	↓
Availability, density and seasonality of resources	Changes in technology and strategy
↓	↓
Technology and strategy	New challenges
↓	
Movement and critical time spent in each zone	

Figure 1.1: Adaptation of the Jarawa

Resource endowment of an area is key for the survival of any community. An inventory of the natural resources, both terrestrial and aquatic as recognised by the Jarawa, has been prepared to know the number and types of resources used by them. Further, these resources have been arranged in order of significance as reflected by their dietary preferences. This explains the relative percentage of animal and plant resources in the total food items collected by the Jarawa. Since the resource distribution over space (physiographic zones) and time (seasons) is not uniform, their distribution in different physiographic zones, viz., coast (shallow sea area), wetlands (area between high and low tides), plains and mountains, has been attempted. The interplay between population and resources has been analysed in relation to foraging technology and strategy.

While discussing foraging strategy, stress has been given to seasonality of resources, location of camps, movement patterns and foraging methods. The role of ecological edges has been discussed to find the determining factors behind the location of camps. Besides, the movement of the Jarawa over time and space has been explained to understand whether there is any pattern in their movement or not, and if yes, what are the determining factors behind such movements. In addition, the foraging methods used in hunting, fishing and gathering have also been discussed in detail. Since the search image, role specialisation and sharing constitute important aspects of foraging strategy, these factors have been elucidated along with other factors. All these factors have been discussed in detail to unravel the nuances of the foraging pursuits of the Jarawa as they are directly related to the question as to how the Jarawa derive their food or eke out their livelihood in the given island environment. Impact of contact of the Jarawa with the non-Jarawa on the resource base and adaptation of the Jarawa to the changing situation have also been examined.

Against the backdrop of the aforementioned aspects of forging, it has been attempted to answer the questions as to what extent the Jarawa are truly a hunting and gathering community and what survival strategies have been adopted by them to cope with the new challenges in the changed situation. Thus the main objectives of the study are:

1. to prepare an inventory of natural resources (both terrestrial and aquatic) as perceived by the Jarawa and also by the non-Jarawa,
2. to analyse human adaptation by finding out technology and strategy of resource utilisation by the Jarawa, and
3. to examine the impact of contact on the adaptation, environment and resource base of the Jarawa and the new challenges therein.

STUDY AREA

Floating in splendid isolation, east of the Indian mainland, the Andaman and Nicobar group of Islands is situated in the Bay of Bengal with Ten Degree Channel separating the Andaman group of Islands from the Nicobar group (Figure 1.2).

It has a wet tropical regime with the predominance of monsoon rainfall. It is characterised by high temperatures and rainfall and has luxuriant growth of tropical forests (for details see chapter 2).

The Andaman group of Islands is home to four Asiatic Negrito hunting and gathering communities, namely, the Great Andamanese, the Onge, the Jarawa and the Sentinelese. They have been living on the Andaman Islands from time immemorial. The North Sentinel Island is home to the Sentinelese, while the Onge, the Great Andamanese and the Jarawa inhabit the Little Andaman, Strait Island and western parts of South and Middle Andaman Islands respectively. The Sentinelese are still unfriendly with the outsiders. Like the Sentinelese, the Jarawa were also hostile to the outside population until October 1997. They have a total population of 534 [Adim Janjati Vikas Samiti (AAJVS), 2019]. The Jarawa territory, which has been declared as 'Jarawa Reserve', covers an area of about 1028 sq km. The resource base of the Jarawa is inclusive of both terrestrial and aquatic ecosystems. They subsist through hunting, fishing and gathering.

Besides the Negrito groups, the Andaman Islands are inhabited by the non-Negrito population also. They include the Andaman Indians (local-born), the Mopillas, the Bhantus, the Burmese, the Karens, refugees from the erstwhile East Bengal and the people from the southern part of India.

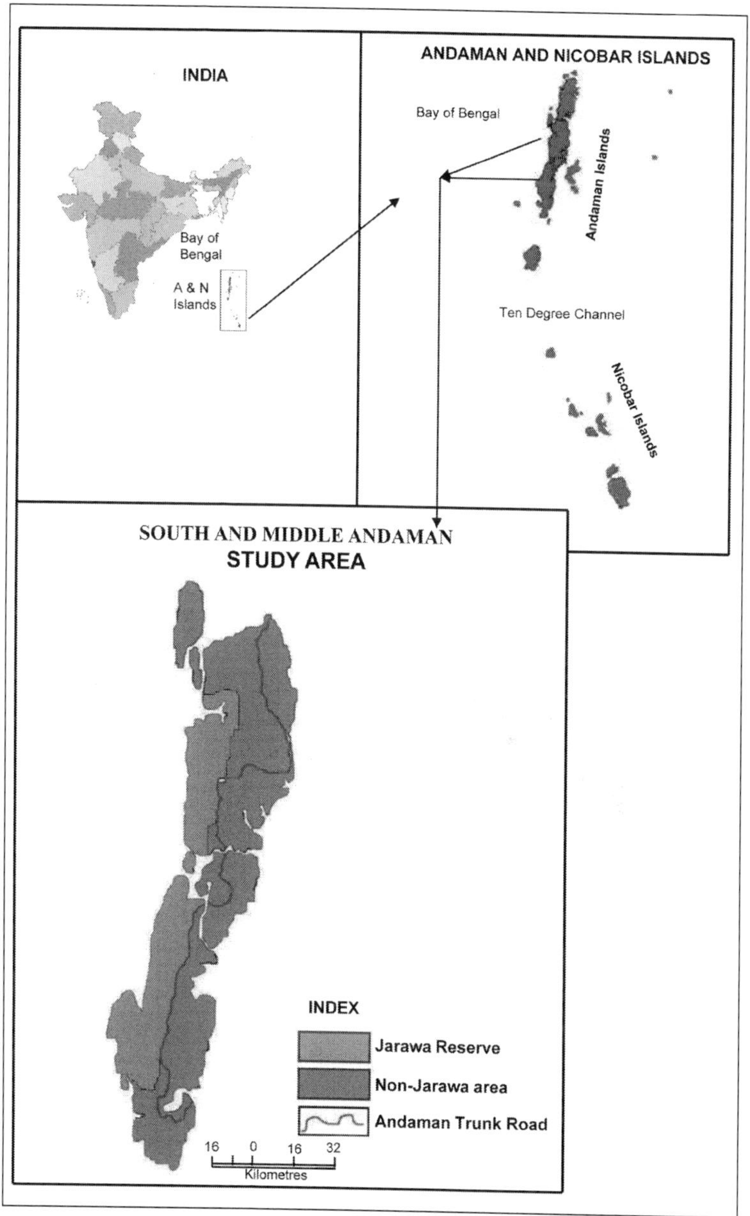

Source: Census, Andaman Adim Janjati Vikas Samiti.

Figure 1.2: South and Middle Andaman: Study Area

In the post-Independence period, the Government of India initiated a programme to rehabilitate persons displaced from the then East Pakistan in the Andaman Islands immediately after Independence. Of all the refugee families, about 2328 families were settled in different parts of the Middle and North Andaman Islands. Interestingly, they were settled on the eastern boundary of the Jarawa territory by clearing the forests. Agriculture has been their main economic activity. Consequent to the cessation of hostility (post-1997), they are sharing the resource base of the Jarawa, albeit illegally. Besides, many people from mainland India who were/are in service have also settled there, mainly in and around Port-Blair— the capital of the Andaman and Nicobar Islands.

DATABASE AND METHODOLOGY

The present study is based on both primary and secondary data. Though the fieldwork in the Jarawa territory had begun from October 1998 and continued until February 2018, detailed fieldwork could only be undertaken from late 2001 onwards. It was because before December 2001 the Andaman Administration did not consider the situation safe enough to allow any persons to stay in the Jarawa territory.

Previously only the estimated population of the Jarawa was available. Through the fieldwork, information was collected about their population. To understand the natural endowment of the area, the biophysical resources of the Andaman Islands, particularly of the Jarawa territory, were identified and recorded. It includes the preparation of a detailed resource inventory of both terrestrial and aquatic resources used by the Jarawa and non-Jarawa. The detailed foraging data of the Jarawa were collected from three locations— Thidong, Boiab and Tanmad between 11 December 2001 and 9 January 2002, 11 April 2002 and 9 May 2002, and 11 August 2002 and 9 September 2002, respectively. It covered the three different seasons—rainy, cool dry, and summer dry seasons. The data on the resources collected and consumed by them were gathered through focal family sampling, in which all the food collection activities of a few families were recorded for twenty-eight days in each season. The data, thus, collected gave quantitative information on the amount and type of the resources collected and the time spent on collection of these resources. It also helped in finding out the per capita availability of resources. This information also helped in explaining the state of health of resources in the Jarawa area. To ascertain the optimality of their foraging behaviour, data on the hunting behaviour of the Jarawa were collected over three different seasons. The data set includes distinct hunting trips undertaken by individuals to capture the game. In order to get information on the location of the Jarawa camp at a particular site and availability of resources therein, altogether 69 Jarawa campsites were visited and the locations of the Jarawa camps were recorded with the help of Geographic Positioning System (GPS) instrument. The information on the movement pattern of the Jarawa, both logistical and residential, was obtained by visiting their locations.

Data were also collected on the Jarawa perception of the resources, intra and inter-family sharing of the resources, division of labour and other socio-economic activities. The data set includes information pertaining to the impact of contact in the post-hostility phase on dress, ornaments, foraging behaviour, addiction to tobacco, exchange of goods between the Jarawa and the non-Jarawa, etc. For the collection of data, structured schedules, participant observation and diary record methods were used. Population data on those individuals who were not present in the camps were collected through the genealogical chart method.

Besides, several published and unpublished records, reports, articles, and books were consulted to obtain relevant data and information on the topic of the research. Topographical information relevant to the study was gathered from the camp office of the Geological Survey of India. As Andaman and Nicobar Islands have about 80 per cent of the area under forest cover, 1C LISS-III, Landsat-TM and IRS-1C-LISS-III-PAN geocoded merged data from 1997 and 2014 were sourced from Indian Institute of Remote Sensing, Dehradun, for visual interpretation to identify types and density of forest resources in the Andaman Islands. In order to prepare a detailed inventory of resources and to know the scientific names of the resources used by the Jarawa, the reports of

Zoological Survey of India, Botanical Survey of India, and Department of Environment and Forest were consulted.

The subsistence activities of the Jarawa involve the hunting of animals, gathering of plants and fishing. The health status of a person is function of food intake and its calorific value. Hence, information pertaining to food intake and its calorific value was sourced from the reports of All India Institute of Public Hygiene and Health, Kolkata and Directorate of Health Services, Port-Blair. Information on the occurrence of diseases due to contact in the pre and post-hostility phases were collected from the Directorate of the Health Services and other published material. The Jarawa have been in regular contact with outsiders since the establishment of the second penal settlement in the Andaman Islands. Data on the history of contact and conflict were obtained from the Census records, published materials and Police Stations. In addition, records of the AAJVS, Port Blair, were used to gather data on the gift articles given to the Jarawa and other related information.

DATA ANALYSIS

Thus, data on the adaptation of the Jarawa to the Andaman ecology have been analysed using various methods. The spatio-temporal resource utilisation pattern in the Jarawa territory has been analysed with the help of the data collected from four physiographic zones. Since the availability and seasonality of resources is distinct in each of these zones, the movement pattern of the Jarawa in these zones has been recorded and analysed.

The 'input-output analysis' has been attempted to explain the ecological context of the subsistence economy of the Jarawa by calculating the 'Index of Subsistence Effort'. The analysis has helped in finding out work input of the economically active Jarawa in a week. In turn, it has given information on how much of their subsistence efforts are oriented toward hunting, fishing and gathering. In addition, it also helps to explain that after hunting and gathering activities, how much time the Jarawa are left with which they devote for leisure-related activities.

The formula used here is taken from Lee (1969), which is as follows:

S = W/C
where S = the index of subsistence effort,
where W = the number of man-days of work, and
where C = number of man-days of consumption.
Mean group size = total man-days of consumption divided by 7.
Man-days of hunting = total man-days of hunting divided by total man-days of consumption.
Work week = the number of work days per adult per week.
Hunting week = the number of hunting per adult per week.
Index of Subsistence = man-days of work divided by man-days of consumption.

To find out the optimality of foraging behaviour of the Jarawa, an encounter distribution for each individual hunter has been derived. The analysis has been accomplished by dividing the time spent by each individual searching for prey into equal units of one hour within which the number of the pray items is encountered. Thereafter, the observed distribution has been compared with an expected Poisson distribution. In order to generate further confidence in the results, the Chi-square goodness-of-fit test has been carried out. The results have helped to explain the hunting behaviour of the Jarawa.

Besides, maps, charts and graphs have been used to give a cartographic representation of necessary information. Photographic coverage has also been done to show important features of the study.

The entire work has been organised in six chapters, viz., background and research issues; physical endowment of the Andaman Islands ecosystem; inventory of resources used by the Jarawa; adaptation of the Jarawa to the Andaman environment; contact, conflict and adaptation; and conclusion.

CHAPTER 2

Physical Environment of the Andaman Islands

Ecology is the study of the relationships between living organisms, including humans and their physical environment. It is, therefore, relevant to understand the physical environment so that ecological interrelationships can be explained in its all-possible details. Moreover, it is from the biophysical environment that a human group derives resources for the subsistence and survival. Against this backdrop, the physical environment of the Andaman Islands, which happens to be the habitat of the Jarawa, has been discussed. The discussion not only highlights the natural endowment of the Andaman Islands but also points out the peculiarities to which the Jarawa have adapted.

LOCATION AND EXTENT

The Andaman and Nicobar archipelago comprises over 534 tropical islands which are spread in the form of more or less an arch for a length of 700 km. The Andaman and Nicobar group of islands cover an area of about 8,293 sq km, and it extends between 6° to 14° North latitudes and 92° to 94° East longitudes in the Bay of Bengal with the Ten Degree Channel separating the Andaman group of islands from the Nicobar group of islands (Figure 2.1). The Andaman and Nicobar Islands are located on the eastern side of the Bay of Bengal. These islands are comparatively at more distance from mainland India then the Myanmar and Malaya Peninsula (Figure 2.2). The Andaman Islands lie 944 km from the Hooghly mouth, while merely 192 km from Cape Negrais of Myanmar. The land area of the Andaman Islands is 6,340 sq km and that of the Nicobar Islands is 1,953 sq km. Interestingly, only 38

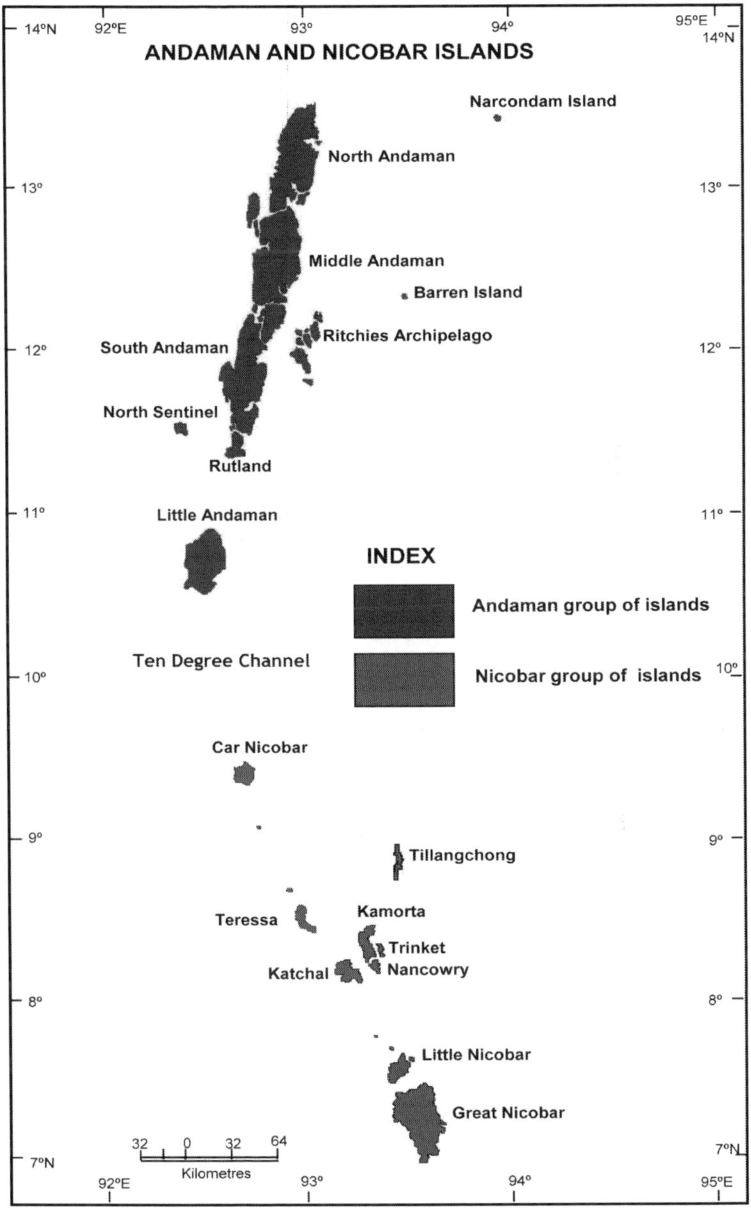

Source: Census.

Figure 2.1: Andaman and Nicobar Islands

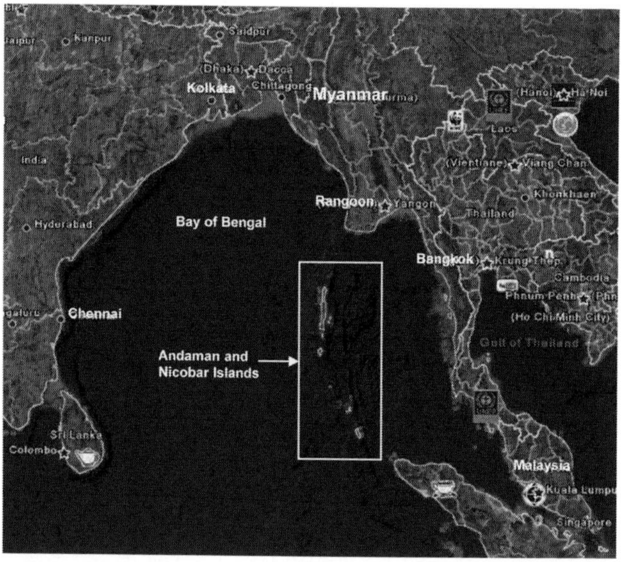

Source: Google Map.

Figure 2.2: Location of Andaman and Nicobar Islands

islands are inhabited, of which 26 are in the Andaman group and 12 in the Nicobar group. In addition, these islands are the habitat of six tribal groups, four of them (including the Jarawa) belong to the Negrito stock, while the remaining two belong to the Mongoloid stock.

The Andaman group of islands lies north of the Nicobar group of islands (Figure 2.1). It extends between 10°30' and 13°30' North latitudes and 92°15' and 95°10' East longitudes. The Andaman group consists of 204 islands. The Landfall Island is at the extreme north of the Andaman group of islands, followed by the three main islands known as the North Andaman, Middle Andaman and South Andaman, all of them separated by shallow seas. At a distance of 64 km from the South Andaman Island stands the Little Andaman Island. Besides, there are innumerable small islands, e.g. Ritchie's Archipelago, Tarmughli, North and South Sentinel islands, etc. (Table 2.1). The Middle Andaman is the largest of all islands in terms of area (561 sq km).

TABLE 2.1: AREAS OF DIFFERENT ISLANDS OF THE ANDAMAN

Name of the Islands	Area (sq km)
North Andaman	490.20
Middle Andaman	561.00
South Andaman	359.51
Landfall and 7 other islands in the North Andaman group	27.92
Interview and 4 other islands in the Middle Andaman group	59.00
Baratang and 4 other islands in the Baratang group	11.34
Havelock and 6 other islands in the Ritchie's Archipelago group	94.20
Rutland and 3 other islands in the South Andaman group of islands	73.86
Tarmughli and 4 other islands in the Labyrinth island	12.20
Little Andaman	289.90
Other islands numbering 166	430.97
Total	

Source: Sen, 1962.

PHYSIOGRAPHY

The first attempt to study the geology of these islands was made by Helfer and Millheil in 1840 which was published in 1859. However, a systematic geological study could begin only from 1870. Thereafter, a number of geological notes were published in the *Records and Memoirs of the Geological Survey of India* and *London Geological Magazin*' (*cf.* Lal, 1976). Since 1958, the Geological Survey of India has been doing a detailed study about geology and mineral resources of the islands. Most of the physiographic information on the Andaman Islands mentioned below, has been sourced from Sen (1962) and Lal (1976).

Oldham (1885) has distinguished two sedimentary formations besides serpentine series – Port Blair series and Archipelago series. In the Port Blair series, the rock types are grey sandstone with interbedded shales, frequently consisting of nests of coaly matter and occasionally beds of conglomerate and pale grey limestone as subsidiary members. The Archipelago series, as the name implies, is dominant in the islands of the Archipelago group. It consists of soft limestone formed of coral, shell and soft calcareous sandstones and soft white clay with occasional bands of conglomerates. Tipper (1904-5) put these series to Eocene (Lower Lutetian) and Miocene formations, respectively. Altogether five formations have been distinguished in the Andaman Islands. These are Pre-tertiary, Cretaceous, Eocene (Lower Lutetian), Miocene Burdigalian, Miocene, recent and sub-recent formations. Of all the formations, the Eocene rocks are most widely prevalent. They occupy the three main islands, i.e. North, Middle and South Andaman Islands. The conglomerate is common in the North Andaman and some parts of the Middle Andaman, while sandstone is common in the South Andaman.

Physiography of the Andaman and Nicobar Islands is dominated by the mountain ranges. The Andaman Islands consist of three parallel ranges, which are, in fact, a continuation of the Arakan Yoma arc—running from the Pataki Range in north-east India to Sumatra Island in Southeast Asia. These ranges run through the islands from north and north-east to south and south-west in an arcuate shape. Along the east coast, the Saddle Range of the North Andaman continues in the Middle Andaman and passes through the Baratang Island to form the Harriet Range of the South Andaman (Figure 2.3). The western range passes through the west coast of Andaman Islands. In the west coast of North Andaman, it forms a series of detached islets as West Islet, Paget Islet, Interview Island, Flat Islet and finally forms the west coast range of South Andaman which continues in the south to form Tarmugli and other small islets. In between the two parallel ranges is Cholunga Range. Cholunga Range and its continuation up to the Ranger Island are one of the highest ranges of the Andaman Islands, attaining a maximum height of 434.64 m at Mt. Ford peak in Rutland. It runs through the middle of South Andaman, where on both its sides are longitudinal bays. Further, the range runs along the west coast of the Middle Andaman and merges into the Ranger Island. The

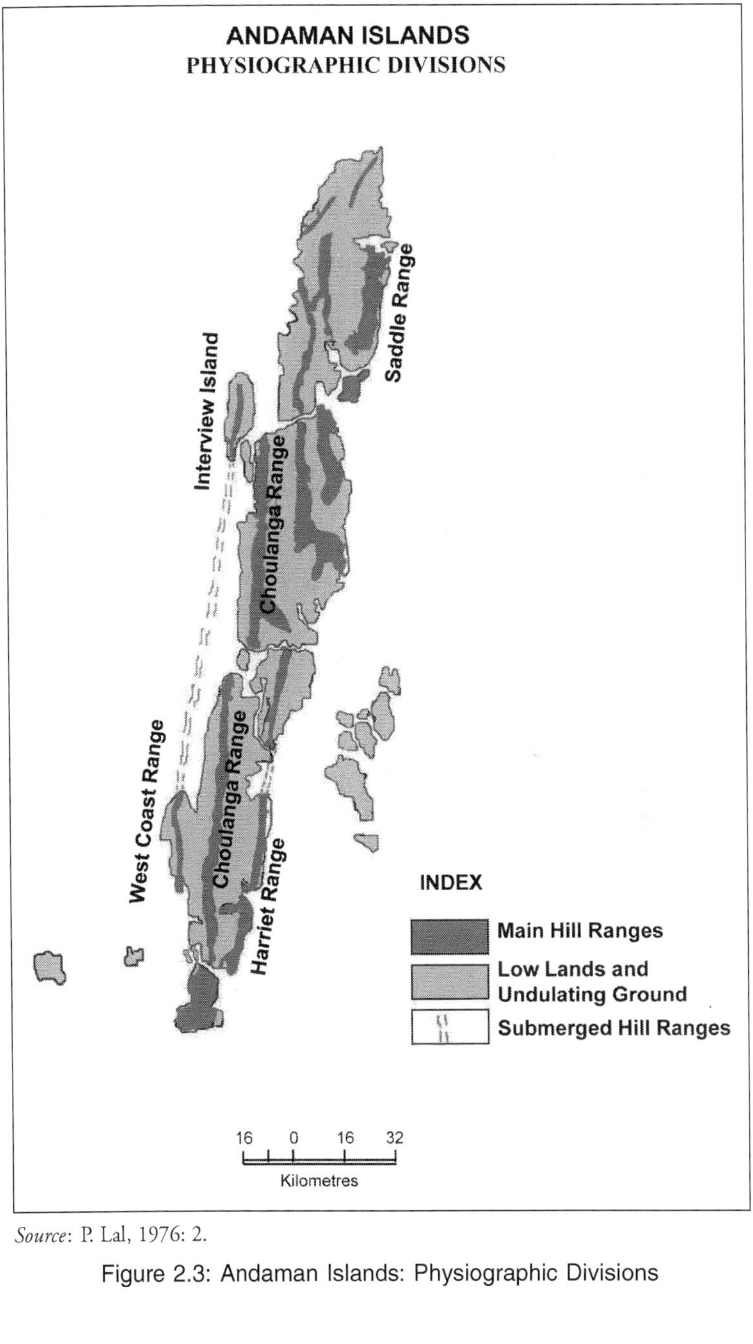

Source: P. Lal, 1976: 2.

Figure 2.3: Andaman Islands: Physiographic Divisions

series of parallel ranges have given rise to ridge and valley topography in the islands. In between the mountain ranges lie the longitudinal bays into which a number of very short distances torrential streams flow from both sides.

In general, the hill ranges are low in height, never exceeding 762 m and they send out spurs in all directions. The highest peak in the whole of the archipelago is the Saddle Peak (732.12 m) in the North Andaman. On average, the east coast ranges are steeper than the west coast ranges. All these ranges are under the deep mantle of forest cover. In between the East-West Range of North and Middle Andaman Islands and Harriet Range continuation in the North, lie the Blair Bay, Kalpong Bay, Kalara Bay, Congo Bay, etc., in the North Andaman and Betapur river valley and Bomlungta river valley in the Middle Andaman.

A profile across North Andaman from west to east gives an idea of the nature of terrain of the Andaman Islands. In the west coast up to Kalara Sea Creek, the relief is undulating. Here the topography is dominated by parallel hills of moderate elevations and narrow valleys. To the east of Kalara Creek, the land for some distance rises gently and then steeply to the highest point at the Saddle Peak (732.12 m). To the east of the Saddle Peak, the slope is very steep and the steepness continues even under the sea after a narrow continental shelf.

The relief of Andaman Islands is striking because, nowhere, the elevation is more than 732.12 m, which is the culminating point in the entire Andaman and Nicobar group of islands. This height is attained by the Saddle Peak along the east coast of the North Andaman. The general elevations of the hills ranges in the Andaman Islands vary from 76.2 m to 381 m (Figure 2.4). A number of ridges and spurs jut out from these hill ranges that enclose narrow and flat valleys and at places have been cut up by streams and their tributaries. The valleys are usually below 15.24 m in their lower part while in the upper part the valleys pass through areas of difficult terrain. Narrow stretches of plain land is available at few places. The hills in most places descend steeply to the water.

A continental shelf that dips steeply seaward bound the seaward

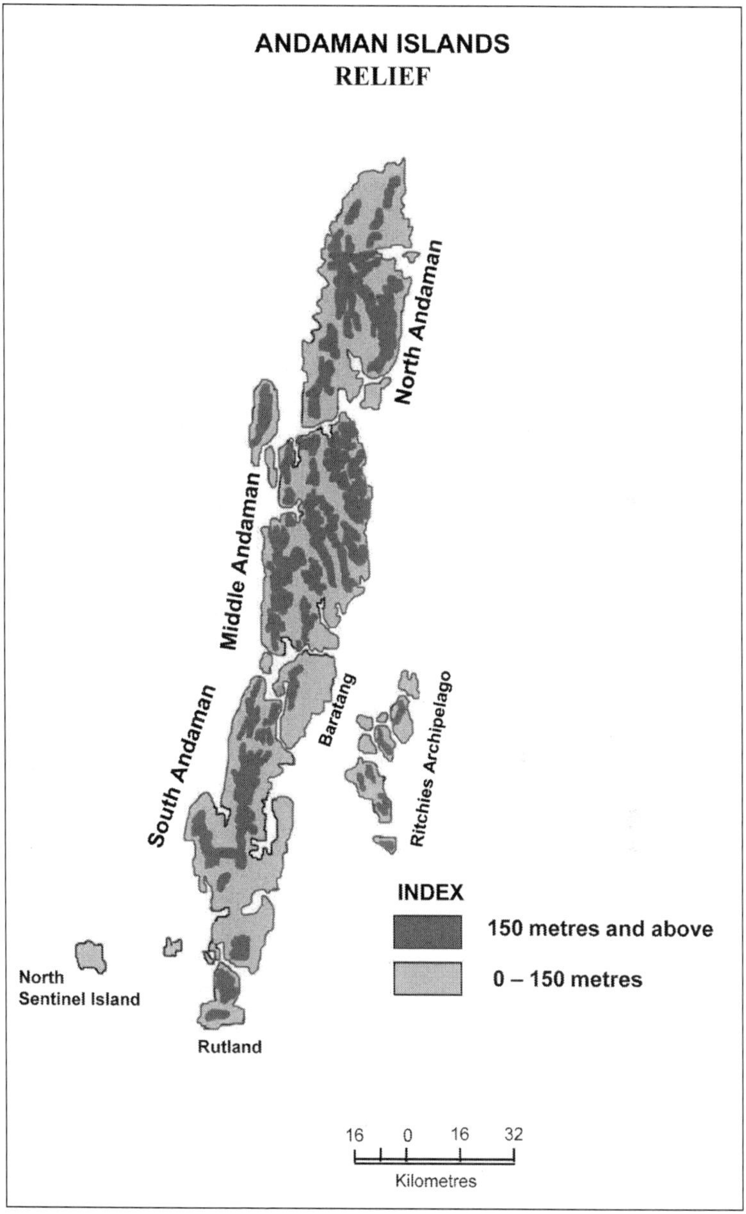

Source: P. Lal, 1976: 4.

Figure 2.4: Andaman Islands: Relief

edge of the Andaman and Nicobar Islands. The continental shelf is wider on the western side than on the eastern side. The western side has several coral banks in the Andaman Islands. The rate of growth and extent of corals formation are richer on the western side than on the eastern side of Andaman Islands. The coral reefs on the west are considered as barrier reefs. On the eastern side, the coral reefs are fringing type. The coastline is highly indented and at many places penetrates the island to make inland bays and deep creeks. Protected harbours are mostly along the east coast of the island. Thus, a wider continental shelf, indented coast and barrier reef provide an ideal breeding and nesting place for many marine resources which are harvested by the different population groups, particularly the Jarawa.

SOILS

The soils of the Andaman Islands have either developed *in situ* on the hill ranges or in the valleys by the materials derived from the hills by erosion and deposited in the valleys or along the sea coast. The following are the three major soil types:

1. *Sandy soils*: This soil type consists chiefly of sand and shingle, mostly calcareous, lumps of old coral and broken shells uplifted by the action of wind and waves just above the reach of high tides. It is extremely porous and the streams coming down the hills disappear here to emerge again at sea level or in the sea. This formation is limited to the sea coast and usually occurs as narrow strips.
2. *Clay and loamy soils*: This soil type occurs in the valleys and the lower slopes of the ridges up to a height of about 76.2 m from the sea level. It is rarely found beyond 91.44 m. This soil is formed by the disintegration of indurated clays and shales, limestones and conglomerates. The soil varies from clayey loam to a coarse rubbly sandy loam and is very shallow in some places. There is no trace of visible humus. It is rich when it is dry and water is less in the dry season.

3. *Hilly soils*: This consists of stiff clayey soil of dark red loam overlying micaceous sandstones. It is moist throughout the year and numerous perennial springs issue from it.

In general, it can be said that the soils of different parts of the Andaman Islands contain a high amount of clay, and are of silty clay to loamy in texture. The refugee population has been settled in the valleys where clay and loamy soil are found and thus conducive for agriculture.

CLIMATE

The location of the Andaman Islands between 10°30' and 13°30' North latitudes makes the climate of the islands tropical which closely approximates to the equatorial climate. The insular position of the islands in the Bay of Bengal in between two land masses in the east and west, location in the tropical zone along the path of travelling tropical storms and cyclones in specific months, considerable north-south extension, broken coastline and peculiar arcuate shape, and the dominant functional control of the south-west and north-east monsoons in the specific months of the year, all together have a combined influence on the climate of the Andaman Islands to give it a distinct feature. With the help of the temperature, rainfall and humidity the peculiarity of the climate of the Andaman has been explained.

TEMPERATURE

The islands have very little annual variation in temperature. The annual mean maximum temperature varies from 29° to 30.5°C and mean minimum from 23.5°C to 25°C and mean annual temperature from 26°C to 27.5°C. The relative humidity is also very high and the average is 80 per cent (Basu 1993). The high temperature coupled with the high relative humidity gives rise to a high sensible temperature. The weather is always warm and very sultry but is ameliorated to some extent by the pleasant sea breezes.

Humidity

The relative humidity varies from 63 to 90 per cent. The highest humidity occurs from May to November, i.e. during the south-west monsoon and the beginning of the north-east monsoon. The lowest humidity is from December to February when it varies from 72 per cent to 75 per cent. The annual variation is about 15 per cent (India Meteorology Department 2003). Comparatively, the humidity in the south is more than in the north.

Rainfall

The islands experience good rainfall from both the south-west and north-east monsoons. The average annual rainfall is 3,400 mm. The highest annual rainfall recorded during the last 60 years is 3,810 mm and the lowest is 2,130 mm (India Meteorology Department 2003). The south-west monsoon brings the maximum amount of rainfall. It begins from the third week of May and ends in October. The south-west region experiences the maximum amount of rainfall because it comes first under the direct impact of the south-west monsoon. This greater amount of rainfall helps in the development of dense tropical vegetation on the western coast. The south-west monsoon bursts over South Andaman by about 20 May, accompanied by thunder and rain. The two periods of maximum precipitation are from May to June, and from August to September, which correspond to the beginning and the termination of the south-west monsoon. Rainfall from the north-east monsoon begins in the month of October, whereas, the months of January and February are almost rainless in the northern stations.

Seasons

As mentioned earlier, there is not much monthly variation in temperature of the Andaman Islands but there is seasonal variability in rainfall. Despite the equable nature of the climate round the year, four seasons are experienced in the islands mainly due to the mechanism of the south-west and north-east monsoons. Moreover, the seasons govern the availability and distribution of certain prey animal species including their nesting and hatching periods, for example, the turtles nest and hatch from November to

February, particularly along the western coast. In accordance with seasons, the Jarawa regulate their movement over space to avail the seasonal resources. The four seasons are as follows:

1. Cool season	From December to February
2. Hot season	From March to mid-May
3. South-west monsoon season	From mid-May to mid-October
4. Post-south-west monsoon season	From mid-October to November

STREAMS

The Andaman Islands is traversed by innumerable streams. The drainage is influenced by the nature and amount of rainfall, the extent of the catchment area and the character of rocks through which they flow. The copious rainfall and hilly terrains help form short and swift streams capable of vigorous erosion. These streams form a close network of drainage over the whole island. The water divide of the Andaman Islands runs in a north-south direction separating the drainage systems of the east coast from that of the west coast. From the main water divide, minor divides shoot off, thus dividing the whole region into a number of drainage basins. Because of the seasonal rainfall, the water level of the streams goes down in the dry season, hence most of the rivers either do not have any water or only a trickle of water. Little water in the rivers may also be partly due to the porous nature of the soils and rocks, whereas perennial streams are mostly confined to the eastern part of the Andaman Islands, thus favouring the establishment of more of human settlements along the eastern coast.

The Middle Andaman Island has only a few small rivers and important among them are the Betapur and Bamlangta rivers. Both of them originate from the hill ranges that are a continuation of Mt. Harriet Range and flow through the longitudinal valleys. The Betapur River and its tributaries drain almost the whole of the north eastern part of the Middle Andaman. A noteworthy feature of the drainage system of these islands is that the perennial rivers are very few. For the aboriginal populations, including the Jarawa, both perennial and non-perennial rivers are very important as the water points are one of the deciding factors for the setting of their camps. It means their camps are wet point camps.

FORESTS

Forests are in abundance in the Andaman Islands except in the areas that have been cleared for settlement and agricultural needs of the settlers. About 77.80 per cent (6,682.17 sq km) of the total area of the Andaman Islands is still covered with thick forests. The original forest cover in many areas has been modified. The growing settlements around Port-Blair, Rangat, Mayabander and Diglipur areas in the South, Middle and North Andaman have encroached upon the forest reserve. Of the total area under forest (6,353.24 sq km) in the Andaman Islands, 86 per cent is reserved, 1 per cent is protected, 5 per cent is unclassified and 8 per cent is under the 'Jarawa Reserve' (Basu 1993). The following are the administrative divisions of the forest:

1. Reserved Forests: These forests cover an area of 5410.74 sq km or 86 per cent of the total forest area of the Andaman Islands.
2. Protected Forests: These forests cover 53.35 sq km. The forests of South Andaman have been declared as 'protected forests' by the government.
3. Unclassified Forests: These forests cover 355.35 sq km.
4. Jarawa Tribal Reserve: About 765 sq km of forests have been reserved for the Jarawa in the South and the Middle Andaman Islands along the western coast.

The forests of the Andaman Islands can be broadly divided into two categories based on edaphic and climatic factors. Based on edaphic factors, three broad forest divisions are (i) tidal forests (mangrove forest), (ii) beach forests, and (iii) riverine forests (low-level evergreen forests). Based on climatic factors two major types of forests are (i) moist deciduous forests, and (ii) wet evergreen forests. Except for the areas cleared for settlements and small Islets which are devoid of natural vegetation, the entire landmass of the islands is covered with lush green forests – a characteristic of the humid and warm tropics.

FOREST TYPES

The standard and most detailed classification of Andaman forests has been given by H.G. Champion (1936). Later, Champion and Seth (1968) gave a revised classification of forest types. They distinguished altogether 14 types of natural vegetation. Some of the forest types merge into each other imperceptibly, hence difficult to identify, whereas others offer a distinct contrast, and can be discerned easily. Major forest types as identified by the Department of Forest have been shown in Figures 2.5, 2.6 and 2.7.

Low Mangrove Forest and High Mangrove Forest

These two types of tidal forests occupy marshy alluvium and stiff clays inundated by salt water. They extend as far as the highest reach of the tide along the sheltered sea coast and up the creeks as far as the influence of the salt water is felt. The low mangrove forests, which form more or less dense evergreen belts, are characterised by *Rhizophora mucronota* and *Rhizophora congugata* species that extend farthest into the sea and take the full blast of the tidal currents. These forests do not grow more than 7 m in height. Next to the low level mangrove belt is found a belt of high mangrove forests which are spread in the higher reaches of the tidal creeks where influence of the freshwater is also felt. The predominant species of the high level mangrove forests are *Brugviera gymnorhiza* and *Brugviera paruiflora.* They grow gregariously and attain a height of 13 m to 21.33 m.

Beach Forest

Beach forests form a narrow belt just above the high tide level in the Andaman Islands. The soil of this belt consists of sands, shingles, shells fragments, etc., and is poorest in mineral contents except for lime. This soil is coarse, porous and more or less dry at the surface. Beach forests are locally known as *Mohwakhari* and have a fairly high girth and a long clear bole. The main species of beach forests are *Colophyllum inophyllum, Terminalia catapa*, etc.

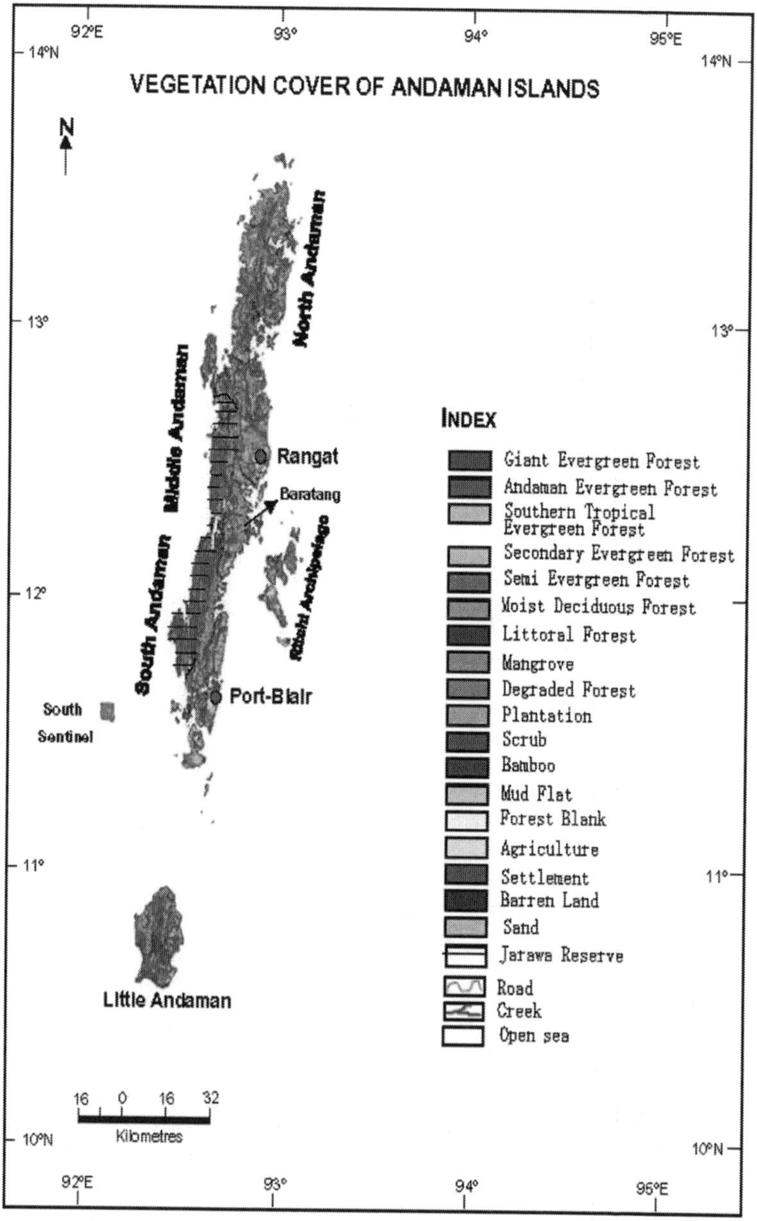

Source: Indian Institute of Remote Sensing, Dehradun, 2006.

Figure 2.5: Vegetation Cover of Andaman Islands

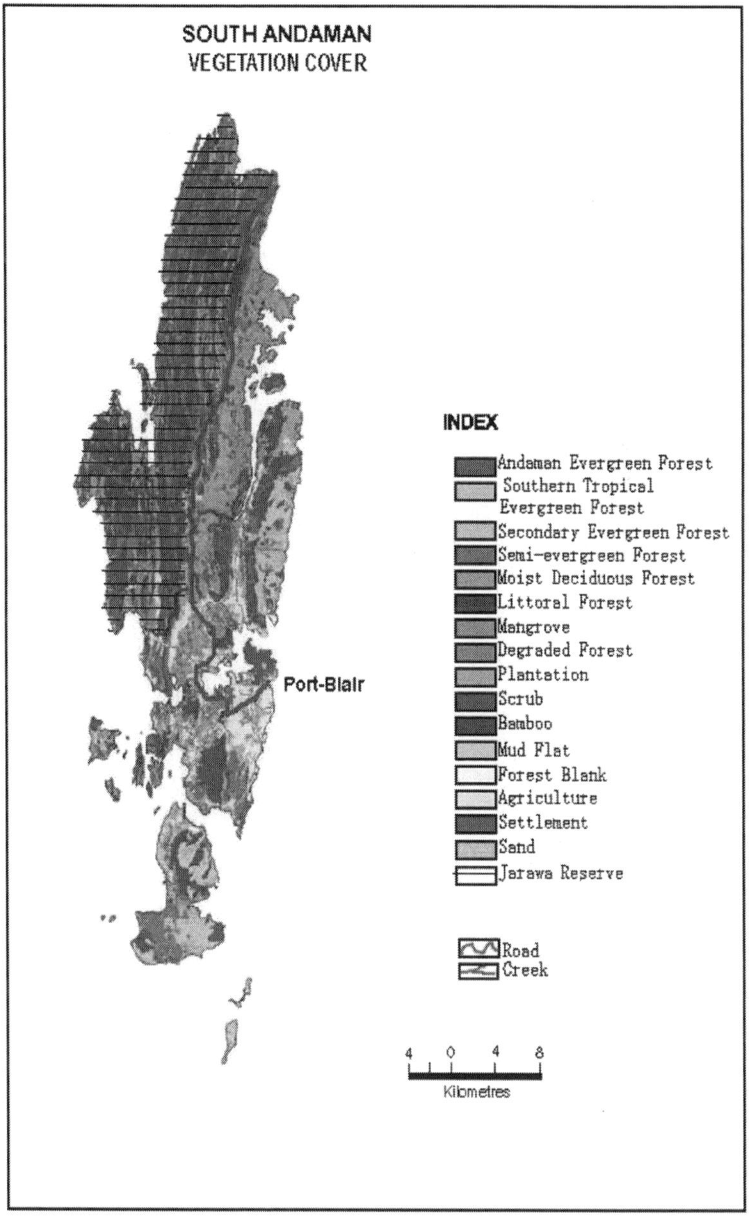

Source: Indian Institute of Remote Sensing, Dehradun, 2006.

Figure 2.6: South Andaman: Vegetation Cover

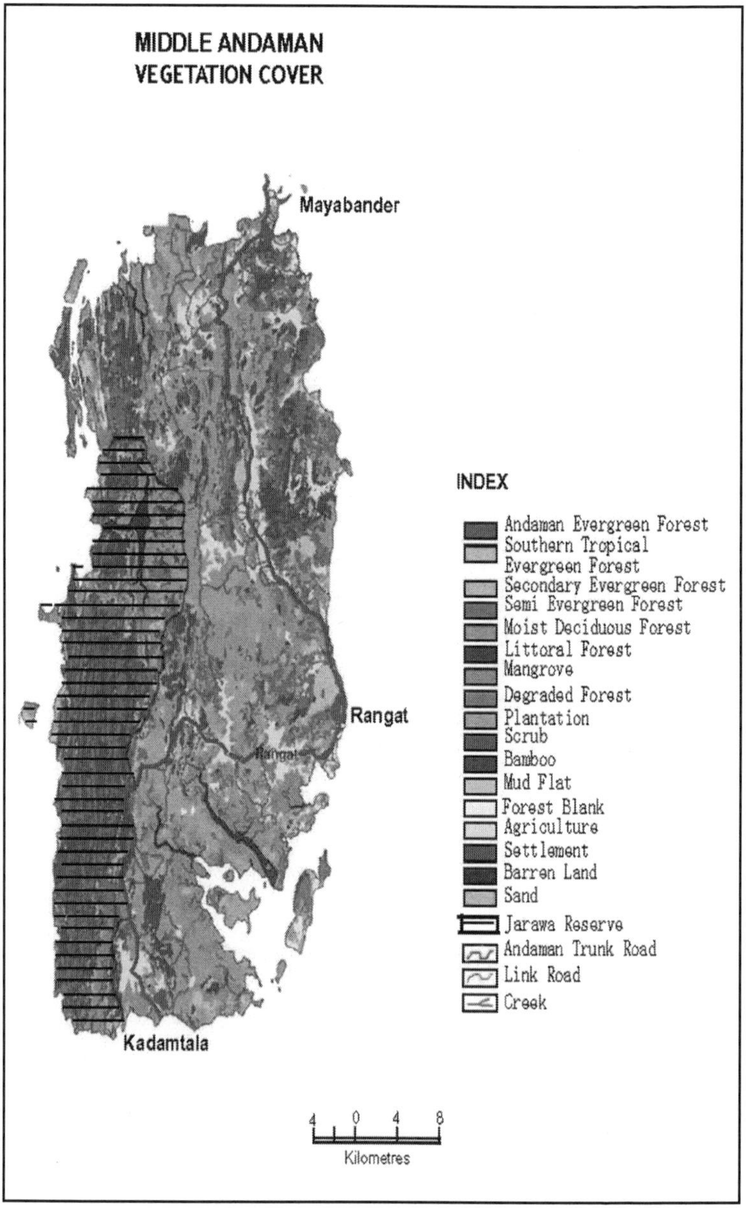

Source: Indian Institute of Remote Sensing, Dehradun, 2006.

Figure 2.7: Middle Andaman: Vegetation Cover

Southern Tropical Moist Deciduous Riverine Forest

This type forms a very small percentage of the forests of these islands being confined to the well-drained alluvium near the banks of the big streams. It grows in the areas characterised by gravelly, sandy and very loose textured soils. The predominant species are *Pyinma, Thitkando*, etc.

Southern Tropical Semi-evergreen Riverine Forest

In the Andaman Islands, these forests are found typically on all alluvial soils along the banks of large freshwater streams which are sufficiently raised above the flood level and are, therefore, fairly well drained having a good sub-soil water supply. The soil is clayey and sufficiently old to let vegetation progress to a climatic climax. The principal species in these forests is *Dipterocarpus alatus*, which grows to the largest size amongst Gurjans (*Dipterocarpus spp.*), often reaching a girth of 9.14 m at breast height and a clear bole of about 304.8 m. Other tree species of importance in these forests are *Sterculia companulata, S. alata, Terminalia procera, T. biolata*, etc. The trees are found scattered and the ground floor is densely covered by shrubs, bamboos, climbers and cane breakers forming a thick tangle of vegetation.

Secondary Moist Bamboo Brakes

This type of forest occurs usually in the upper parts of steep hill slopes, particularly on their hotter (sunny) sides. It is found characteristically in parts of the North Andaman Island along the higher ridges of Saddle Range. This type of forest consists of a gregarious growth of bamboo brakes with a few scattered trees of *Dipterocarpus turbinatus, Terminalia procera, Sterculia companulata*, etc.

Andaman Moist Deciduous Forest

This is the subsidiary edaphic type of moist tropical forest, locally known as the *Padauk* (*Pterocarpus dalbergioides*), which is found on the undulating surface and gentle slopes up to about 91.44 m in height and covers about 45 per cent of the total area of the Andaman. *Padauk* is the most important timber species of these forests. There are many other valuable deciduous species such as *Terminalia biolata, T. procera, Canarium euphyllum*, etc., and a number of species valuable to the match, plywood and packing case industries.

Cane Brakes

They grow in dense shadows and wet hollows where the soil is permanently wet, consisting of fine clay rich in humus. This type of forest mostly grows in association with evergreen and semi-evergreen climaxes than the deciduous ones. It forms an impenetrable thicket of long trailing stems with a few erect species also. Some of the important species of cane present in these brakes are *Calamus andamanicus, Calamus pheuborivalsis, Calamus palustris*, etc. The creeping bamboo is also invariably found there.

Southern Wet Bamboo Brakes

This type is also connected with the evergreen and semi-evergreen climaxes along sheltered valleys. Dense clumps of *Oxylenanthera nigso-ciliata* are found with scattered trees of *Dipterocarpus incanus, Planchonia andamanica, Pisonia excelsa*, etc.

Southern Moist Bamboo Brakes

This type grows on the moist shady and gentle slopes. The species forming such brakes are *Oxylenanthera nigsociliata* with scattered trees of *Dipterocarpus incanus, andamanica, Pisonia excelsa, Hopea odonata*, etc.

Southern Tropical Semi-evergreen Forest

This type of forest is found more or less in transitional pre-climax form, between the tropical evergreen and the moist deciduous forms. It is not as dense as the southern tropical semi-evergreen riverine type, though it resembles it very much in its floristic composition. It has a mixture of both the evergreen and deciduous trees, the former predominating.

Southern Low Tropical Evergreen Forest

This type is found in steep hill slopes exposed to strong winds and having a hard, reddish-brown, infertile thin layer of soil. In the region where it is found, there is usually heavy rainfall of over 2,540 mm and very often, the atmosphere is cloudy and misty. It is typically found on the steep slopes of Saddle Hill and surrounding peaks in North Andaman, Mt. Ferrington in Middle Andaman, etc. The characteristic feature of this type is the presence of stunted trees which rarely exceed 9.14 m in height and 0.9 m in girth. The floristic composition in the overhead canopy is of *Dipterocarpus costatus, Mesua ferras, Canarium mannii,* etc.

Eastern Tropical Evergreen Forest

This type forms the climax vegetation in areas of heavy rainfall having more or less shallow soil overlying serpentine intrusions. It is found on the steeper slopes of the higher ridges where the tree growth is less luxuriant than in the evergreen *Dipterocarpus* type.

Evergreen Dipterocarpus Forest

Andaman forests reach their climax in this type of forest and it constitutes the most luxuriant evergreen forests of the islands. These forests are found on the high hill slopes and ridges in which outcrops of igneous rocks predominate. The rainfall here is the heaviest being well over 3040.8 mm per annum. The soil consists of a deep clayey loam which is always wet, having a thick humus layer. The principal tree species is *Dipterocarpus grandiflorus* which attains maximum height and growth among the trees in the Andaman island ecosystem.

Characteristics of Andaman Forests

The dense forests consist of a tangled mass of climbers, lianas, canes, bamboos, etc. Mangrove forests are confined to low lying banks of creeks and sheltered portions of the coastline subject to tidal action. On the uppermost part of the higher hills and sometimes on steep slopes with poor soils, which are usually exposed to speedy winds, the vegetation is comparatively stunted in growth. Such areas contain mainly bushes, shrubs and stunted trees, which are not presently of commercial importance. In various types of forests, excluding mangroves, the trees grow in an intimate mixture of different species, many of which are of commercial importance.

In virgin deciduous forests, fresh regeneration and the younger age classes are practically absent except to a small extent in giant evergreen and Andaman tropical evergreen forests. The reason for this is that in deciduous forests, the top storey trees are deciduous whereas vegetation below the top storey is often evergreen. Without human assistance, the deciduous species would find it difficult to regenerate themselves through this evergreen under storey. In fact, the climax vegetation of the Andaman Islands belongs to the giant evergreen forests.

The lack of gregariousness in the Andaman forest is well known. An absolute preponderance of one species or even an assemblage of species rarely marks the floral landscape on these islands. There are several key features of the tropical rainforest ecology of the Andaman Islands, some of which are as follows:

1. The tropical rain forests of the Andaman Islands have one of the most productive terrestrial ecosystems with very high gross and net primary productivity;
2. It is extremely efficient in rapidly cycling most of the nutrients; and
3. It has a very great biomass.

A notable feature of the resource availability in the tropical rain forest is that the species with edible parts are widely dispersed. It is, therefore, implied that the tropical rain forest environment of the islands is extremely diverse floristically. The members of a particular species tend to be widely dispersed than clumped together. In addition, there are limited numbers of edible plant species. It is also reflected in the dietary composition of the Jarawa. The

Jarawa, despite inhabiting an ecosystem with the diverse biotic environment, rely upon a limited range of edible plants. However, there are enough non-edible plant resources to meet their other requirements.

FAUNA

Despite the abundance of forests in the Andaman Islands, wildlife is peculiarly deficient throughout them. The deficiency is more pronounced concerning mammals. There are only 20 identified species of mammals, of which again about 12 are peculiar to these islands. The Andaman species of mammals and birds differ significantly from those of the adjacent islands like Nicobar, Sumatra and Java, etc.

Mammals

The Andaman Islands are endowed with rich floristic composition but they are poor in faunal wealth. The large mammals and monkeys are entirely absent from the Andaman Islands. The largest indigenous wild mammal is only the Andaman pig (*Sus andamanensis*) which is much smaller than the mainland pig. The other indigenous mammal found in the islands is the civet cat (*Paguma larvata tytlery*). Bats and rats constitute nearly three-fourths of the known mammals. A number of deer species were introduced in these islands in the early 1920s. Of these, the spotted deer (*Axis axis*) has acclimatised well and spread in almost all the islands. Barking deer (*Muntiacus muntjak*) has also survived on these islands, and have been breeding successfully but they are comparatively rare. Hog deer (*Axis porcinus*) have also been reported on the islands but they are rare. Of the introduced mammals, another interesting species is the wild goat on Barren Island. Queerly enough, they have adapted to saline water. Two marine mammals, viz., sea cow (*Dugong dugong*) and dolphins (*Dolphinus dolphis*) are found in the surrounding sea waters. While dolphins can be seen very frequently, the *dugong* is very rare. All mammals, except deer, are an invaluable source of food for the tribal peoples of the Andaman Islands.

Reptiles and Amphibians

There are several lizards and snakes species including the viper and cobra inhabiting the island ecosystem. However, cobras are very rare. Salt water crocodiles (*Crocodiles palustris*) are widely distributed in almost all the creeks and backwaters. Among the reptiles, only monitor lizards are game animals for the tribes of the Andaman Islands.

Birds

The Andaman Islands are not very rich in bird fauna, but there are a few species indigenous to these islands, which are rare and quite interesting. Amongst birds, the Andaman green pigeon, hawk, eagle, scarlet minivet, black head bulbul, white head mynah and Indian cuckoo are common. Based on his survey and the recorded evidence available, Abdulali (1962) has listed 112 species and sub-species of birds. The list also includes several introduced species that have adapted to the environmental setup of the islands. Birds are occasionally eaten by the Negrito tribal population.

COASTAL ENVIRONMENT

In terms of an assemblage of animal species, the Andaman and Nicobar Islands occupy a unique position. They are close to the 'Indo-Malayan Region' which is considered to be a 'faunastic centre' from which other sub-divisions of the Indo-West Pacific region recruited their fauna (Tikader et al. 1986). Therefore, some of the typical Indo-West Pacific groups of animals are found on these islands. Some of the animals are giant clams (*Tridacnidae*) among molluscs and sea moths (*Pegasidae*), whitings (*Silligindae*), rabbit fish (*Siganidae*) and plesiopdae (*Plesiopidae*) among fishes. There are many more such marine animals. Although the islands have a great diversity of marine fauna, many groups are yet to be identified in detail. The Andaman sea is in the tropical belt. With an area of 0.602×10^6 km^2 (average depth of 106 m) and enclosing water of the volume of $0.660 \times 10 \times$ km^3 (Tikader et al. 1986:

14), it provides a vast ecosystem for the existence of rich marine life that can be converted into resources for various uses. The intertidal and neritic zones of the Andaman Islands, together called as the coastal sea, are the happy abodes of almost four fifths of all the plants and animals. They are abode to a variety of fish, molluscs, crustaceans and reptiles. Around the islands, the littoral and sublittoral zones are occupied by underwater coral populations, which display the flamboyancy of tropical life. The seashore of Andaman Islands can be divided into rocky, sandy and muddy shores. It is often interspersed with mangrove vegetation.

Rocky Shore

In several of the islands, the coasts are rocky. The life forms on the rocky shore are mainly governed by the tides. The sea animals found in the rocky shore zone are limpets, chitons, neritides, top shells, turban shells and certain species of crabs, molluscs and shrimps.

Sandy Shore

The flourishing of life on the sandy shores is not so marked as on rocky shore. The fauna of sandy beaches are *polychaetes*, molluscs, amphipods, *sea-anemones*, etc. *Polychaetes* of the phylum *Annelida* are the most abundant of the sandy intertidal animals. Among crustaceans, the dominance of copepods has been seen. Other important crustaceans are snapping shrimps, fiddler crabs, bivalve shells, cockles, and calms. The turtles prefer to visit the sandy shores during the winter season to lay eggs.

Muddy Shore

The muddy shores have developed where sea currents are slow and weak, allowing settling of fine particles on the relatively calm beaches. Such conditions are found in sheltered bays and in the mouths of coastal streams. The fauna of muddy shore consists predominantly of pelecypod molluscs, worms, a few crustaceans and some fish that spend at least part of their lives in the habitats below the ground.

MANGROVES

Two types of forest, namely mangroves or tidal swamps and littoral forests or beach forests influence seashore topography of the islands. The mangrove ecosystem supports many brackish water and freshwater fishes. Many of the animals of mangroves are common to mudflats. These include different types of crustaceans like fiddler crabs and hermit crabs. Among molluscs gastropods, bivalves and edible oyster are common. It can be said that the paucity of terrestrial fauna is compensated by the abundance and diversity of marine animals. In fact, the coastal zones are the major food gathering zones for the tribal peoples of the Andaman and Nicobar Islands. Interestingly, the Jarawa do not relish the sea cucumbers which are available in abundance near the shore.

THE PEOPLE

A discussion on the physical environment of the Andaman ecosystem will remain incomplete if the people of the islands are not mentioned. An ecological study of the people of the Andaman Islands is rendered extremely interesting by virtue of the great diversity of the people inhabiting the island ecosystem. The Andaman Islands have found a place in the accounts of sailors, travellers and traders from long past like that of Ptolemy in the second century, of the Chinese in the seventh century, of the Arabs in ninth century, and the Europeans in the thirteen century (Mathur 1968: 7). However, a systematic and detailed account about the islands and the people has been found since 1858 when the British occupied these islands the second time to establish the penal settlement. In the post-Independence period, some detailed studies were carried out on the environment and people of the Andaman Islands (Majumdar 1975, Pandit 1974, 1976, and 1989, Sarkar 1985 and 1987, Sarkar 1987, 1990, 1993 and 1996). In the post-1998 phase, the major works are by Sreenathan (2001), Mukho-padhaya et al. (2002) and Sakseria and Pandya (2010).

The Andaman and Nicobar Islands are home to six tribal groups, namely the Sentinelese, the Jarawa, the Onge, the Great Andamanese, the Shompen and the Nicobarese. Of the six tribal groups, the first four tribal groups belong to the Negrito stock (Plates 2.1, 2.2, 2.3, and 2.4) while the latter two belong to the Mongoloid stock. Interestingly, the Andaman Islands are home to the Negrito people while the Nicobar Islands are to the Mongoloid people.

Before the colonisation of these islands by the British, particularly after 1857, the Andaman Islands were the exclusive abode of the Negrito people. However, it was only at the end of the eighteenth century, with the attempt of the formation of the settlements and later, of the penal settlement, that there could begin an influx of the foreign people, mainly from different parts of mainland India. Since these people were from different parts of India, their diverse social and cultural traits gave a character of heterogeneity to the human fabric of the islands. In the post-Independence period, the settlement of the refugees from the erstwhile East Bengal and some of the people from south India took place in the islands. It was mostly at the displeasure of the tribal (Negrito) people. Hence, the people of the Andaman Islands could now be divided into two groups, viz., the tribal (also referred as aboriginal) and the non-tribal people.

Source: Anthropological Survey of India.

Plate 2.1: A group of Sentinelese receiving coconut from the contact party

Source: Anthropological Survey of India.

Plate 2.2: A Jarawa family

Source: Anthropological Survey of India.

Plate 2.3: An Onge couple

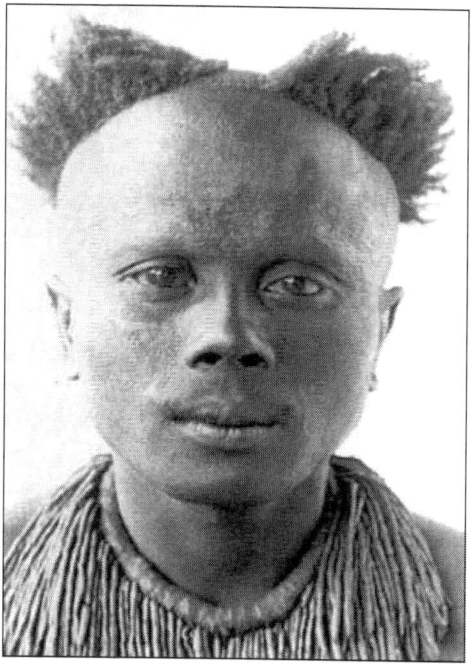

Source: Anthropological Survey of India.

Plate 2.4: A Great Andamanese man

THE NEGRITO PEOPLE

Nothing more deserves a special note on the islands than the Negrito population. Because of the insular nature of the islands, the Negrito population is considered as one of the purest. Their way of life may be considered as the living form of the most ancient way of life. They are short in stature; their skin is black and their hair frizzy. There is some biological and cultural affinity of these tribes with the Negrito groups of Southeast Asia like, the Semang of Malaysia Peninsula and the Aeta of Philippines. Thus, it is believed that Andaman Negrito groups migrated to their present habitat from Southeast Asia in the remote past either by sea or by land route. Nevertheless, evidence to establish this hypothesis is not yet sufficient. Regarding distribution of the four Negrito tribes on different islands of the Andaman, there are a number of assumptions, but all these have a common proposition that for their nomadic nature either these tribes moved to different islands or some of them drifted to present habitat by the sea waves while moving from one place to another in canoes. Their movement further south below Little Andaman was most probably hindered because of the presence of fast flowing turbulent ocean currents at 10° North latitude which is also known as 10° Channel.

The intrusion and decades of contact with the non-tribal population have brought about a rapid impoverishment and decline of two of the Negrito groups of the islands, i.e. the Onges and Great Andamanese. The other Negrito population, i.e. the Jarawa have been experiencing a gradual shrinkage in their total command area because of the gradual expansion of the area of influence of the new settlers. The Jarawa are today confined to the western part of the Middle and South Andaman Islands and the Onge in the Dugong Creek and South Bay areas of the Little Andaman. After the tsunami which struck the Andaman Islands on 26 December 2004, the Onge residing at the South Bay were also settled at the Dugong Creek. The Great Andamanese have been resettled at the Strait Island. They have the lowest population among all the tribal groups, i.e., 75 and the Sentinelese are on the North Sentinel Island with an estimated population of 100 souls only (Table 2.2). The relationship of the tribal people (Negrito group) with the outsiders have had been one of deep distrust and hostility, which has rightly been explained by Portman (1899) as an outcome of unfriendly attitude of the outsiders. While the Great Andamanese and the Onge were coerced to be friendly with the use of force during the colonial period, the relation with the other two Negrito groups continued to be sour even in the post-Independence period. Decades of friendly gestures by the Andaman Administration ultimately succeeded in befriending the Jarawa in 1997, but this is not the case with the Sentinelese. They are still outside the ambit of friendly relations. However, the acceptance of friendliness on the part of the Negrito group has proved to be a bane for them as their numbers have drastically decreased after the friendly contacts due to various reasons.

TABLE 2.2: TRIBAL POPULATION IN ANDAMAN AND NICOBAR ISLANDS

Tribes	Location	Population	Remarks
Great Andamanese	Strait Island	75	On the verge of extinction
Onge	Little Andaman	121	Earlier the Onge were settled at Dugong Creek and South Bay. After the tsunami, South Bay group has also been settled at Dugong creek.
Sentinelese	North Sentinel Islands	50*	No breakthrough till date in establishing a friendly relationship with them, but efforts are on.
Jarawa	Western coast of South and Middle Andaman Islands	534	Till 1997, they were unfriendly to outsiders.
Nicobarese	Car Nicobar, Chowra, Teresa, Nancowry, Katchal, Trinket and Great Nicobar	36,842**	Relatively well advanced.
Shompen	Great Nicobar	237	A shy tribe living in the interior.

Source: Directorate of Economics and Statistics 2007; Census 2011; AAJVS Records, 2019.

* Approximate population.

** Population figure as per 2011 census, while all other figures are as per AAJVS record 2019.

Antiquity of the Negrito People

The antiquity of the Jarawa or for that matter of the Negrito people of the Andaman Islands is still shrouded in mystery. In this regard, one has to depend on the materials obtained from the excavation of the kitchen midden sites (shell mounds), which are an assemblage of shells, pottery, implements, equipment, etc., buried in successive layers at Beehive Island and Chouldhary, and considered to be the earliest sites of human occupance of the islands (Man 1883, Portman 1899, Holland 1904, Cipriani 1966, and Dutta

1974). Chatterjee excavated one kitchen midden site at Beehive Island of Middle Andaman in 1952, and Cipriani also carried out study of the shell mounds (cf. Dutta 1974: 13-15). In comparison to the Beehive, *lithic* industry at this site was richer. Here the flakes were predominant (65 per cent) than core (2.03 per cent) and finished tools (32.93 per cent). On the basis of faunal evidence, flakes, etc., and comparing them with the blade industry found at different Toalean sites of Southeast Asia, Dutta (1974: 35-8) opined that the Andaman Islanders would not have arrived prior to 300-100 years BC. The radiocarbon dating of these materials put them to be 2,280 years old (Cooper 1990). The Mesolithic culture of the Andaman Islands was associated with the pottery. When the Andaman findings are compared with those of the Southeast Asian ones, it seems improbable that the bearers of this culture existed on the Andaman Islands earlier than 300 BC. It must be noted that pottery could be found in the Upper Toalean layer in Indonesia, allowing some time for the spread and drift of the culture, the Mesolithic culture '. . . possibly arrived in the Andaman Islands sometimes around the beginning of the Christian era . . .' (Dutta 1974, 35). Thus, the archaeological evidence suggests of a cultural link between the Andaman Islands and Southeast Asia around that period. Interestingly, the Great Andamanese oral tradition bears the memory of a period when they were inhabitants of a large landmass where there were many other people speaking the same language and large animals used to roam in that land. Then there was a great cataclysm that submerged the large mass of land with man and animals (Portman 1899: 8).

Genomic studies suggest that they arrived at these islands much earlier. The identification of M31 lineage among the tribal community of Andaman Islands establishes the proposition that Andaman islanders are descendants of the first humans to migrate out of Africa (Thangaraj et al. 2005). However, the later studies by the Anthropological Survey of India and others suggest that the Jarawa, the Great Andamanese and the Onge along with the Rajbanshi, the Paudi Bhuyan, the Munda, the Bhoi Khasi and the Savara belonged to the same stock, i.e., M31 lineage around ~45,000 years ago.

Around ~37,000 years ago, the Andaman tribal communities migrated toward Andaman Island (Palanichamy et al. 2006, Barik et al. 2008 and DNA Polymorphism Consortium 2018). Around 24,000 years ago, they gave rise to the sub-linage M32 in the Andaman Island (Barik et al. 2008).

The Jarawa

The tribal population of the Andaman and Nicobar group archipelago can be broadly divided into two categories, viz., Negrito and non-Negrito. The Negrito population of the Andaman Islands in yester years could be divided in three groups: the *ar-yoto* (coast dwellers), the *erem-taga* (jungle dwellers) and *adajig* (creek dwellers). The Jarawa were considered *erem-taga.* Interestingly, the group known to outsiders as the 'Jarawa' identifies itself as 'Ang'. It is generally agreed that the term 'Jarawa' originated from the *Aka-Bea-da* dialect, which means 'the other people'. During the colonial period, the Jarawa were given other names also such as, 'Jungli', 'Minicopie', 'Yerewa', 'Ya-eng-gna', etc. (Portman 1899: 701).

The Jarawa are one of the five PVTGs and one of the four Negrito groups of the Andaman Islands. Their habitation area, also known as 'Jarawa Reserve', is spread over the western part of the South and Middle Andaman Islands and measures approximately about 1,028 sq km (see Figure. 3.1 in Chapter 3). The total population of the Jarawa is 534 as per the last survey in March 2019 (AAJVS). They subsist through the hunting of wild animals, gathering of wild plant foods and fishing, with no domestication of plants and animals. The tools used for the collection of resources are simple, which include bow and arrow, fishing hand net, digging rod, metal knife, iron *dao* (a kind of chopper), wooden bucket and baskets. The resources are collected from both terrestrial and aquatic ecosystem. There are three territorial groups of the Jarawa, viz., Tanmad group, Thidong group and Boiab group (see Figure 3.1 in Chapter 3). The immediate neighbours of the Jarawa are the non-tribal population, who have also been referred to as 'non-Jarawa' in the present discussion.

The basic unit of the social organisation of the Jarawa is a band.

Members of a band are related by blood or by marriage and their numbers vary from fifteen to fifty persons. The Jarawa practice monogamy. Marriages are either inter-band or inter-territorial. Marriage between widow and widower is permitted. Most members of the local groups are related either through consanguinal or affinal relations. Children can be from an earlier marriage of the couple or born from present marriage. The community hut is shared by all the social units. The average family size comprises of four persons. Nuclear family is the norm. The community hut is the place where most of the economic and social activities take place. On attaining adulthood, the initiation ceremony, *lepa*, is observed. In the Jarawa society, every able bodied person above the age of 15 is an economically active member of the society supporting himself. There is no dependent population except the children.

The Jarawa are egalitarian. There is no formal leadership either at the band level or at the territory level. Seniors in the band are consulted for solving the disputes, organising foraging expeditions, etc. However, they have an informal political structure with regard to governing the rights of a territorial group over its territory. Individual tribesmen are free to forage within their territory. They are not supposed to transgress into the territory of other groups for foraging. In case some of their people are interested to forage in other's territory, they must meet the concerned group and seek their consent. Generally, the hosts escort the guests to pig hunting or honey collection and the foraged items are shared. Whenever a group or a person visits another area, the hosts take the chance of inviting them to forage with them, which is considered a gesture of hospitality. When the guests depart, it is a norm for the hosts to offer parting gifts like meat, honey, etc.

In the Jarawa society, except hunting of wid pig, there is no specific division of labour between males and females. Both males and females are found to be engaged in all kinds of foraging activities. Most of the gatherings including fishing is done by the womenfolk. Though men also take part in the gathering, it is comparatively less. Females bring in the bulk of edible resources. As regards the making of the foraging implements, it has been observed that the process of making some of these implements is gender-specific. For instance, hunting objects (like bow and arrow) are always made by the adult male folk while adult female folk makes the basket and fishing net. Both males and females make wooden buckets. The bows and arrows are exclusively used by the male Jarawa, while the fishing net is used by the female folk only.

The Jarawa, like many other hunter-gatherers, have the notion of the 'giving environment', that the land around them is the source of everything. Nature is seen as a living entity having a mystical force. They also believe in the existence of malevolent and benevolent spirits. The world of the Jarawa is a multi-layered world composed of two-layered planes: one exists above the present world which they inhabit while the other is underground. The above and below worlds of myth are in intimate contact with the normal plane of existence. The *shaman* possesses the mystical power to transcend the worlds of myth.

Non-Tribal People

In addition to the Negrito groups, the islands are also inhabited by those who came or were brought to the Andaman Islands after the arrival of the British. The convicts of the penal settlements have settled in these areas by bringing members of their families from the mainland or by getting married to the convict women. They are now called the 'local born'. The settlements of these people have grown exclusively in the South Andaman Island, particularly in Port Blair and the neighbouring villages. Despite having hailed from different parts of India and speaking different languages, they have become an integrated community and Hindi is their spoken language. Such formation of a homogenous community is verily an example of fusion under a given set of geographical setting, i.e. isolation of the islands from mainland India. Apart from them, a few groups of the Bhantus and the Mopillas and a few Burmese and Karens have also settled on these islands. Except for the Karens, who have settled through free enterprise in the northern part of the Middle Andaman Island, all other groups were brought to the islands to serve the terms of their conviction. After termination of colonial rule, very few of them opted to go back to their native place. However, all these groups have settled quite peacefully on these islands. Initially, agriculture was the basis of the economy. Now many of them are engaged in other enterprises (like service, business, transport, etc.). Besides, in the post-Independence period, many displaced families from the then East Bengal were resettled in different parts of the South, Middle and North Andaman Islands and were given lands for agriculture and horticulture. They are the immediate neighbours of the Jarawa.

CHAPTER 3

Inventory of Resources Used by the Jarawa

Human beings have varying needs and want. Various efforts are made by human beings to meet these needs. Resources are the means of satisfying those needs and wants. However, a natural thing or a substance does not become a resource unless man recognises its utility. In fact, it is the function of a thing or a substance in relation to human wants that makes it a resource. Zimmerman (1951), in his 'functional or operational theory of resources', has described that resources do not mean a thing or substance, but the function which a thing or substance may perform or the operation in which it may be used. While nature provides the necessary physical base for man's efforts in the creation of resources, the culture influences the environmental perception, preferences and decision making of a human group. Therefore, unless perceived as 'resource' a matter or substance remains part of nature. It is human perception that turns a thing or substance into a resource. In addition, the availability and seasonality of resources also determine the pattern of resource utilisation.

The Jarawa are a hunting and gathering community with a distinct culture. In order to meet their needs, they utilise different types of resources of the island ecosystem. It is, thus, important to understand how a hunting and gathering community like the Jarawa perceives resources in the island ecosystem. Before elucidating in detail the inventory of resources of the Jarawa, it is worth mentioning about the Jarawa and their territorial groups, as they are directly or indirectly related to the distribution and availability of resources.

TERRITORIAL GROUPS OF THE JARAWA

As stated previously, though the Jarawa are homogenous, there are three territorial groups among them. Before 2001, there was no information about the territorial division among them. A later study by the Anthropological Survey of India reported about the existence of three territorial groups among them. These territorial groups are *Tanmad*, *Thidong* and *Boiab* groups (Figure 3.1). The *Tanmad* group inhabits the south-western part of Middle Andaman Island (Kadamtala area), while the *Thidong* groups inhabit the north-western part of South Andaman (Middle Strait area) and the *Boiab* groups south-western part of the South Andaman Island (Tirur area). Territories of the *Boiab* (Tirur area) and *Thidong* (Middle Strait area) are contiguous to each other, only punctured by the inland creeks, while the third territory, i.e. *Tanmad*, is on a separate island. Besides, there are some buffer zones also, like Baratang Island, in between the *Thidong* and *Tanmad* areas. Resource acquisition in a particular territory by a particular group of the Jarawa is the basis for grouping the Jarawa into three territorial groups and demarcating their respective territories. Since the *Boiab* and *Thidong* territories are contiguous, it is difficult to draw a boundary between the two. However, to solve this problem, the huts of the Jarawa of both territories were plotted on the map and it was found that the 12° North latitude roughly divides them. The line, dividing the *Boiab* and *Thidong* territories, runs from Putatang on the eastern side to Petchhleg on the western side of the Jarawa territory.

The movement of different groups of the Jarawa is territory specific in relation to hunting and gathering activities. Though within the same territory, there are sub-groups also, there appears to be no restriction on the movement of these sub-groups within the territory for the purpose of food acquisition. But this rule is not applicable when they move for social purposes, for example in case of marriage alliances as inter-territorial marriage alliances exist among them. It clearly shows that each group has access to resources of its territory only, and inter-territorial sharing of resources is strictly prohibited. The Jarawa as a whole also display

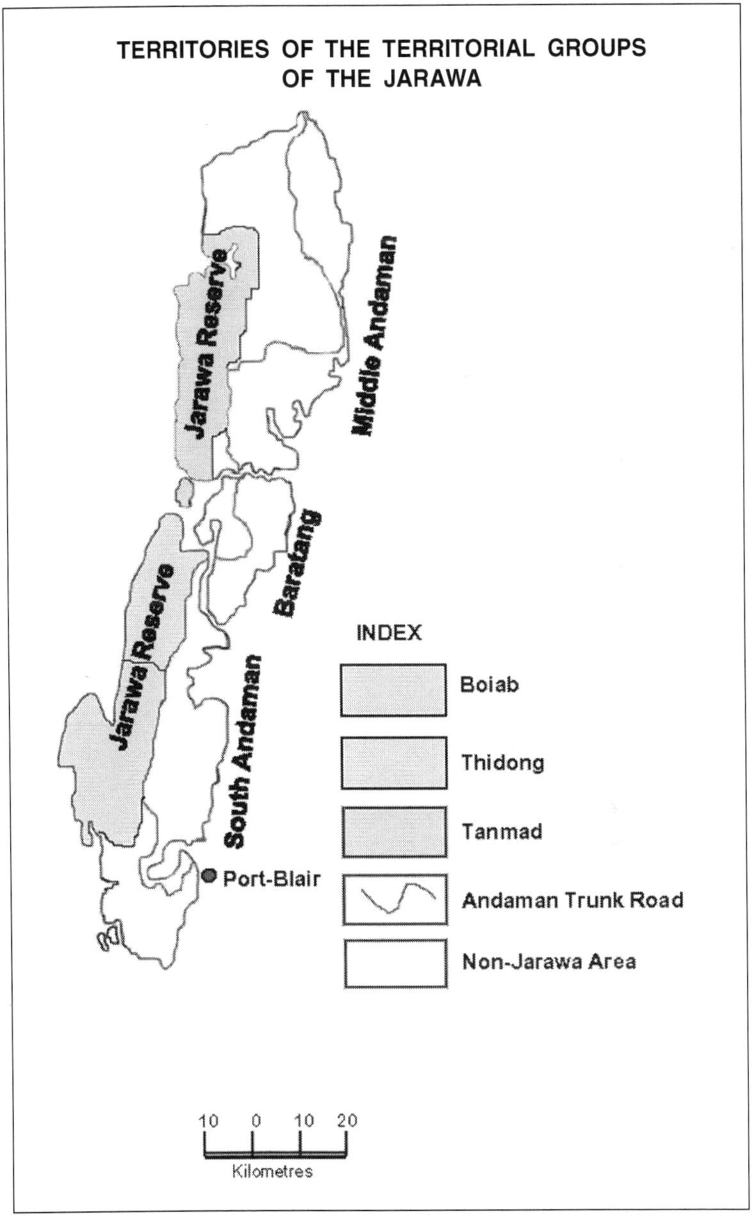

Source: Based on Field Investigation, 2002.

Figure 3.1: Territories of Territorial Groups of the Jarawa

a strong sense of possession for resources of their territory when the question of sharing of resources of their territory by the non-Jarawa arises (details are discussed in Chapter 5). Thus, it can be said that the concept of territoriality at the subsistence level is very strong in the Jarawa and it flows from the topophilia (sense of attachment). It is quite natural in a foraging society.

For the first time in 2002, the Jarawa population was head counted and it reported a total population of 265 (Table 3.1). The *Tanmad* had the largest concentration of the Jarawa (103) followed by *Boiab* (84) and *Thidong* (7). Now the *Thidong* has the largest concentration of the Jarawa. Besides, in a span of 17 years (2018), the Jarawa population has doubled (Table 3.2). The present population of the Jarawa as on March 2019 is 534 as per the record of Andaman Adim Janjati Vikas Samiti (AAJVS). As regards the sex ratio, it is observed that it was almost equal in 2001. But over the years the gap between male-female ratio has widened. It was 909.34 females per thousand males in March 2018. In 2019, it has further declined to 860.63 females per thousand males (Table 3.2). In absolute terms, the Jarawa have 53.7 per cent male population compared to 46.3 per cent female population. Table 3.2 reveals that the age group 0-10 years has 58.71 per cent male children compared to 41.29 female children. The same trend is observed in the age group of 41-50 years.

TABLE 3.1: THE JARAWA POPULATION IN DIFFERENT TERRITORIES

	Jarawa Population in 2002			Jarawa Population in 2018		
Territory	Male	Female	Total	Male	Female	Total
Boiab	39	45	84	61	64	125
Thidong	45	33	78	101	92	193
Tanmad	51	52	103	103	85	188
Total	135	130	265	265	241	506

Source: Anthropological Survey of India, 2002; Andaman Adim Janjati Vikas Samiti (AAJVS), Port Blair, 2018.

TABLE 3.2: DEMOGRAPHIC PROFILE OF THE JARAWA AS ON 31 MARCH 2019

Age Group (In years)	Male	Female	Total
0-10	118	83	201
11-20	48	46	94
21-30	48	52	100
31-40	28	28	56
41-50	27	19	46
51 and above	18	19	37
Total	287	247	534
	(53.7 %)	(46.3 %)	

Source: Andaman Adim Janjati Vikas Samiti (AAJVS), Port Blair, 2019.

THE JARAWA RESERVE

The present day 'Jarawa Reserve' territory corresponds roughly to the area under the occupation of the Jarawa. The Jarawa, however, colonised their present territory a little more than a century ago under certain compulsions. Before that, they had occupied the areas lying in the southern part of the South Andaman Island. According to late nineteenth century British chronicles, the people inhabiting areas on the east coast of the South Andaman Island in the late eighteenth century were the Jarawa. This area is close to where the present day town of Port Blair stands. When the second British settlement was established at the same spot in the South Andaman Island in 1858, the Jarawa were not found in the vicinity of the settlement. They had moved further west, probably as a result of their continuous feud and competition over resources with the Aka-Bea-da, a Great Andamanese tribe (Portman 1899: 765). Radcliffe-Brown (1922, 1948: 15, 19, 25) also observed that while all the tribes of the Andaman Islands were restricted to their respective parts of the islands, the Jarawa and the Aka-Bea-da were often found in a common area of the island and were continually at war with one another. However, while the Aka-Bea-da occupied the coastal parts of the island, the Jarawa were restricted to the interior forest regions.

Various colonisation programmes and punitive expeditions during the late nineteenth and early twentieth century pushed the Jarawa northward from the South Andaman, but they did not vacate the South Andaman Island completely. Lidio Cipriani found them in both South and Middle Andaman Islands around the middle of the twentieth century (1966: 2, 6). Due to opening of the area inhabited by the Jarawa for colonising activities, like establishing villages and forestry operations, violent conflicts between the Jarawa on the one hand and the police, self-supporting convicts and the friendly Andamanese tribes on the other, became common.

The Government of India declared the Jarawa habitat as a 'Reserved Area' in the year 1956 to ensure that members of the tribe get exclusive access to land, water and all the resources of the Reserved territory. It is spread over the western side of the South and Middle Andaman Islands. It may be noted that settlements of the non-Jarawa were coming up almost all around the Jarawa territory by this time. Although the settler population was exploiting the resources of the reserve occasionally in the initial years, the exploitation grew manifold in subsequent years as the settler population increased. The protective measures taken for the Reserve could not stop poaching and extraction of resources completely from the Jarawa territory; however, it has been effective to a certain extent. In the subsequent notification, there was some change in the total area of the 'Jarawa Reserve' (Mukhopadhyay 2002). Before the Gazette Notification of 2004, it measured about 765 sq. km. After the 2004 notification, it has expanded to approximately 1028 sq km (Gazette 2004). Their movement within the habitat is confined to a reserved forest having approximately an area of 1028 sq km. Earlier, 200 m on both sides of the Andaman Trunk Road (ATR) in the 'Jarawa Reserve' were not reserved. Now it extends to 30 m only on both sides of the ATR in the 'Jarawa Reserve'. A scrutiny of the notification reveals that this increase in the territory has not much of significance for the Jarawa as they have been using that territory before the notification. Second, an increase in the area of Jarawa territory does not make any significant change in terms of the increase in resource availability. However, the beneficial aspect of this notification is that now there is a prohibition on fishing and extraction of timber and other forest produce from the newly added territories by other people or non-Jarawa. This, in turn, would protect the main Jarawa territory by functioning as a shock absorbing zone in the event of extraction of resources by the non-Jarawa from the eastern side of the Reserve in the South Andaman. Interestingly, unlike many hunter-gatherers of the world, the immediate neighbours of the Jarawa are people engaged in business, trade, service and agriculture. In case of most of the hunter-gatherers of the world, their immediate neighbours happen to be people who are at the next higher level of sociocultural and economic development, such as cattle herders or cultivators engaged in subsistence agriculture.

RESOURCE BASE OF THE JARAWA

The resource base of the Jarawa is inclusive of both the terrestrial and aquatic resources. At the cognitive level, the Jarawa classify the space into four categories. These are *pilleh* (coastal area), *tagidh* (marshy area), *chanhannap* (plain forest land), and *tinon* (hilly dense forest). Of course, *wa* (streams, inlets) is considered an important resource by them. Through a schematic diagram, the location of four physiographic zones and the types of resources available in each zone have been shown (Figure 3.2).

Terrestrial resources are exploited from the *Chanhanap* and *Tinon* areas, while *Pilleh* and *Tagidh* areas are used for the exploitation of aquatic resources. The freshwater need is met from *wa* (streams). However, the availability of many of these resources is season-specific. So far the Jarawa has been observed using about 139 species of plants as a resource, of which 54 are edible resources and the remaining are non-edible resources. The collection of aquatic resources is mostly for food purpose. Aquatic resources consist mostly of different varieties of fish, crabs, shells, molluscs, turtles and turtle eggs. The resources gathered by the Jarawa can be put under two broad categories, namely edible resources and non-edible resources. The edible resources can further be sub-grouped

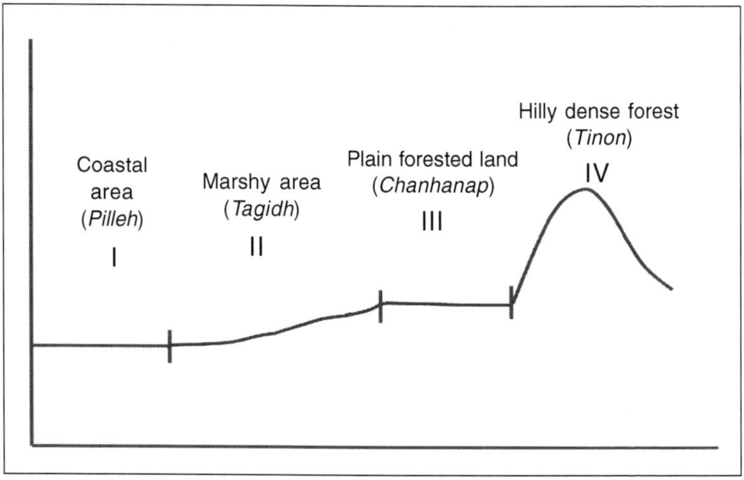

Source: Based on Field Investigation, 2002.

Figure 3.2: Schematic Presentation of Cognitive Space of the Jarawa

into two categories namely (i) plant resources, and (ii) animal resources.

EDIBLE RESOURCES

The edible resources of the Jarawa consist of both animal and plant resources. The plant resources are gathered from the terrestrial ecosystem only, while animal resources are procured from both terrestrial and aquatic ecosystems. Thus, both terrestrial and aquatic ecosystems provide food resources to the Jarawa..

EDIBLE PLANT RESOURCES

There are numerous plant species available in the 'Jarawa Reserve', which are yet to be fully documented. Of the total edible plant species used by the Jarawa, so far only 54 have been documented (Table 3.3). The edible plant resources of the Jarawa can be put under three broad groups. These are (a) tubers, (b) fruits, pulp and tender leaves, and (c) seeds. Further, the edible plants and their products are classified into three categories as per their utility.

TABLE 3.3: EDIBLE PLANTS USED BY THE JARAWA

Tyep of edible plants	No. of species	Availability of edible plant resources		
		Plenty	Adequate	Occasional
Tubers (*Dioscorea sp.*)	3	3	0	0
Fruits, pulp and tender shoots	41	16	18	4
Seeds	5			
(a) *Artocarpus chaplasha* (Jackfruit seeds)	1	1	0	0
(b) *Cycas rumphii*	1	1	0	0
(c) *Nypa fruticans*	1	1	0	0
(d) *Sterculia Rubiginosa*	1			
(e) *Entada rheedei*	1			

Source: Field Investigation, 1998-2004; and Department of Environment and Forests, 2002.

1. Major foods: There are only five plant species which provide for a major part of the Jarawa diet in a certain season. Among them are honey (produced by large bee), two species of *Dioscorea*, jackfruits (*Artocarpus chaplasha*), *Nypa fruticans* and seeds of *Cycas rumphii* (Plates 3.1, 3.2 and 3.3).

Source: Anthropological Survey of India.

Plate 3.1: Collection of tubers

Source: Anthropological Survey of India.

Plate 3.2: A Jarawa man processing wild jackfruits

Source: Anthropological Survey of India.

Plate 3.3: A Jarawa woman with collection of seeds of *Cycas rumphii*

2. Minor foods: Under this category come those plants which are eaten in less quantity compared to the above mentioned five species, and their period of consumption is also short. There are about fourteen minor food resources/items. These are *Artabotrys speciosus, A. lacoocha, Baccaurea ramiflora, Clamus andamanicus, Diospyros andamanica, Ficus racemosa, Garcinia cowa, Mangifera andamanica, Pinanga manii, Donax canaeformis, Pometia pinnata, Terminalia catappa, Sterculia rubiginosa* and *Entada rheedei.*
3. Supplementary foods: This category includes those plant resources that are not eaten regularly in any season, but these are consumed on the spot as and when found in the course of their foraging activities. Seasonal fruits and the shoots of the tender plants come under this category (Plates 3.4 and 3.5).

Both minor and supplementary foods are consumed in less quantity and generally at the place of gathering itself. These edible plants are the source of carbohydrate, vitamins and other nutrients for the Jarawa. Most of the fruits are eaten fresh and raw. A major portion of them is consumed on the spot of gathering without

Source: Author collection.

Plate 3.4: A Pandanus fruit, occasionally consumed by the Jarawa

Source: Author collection.

Plate 3.5: A variety of citrus fruit, occasionally consumed by the Jarawa

cooking. However, there are two plant resources which are processed before eating. These are the seeds of the wild jackfruit (*Artocarpus chaplasa*) and the *Cycas rumphii.* The seeds of the jackfruits, both ripe and unripe, are processed. They put the seeds in a net bag and bury it under mud in a creek for about three weeks. Afterwards, it is taken out and sun dried. Thereafter it is eaten. The seeds of the *Cycas rumphii* are also put under the seawater for about a week before consuming. According to the Jarawa, this process helps to remove the toxic elements present in the seeds. However, it is yet to be established scientifically. Besides the seeds, the pulp of the wild jackfruit is also eaten (Plate 3.2). Pulp of the ripe jackfruit is eaten immediately, while unripe jackfruits are broiled in the fire. For broiling, they make a shallow elliptical depression in the ground. It measures about 100 to 150 cm in diameter and about 50 cm in depth. Thereafter, burning firewood is placed inside it. Then it is covered with an interrupted layer of stone-chips above which the food material is placed in heaps. After three to four hours of baking, the fruits are taken out and the pulp is relished.

EDIBLE ANIMAL RESOURCES

The edible animal food items are collected from both terrestrial and aquatic ecosystems of the Islands. The animal resources from terrestrial ecosystem consist of wild pigs (*ovu*), monitor lizards (*orrugu*), grub larvae, honey and a few species of birds, while the resources of the aquatic ecosystem comprise of turtles (*ukkele*), turtle eggs, fish (*naappo*), molluscs, crustaceans, etc. (Table 3.4). So far the Jarawa have been found consuming 82 types of edible animal resources.

Although numerous edible items are collected through hunting, fishing and gathering, the Jarawa have a dietary preference for the meat of wild pig, monitor lizard, turtle, fish and molluscs (Plates 3.6, 3.7, 3.8 and 3.9). This means that when these items are available in plenty, other items are eaten less. The flesh of the Andaman feral pig is the most relished of all items. Culturally also, the wild pig is very significant and holds a special importance for the foraging communities of the Islands including the Jarawa. Flesh of the wild pig has importance in almost all the rites and

TABLE 3.4: EDIBLE ANIMAL RESOURCES OF THE JARAWA

Type of animal resources	No. of species	Availability of animal resources		
		Plenty	Adequate	Occasional
Wild pigs (*Sus scrofa andamanensis*)	1	–	1	–
Monitor lizards (*Varanus salvator andamanensis*)	1	–	1	–
Sea cow (*Dugong dugon*)	1	–	–	1
Birds	9	–	–	–
Turtle	3	–	–	–
Fish	29	15	–	–
Crustaceans	15	–	–	–
Insects	3	–	–	–
Molluscs	17	4	–	–
Grub Larvae	1	–	1	–
Honey	2	1	0	1

Source: Field Investigation, 1998-2004; Z.S.I., 2002, Port Blair.

Source: Anthropological Survey of India.

Plate 3.6: A Jarawa boy dressing the roasted pig

Source: Anthropological Survey of India.

Plate 3.7: A Jarawa processing the monitor lizard

Source: Anthropological Survey of India.

Plate 3.8: A Jarawa girl with her fish catch

Source: Anthropological Survey of India.

Plate 3.9: Bivalve shells collected from the creek

rituals. Oliver (1984) and Whitaker (1988) have drawn an analogy between the density of wild pig and the general health of other resources in the forest. Their analysis suggests that by taking one variable, i.e. wild pig population, the status of the other resources (mostly the forest based resources) of the area can be inferred. The high density of wild pigs means a healthy status of other resources, whereas a low density indicates thinning and dwindling of other resources, meaning poor status. Since the foraging communities of Andaman Islands are dependent on natural resources for their sustenance, the status of resources affects them directly.

It is interesting to note that the Jarawa do not hunt deer that are in abundance in the Jarawa territory (Plate 3.10). The apparent reason may be that it is an introduced species in the Andaman Islands ecosystem. When the Islands were occupied for the second penal settlement, the British introduced the deer. Since it was an alien species, it was not in the list of prey animals of the Jarawa; hence, they desisted from hunting the deer. Being an introduced species, the deer did not find any mention in their traditional

Source: Anthropological Survey of India.

Plate 3.10: A Jarawa boy playing with a fawn (deer) caught by him

world view and knowledge system. As such, the deer was not included in the category of food items. Besides, the Jarawa have the notion that eating deer meat would make them sick. Moreover, they do not find the meat of the deer delicious as that of wild pig and monitor lizard for it contains comparatively less fat.

Honey is collected mostly during the dry season between December and early May. The entire contents of the beehive are relished by the Jarawa, which consists of honey, eggs, larvae and pollen. At times, when honey is collected in plenty, it is stored up also. For this purpose, a small trench is dug and the wooden bucket of honey is put into it. Thereafter, it is covered with soil and leaves. However, such storing up of honey is occasional. Generally, most of the honey is consumed within two to three days of its procurement.

Edible aquatic resources consist mostly of different varieties of fish, crabs, shells, molluscs, turtles and turtle eggs (Table 3.4). In the aquatic resources, fishes and molluscs are important food items for the Jarawa, and both are found in abundance in the coastal region of their habitat, hence easy to catch. Of particular importance are bivalve shells and fish found in the creek and shallow water near the shoreline. Male members fish with the help of bows and arrows while female members do it with hand nets. However, females do most of the fishing. In the case of such simple tools, the success rate is directly related to the abundance of fish. The fish are not only the source of protein but of fat too for the Jarawa. The edible marine resources, particularly the fish and molluscs, are the keystone resources for the Jarawa. The keystone resources (Terborgh 1986) are those resources, which are available round the year and enable the population to survive through the lean period. In case of the Jarawa, the above mentioned marine resources are available throughout the year and regularly consumed by them. The aquatic animals can be classified into the following three categories according to their importance as food items.

1. Major foods: The major foods of the Jarawa consist of the meat of wild pig and monitor lizard, bivalve shells, turtle eggs, and different species of fish. The availability of turtle eggs and many

of the fish species are seasonal. Significantly, honey is also included in the major foods.

2. Minor foods: Under this category come those animals that are eaten in less quantity compared to the major foods. Numerous sea animals come under this category. Important ones are turtle, grub larvae, prawn and certain species of fish and crab.
3. Supplementary foods: Animals, which are not eaten regularly in any season, are included in this category. In fact, the occasionally eaten animal food items are sea cow (dugong), lobster, birds and certain species of shell and fish.

FRESH WATER SOURCES

Apart from the edible plant and animal resources mentioned above, water is a basic resource for the Jarawa, like any other life forms. The Andaman Islands have a wet tropical climate with an average rainfall of 2,900 mm per annum. Due to high rainfall and mountain ranges, there are a number of streams (a major source of freshwater) in the Jarawa territory. During the study, few freshwater sources have been identified. Three of these sources are in the Middle Andaman Island, one each near Panighat, Lekera Lunta and Dhaninala, while two are in the South Andaman Island, one each near Middle Strait and R.K. Nallah area. Besides, there are freshwater streams near Constance Bay area, Dalrymple Beach area, Port Campbell and Blair Beach. The Foul Bay, Rocky Points, Bay Flat Island and Robert Bay also have a number of seasonal streams. Robert Bay is also a camping site of the Jarawa, mainly for turtle hunting, as this area happens to be a turtle nesting ground. Two types of turtles—green turtle (*Chelonica mydas*) and hawksbill (*Eretmochelys imbricate*) come here to lay eggs. Other places of freshwater streams have been found in Cape Bluff, Spike Islands, Port Anson, Foul Bay area, Louis Inlet, the coastal belt along Palmer Point, Cape Barwell and south of Montgomery Island, Melagar Boilya and Wologa Boilya system. The Melagar Boilya and Wologa Boilya system have an extensive wetland area that is also fed by a fresh-water stream. Yeratiljig is the only wetland and creek system in the Andaman Islands with the most extensive *nypa* palm (*Nypa fruticans*) habitat. Freshwater streams have also been found near Hiran Tikri and Badabalu.

There are probably some more freshwater sources inside the Jarawa territory because water is one of the few important factors taken into consideration by the Jarawa while setting up a camp at any place and all campsites have not yet been studied due to various reasons. Observations made during field investigation suggest that there is no scarcity of potable water in the Jarawa territory. However, it may be noted that the perenniality of the water sources in this area is a function of a high density of forest cover. Water sources will remain perennial only so long as the forests are undisturbed.

NON-EDIBLE RESOURCES

In addition to edible resources, there are many non-edible resources used by the Jarawa to meet their other requirements. It consists mostly of plant and non-plant resources. The non-edible usage of plant resources is mainly for shelter, medicines, ornamentation, repellent for honeybees and implements. It has so far been found that the Jarawa make use of 85 plant species (Table 3.5) for non-edible purposes. The actual number could be much more than the observed figures. In addition to the plant resources, there are a few things which are also important for the Jarawa. Important among those are ochre, iron and metal utensils. While the ochre is used to paint the body, iron is used to make various implements. Besides, metal utensils are also used by them for storing and cooking

TABLE 3.5: NON-EDIBLE PLANT RESOURCES OF THE JARAWA

Type of Non-edible Plant Resources	No. of Species
Medicinal plants	15
Plants used in hut making	19
Plants used in ornamentation	41
Plants used in implements making	7
Plants used as repellents	3

Source: Field Investigation, 1998-2004.

purposes. It is interesting to note that except the iron and other metal utensils, all other resources are naturally available in the Jarawa area. The iron and metal utensils are supplied presently by the AAJVS.

PLANTS FOR SHELTER

Shelter is one of the basic requirements of human beings. For shelter, the Jarawa construct huts made of parts of the plant or tree. Based on the size, the huts of the Jarawa can be placed under two categories, namely the large beehive type huts and lean-to type huts. While the former is a community hut, bigger in size and stronger, the latter is an individual family hut, small in size. In the construction of huts, plant or tree products are used as poles, strips and thatching materials.

The Jarawa use parts of many plant and tree species. Some of the common uses have been discussed here. For poles, the Jarawa generally use stems of trees like *Baccaurea ramiflora, Knema andamanica, Leea angulata, Lagerstroemia, Speciosa, Areca triandra, Antidesma velutinum, Sterculia alata, Mussaenda macrophylla,* bamboo, etc. Selection of the plants or trees generally depends on their availability in a particular area. For thatching purpose, the leaves of *Licuala peltata, Caryota mitis, Daemonorops, Calamus grandis, Calmus pseudorivalis, Daemonorops kurzianus* and *Musa sapientum* plant species are used. Interestingly, the Jarawa were never seen using the leaves of the *Nypa fruticans* for thatching purpose while the other tribes of the Andaman Islands use it.

For making bark strips, the plants used by them are *Anodendron manubrium (Apocynaceae), Antidesma velutinum (Euphorbiaceae), Calamus longisetus (Arecaceae), Dendrobium spp. (Orchidaceae), Desmos dasymaschalus (Annonaceae), Hibiscus tiliaceous (Malvaceae), Planchonia valida (Lecythidaceae), Pterocymbium tinctorium (Sterculiaceae), Sterculia villosa, Combretum latifolium (Com bretaceae)* and *Calamus.* For twigs they generally use *Combretum* plant species. The floor of the huts, especially the place earmarked for sleeping, is usually covered with leaves of *Licuala peltata* or *Pterospermum acerifolium.*

PLANTS FOR MEDICINES

For ages, the Jarawa have been using ethnomedicine to cure different ailments. By continuous practice, elders of the Jarawa community have developed expertise in identifying and applying different plant products for curing various health disorders like cough, cold, headache, body ache, abdominal pain, etc. Further, the Jarawa also use leaves and barks of some of the plants and trees (*Dracaena angustifolia* and *Enpatorium odoratum*) during menstruation period to stop excess bleeding. So far, about 16 species of medicinal plants have been identified, whose different parts are used by the Jarawa for the medicinal purpose (Table 3.6). Significant to mention that all plant products are applied externally either as intact material or in the form of a crushed paste. Interestingly, there is no oral ingestion of any medicinal plant product.

PLANTS FOR ORNAMENTATION

The Jarawa have high aesthetic value. They are fond of flowers and they adorn themselves with several wildflowers, floral buds, leaves, etc. They adore bright colours and apply white ochre on the face. They wear girdles made from finely dissected tender leaves of plants. Besides, they also wear ornaments made of flowers seasonally available in the forests. These are put on as headbands, necklace, garlands and armlets.

PLANTS AS REPELLENT FOR HONEYBEE

At the time of honey collection the Jarawa use the sap of leaves and stems of *Orophea katschallica* called *tangopa jath*, *Pseuduvaria prainii* called *hoomal* and *Amomum aculeatum* called *uiyaw* as bee repellents. External application of these plant products ensures safety from the bees while collecting honey from the hives.

PLANTS FOR MAKING IMPLEMENTS

The foraging pursuits of the Jarawa involve hunting, fishing and gathering. The implements used by them are simple and few. While

TABLE 3.6: MEDICINAL PLANTS USED BY THE JARAWA

Name of the Plant	Family	Jarawa Name	Part Used	Purpose
Amomum aculeatum	*Zingiberaceae*	Uiyaw	Leaf, stem	Tied around chest for cough and fever, leaf is applied on scars.
Angiopteris lygodiifolia	*Angiopteridaceae*	Tikalu	Fronds	Fronds are worn around chest for cough & cold.
Caryota mitis	*Arecaceae*	Endau	Stem pith	Stem pith is eaten to stop vomiting & for stomach pain.
Chromolaena odorata	*Asteraceae*	Auth	Leaves	Leaves used as coagulant particularly on leech bite, cold & cough.
Curcuma zedoaria	*Zingiberaceae*	Ooyekuchin	Leaves	Used in cold and cough.
Cucurbita sp.	*Cucurbitaceae*	Uru	Leaves	Used in neck pain and fever.
Dracaena angustifolia	*Agavaceae*	Tidba	Young twigs	Used to clean genitals during menstruation period.
Enpatorium odoratum	*Zingiberaceae*	Aath	Leaves	Used during menstruation.
Gnetum scandens	*Gnetaceae*	Ehole	Stem, sap	Stem sap is used externally to get relief from stomach pain.
Knema andamanica	*Myristicaceae*	Aure	Stem, leaves	Used as coagulant.
Kunstleria keralensis	*Fabaceae*	Quato	Bark	Used in headache.
Myristica andamanica	*Myristicaceae*	Oro	Leaves, twigs	Leaves and twigs are used as garland when sick.
Piper betle	*Piperaceae*	Tole	Leaves	Used in cold and cough.
Pseuduvaria prainii	*Annonaceae*	Hoomal	Leaves	Leaves are wrapped around body in cough and fever.
Thottea tomentosa	*Aristolochiaceae*	Udupet	Whole plant	Used in cough and fever.
Trichosanthes tricuspidata	*Cucurbitaceae*	Urubethe	Whole plant	Used in throat pain.

Source: Field Investigation, 1998-2004; B.S.I., 2002, Port Blair.

the hunting implements consist of bows and arrows, pointed wooden sticks and iron rods, the fishing and gathering implements comprise the fishing nets, buckets and baskets. The process of making some of these implements is gender-specific. For instance, hunting objects like bows and arrows are always made by the adult male folk while adult female folk make baskets and fishing nets. Both males and females make wooden buckets. A bow and arrow is exclusively used by the male Jarawa, while the fishing net is used by the female folk only. The other implements used by the Jarawa are knives and *dao*, which are obtained from the AAJVS or settlers.

Bows and Arrows

Bows and arrows are of cardinal importance to the Jarawa. For making a bow, good quality wood with high elasticity is required (Plate 3.11). To meet this requirement, the Jarawa use the stems of *Calamus andamanicus, Dinochloa scandens and Sageraea elliptica* plants. The strings of the bows are made from the bark of *Ficus scandens, Desmos dasymaschalon, Anodendron manubrium* and *Polyalthia parkinsonii* plants. The Jarawa make arrows of different types and sizes for different purposes (Plates 3.11 and 3.12). The

Source: Anthropological Survey of India.

Plate 3.11: Foraging implements of the Jarawa: bow, arrow, digging rod and knife

Source: Anthropological Survey of India.

Plate 3.12: Arrows with fixed and detachable arrowheads

stem of *Murraya paniculata* is chosen for preparing the wooden arrow, while the stem of *Areca triandra*, *Dinochloa*, and *Ancistrocladus* are used for making hunting arrows. Iron is used for making the arrowhead. The arrowhead is tied to the stick with a string made of plant fibre from *Dendrobium.*

Chest Guard

While going out for hunting, the Jarawa wear a chest guard called *kekad* made from the bark of *Planchonia valida, Polyalthia parkinsonii* and *Sterculia villosa* (Plate 3.13). It protects them from injury during hunting. It is also used for keeping knives during hunting. There are two layers of bark strip in a chest guard and it is 20-30 cm in diameter. The ends of the bark strip are neatly stitched together with bark string. The surface of the *kekad* is decorated with a dye obtained from the stem juice of *Myristica andamanica* plant.

Source: Anthropological Survey of India.

Plate 3.13: A Hunter with bow, arrow and chest guard

Basket

The Jarawa also use baskets called *taaiku* for collection of food, leaves, shells, etc. (Plates 3.14 and 3.15). These baskets are of various sizes and more or less conical in shape with a wide mouth and narrow bottom. These are made from the strips of cane and *Korthalsia laciniosa.* The leaves of *Licuala* palm are spread inside the basket.

Wooden Bucket

For the collection and storage of honey and for keeping and carrying other articles, they use dug-out wooden buckets, which they call *uuhu* (Plate 3.15 and 3.16). For making the bucket, wood of the *Pajanelia longifolia, Oroxylum indicum* and *Sterculia villosa* plant species is used. Making of the wooden bucket is an exclusively adult male activity. While making the wooden bucket, the wooden block is scooped out and given the shape. Thereafter, the wax is plastered both inside and outside of the bucket to avoid any

Source: Anthropological Survey of India.

Plate 3.14: A Jarawa woman making a cane basket

Source: Anthropological Survey of India.

Plate 3.15: Baskets and buckets of the Jarawa

Source: Anthropological Survey of India.

Plate 3.16: A group of Jarawas busy making dugout buckets from the trunk of a tree

leakage from it, which guarantees the safe storage of valuable food items, particularly honey, derived through strenuous labour, sharp skill and tactful strategy.

Bark Strips

The Jarawa use bark strips of plants for various purposes like cordage, lifting baskets, carrying babies, transporting the hunted pigs, etc. For preparing strips, they often use the bark of *Anodendron manubrium (Apocynaceae), Antidesma velutinum (Euphorbiaceae), Calamus longisetus (Arecaceae), Combretum latifolium (Combretaceae), Dendrobium spp. (Orchidaceae), Desmos dasymaschalon (Annonaceae), Hibiscus tiliaceous (Malvaceae), Planchonia valida (Lecythidaceae), Pterocymbium tinctorium (Sterculiaceae)* and *Sterculia villosa* plants.

Torch

The torch, called *pone*, is used by the Jarawa while moving during the night. To prepare the torch the powdered resin of *Canarium euphyllum* (*Burseraceae*) plant is put into the leaves of *Licuala peltata*. Thereafter, the leaves are rolled and tightened with a string obtained from the bark of any plant. Thereafter a thin coating of clay is applied on the outer side of the torch to prevent the leaves from burning quickly. To lit the torch nowadays they use match sticks. In the past, they produced fire by rubbing two stones.

Ochre

The Jarawa use two types of ochre—red and white—that are naturally available in their territory. They mix pig fat in the ochre and prepare the paste. Thereafter, it is applied to the body. The ochre is applied either for medicinal purposes or in relation to any ritual or for decorating the body (Plate 3.17).

Source: Anthropological Survey of India.

Plate 3.17: A fully decorated Jarawa (painted body, headgear and chest guard)

IRON PIECES AND METAL VESSEL

For the Jarawa, the acquisition of iron, a material that is the basis of their hunting and gathering pursuit, is of cardinal importance. It is not naturally available in their habitat. They do not know of any other easy source for this material but the settlements of the non-Jarawa. In the past, they used to collect iron from jetsam, and parts of broken ships washed ashore. The iron is used for making arrowheads, knives and digging rods. These implements are of vital importance to the Jarawa. Besides, they also make machetes for clearing the vegetation. For hunting pigs, arrows having elongated leaf-like iron head are used, while arrows with the pointed iron heads are used for fishing. In addition, they also procure metal utensils. These utensils are used for storing and cooking. Of course, these articles have lately found their way in the material culture of the Jarawa. Now, these items have become a necessity. For procuring the metal, earlier (before 1997) they used to visit the settlement areas, sea coasts and the motorable roads. Such activities had led to the development of a kind of relationship between the Jarawa and the settlers, arisen historically out of a one-sided necessity, i.e. acquisition of iron implements and aluminium pots from the villages of the non-Jarawa. The relationship that continued in the ambience of hostility was one of necessity and not of choice. In the post hostility phase, i.e. after 1997, the Jarawa are getting a regular supply of iron and utensils of aluminium from AAJVS, an organisation functioning under the Andaman and Nicobar Administration.

SEASONALITY OF FOOD RESOURCES

The harvesting of terrestrial and aquatic resources is mostly for food purposes. However, the availability and in some cases density of many of these resources is season-specific, it means availability of these resources vary from one season to another. The collection of resources by the Jarawa is, therefore, subject to the abundance of certain resources in a particular season. The availability of a few edible resources is inter-seasonal also. There are three broad resource seasons as given below:

1. Mid-March to mid-May (dry summer season): It is the season for collection of wild jackfruit. The fruits of wild jackfruit are collected in large quantities during the dry summer season. The pulp of ripe fruit is eaten instantly. The unripe fruit is cooked in the fire and thereafter, its seeds are taken out. Some of the seeds are eaten immediately, while the remaining ones are stored. The stored seeds last until August. Coincidently, this period happens to be the lean season of pig hunting due to some reasons discussed elsewhere. There is an occasional collection of honey also in this season.
2. Mid-May to November (rainy season): The rainy seasons include both the south-west and the north-east monsoons. During this season, the thrust is on pig hunting and collection of the seeds of *Cycas rumphii and Nypa fruticans.* During this period, roots and tubers, the food of the feral pigs, are available in abundance. As a result, the pigs grow heavier during this period. The collection of the seeds of *Cycas rumphii* continues until the end of November.
3. December to mid-March (cool winter season): This is the main season of collection of honey and turtle eggs, followed by pig hunting. The turtles start coming ashore to lay the eggs from November onwards. Thus, the turtle hunting together with the collection of eggs begins from November and continues until the end of February, though egg collection diminishes gradually. There are a few species of turtles that lay eggs in other seasons also. The honey collection begins when the rain stops, i.e. from December and lasts until May.

In the case of wild pigs, seasonality does not hold true, except that fewer pigs are hunted between March and May. There appear to be two reasons for it. Firstly, there are other edible resources available in abundance during this period. During this period, the roots and tubers eaten by the wild pigs are available in less quantity and as such pigs become thinner and have less fat on their bodies. According to the Jarawa, during this period, wild pigs turn black and their meat does not taste good as it has less fat. In other words, the Jarawa relish flesh of the pigs when it is rich in fat contents. The fewer hunting efforts in this period are related to lesser fat in the pigs. However, no seasonality is observed in case of the fish, molluscs and crabs as they are available throughout the year. Thus fishing goes on round the year and the supply of the aquatic edible resources is in plenty. The same is the case with the availability of edible tubers (*Diascorea* sp.) also. Plants of a single species can be found in all stages of growth at the same time. At least two species of tubers (*woh*) sometimes have mature and immature tubers on the same plant at a particular time. The data from 1999 to 2004 show that wild tubers were available round the year, though the rate of return varied to some extent. Interestingly, a similar kind of observation was made for edible tubers available in the Malay Peninsula (Rambo 1982: 263, Van der Schot 1986: 12, cf. Hart and Hart 1986: 41). Those tubers were also of *Dioscorea* sp.

RESOURCES OF THE NON-JARAWA PEOPLE

Agriculture is the primary occupation of the non-Jarawa population in rural area while the urban population is engaged in secondary and tertiary occupations. To meet their needs for timber and minor forest produce, concessions have been granted to them under Government Notification No. 13/87-F(T)/27/25 dated 24 April 1987, but they are supposed to procure these items from the forests on the periphery of the Jarawa territory. Owing to the degradation of the forests in the non-reserved forest area, they have to depend on the forest resources of the 'Jarawa Reserve'. Over the years, their population has increased and so have their needs. Consequently, many of them are inadvertently using the terrestrial and aquatic resources of the 'Jarawa Reserve'. Though entry to the 'Jarawa Reserve' is restricted and the extraction of the resources prohibited, many of the non-Jarawa stealthily and illegally indulge in poaching and extraction of forest resources. Until 1996, the Department of Forests was the chief agency involved in the extraction of timber and minor forest produce from the Jarawa territory. The rural as well as urban population meet their requirements by purchasing sawn timber from the sawmills of the Department of Forests at Chatham or the privately owned small sawmills operating in and around Port Blair. Besides forest resources (plant and plant products), animal resources are also extracted by the non-Jarawa which consist of terrestrial as well as animal resources. Against the aforementioned background, the resources collected by the non-Jarawa from the Jarawa territory have been discussed. Further, many of the points discussed here are related to aspects of the conflict between the Jarawa and non-Jarawa.

FOREST RESOURCES

A large variety of forest products are extracted by the non-Jarawa from the forests of the Jarawa territory to meet domestic as well as commercial needs. This very act has caused ripples in the relations between the Jarawa and the non-Jarawa. The forest resources extracted by the non-Jarawa consist of both minor forest produce and commercially important wood.

Firewood

Firewood is one of the important minor forest products procured by the non-Jarawa people to meet the basic requirement of fuel for domestic or cooking purposes. The Forest Department issues licenses for firewood to the local people as well as to the contractors for the extraction of fuelwood on payment of royalty. Besides, firewood is also obtained from both private and government owned sawmills. Earlier the leftover lops and tops from the areas of timber extraction by the government provided a good source of fuel to them.

Cane

Eight species of canes are available in the forests. The Forest Department uses cane for making coupe holders. Besides, it also makes cane-rafts to transport the logs, and as the coupe holder. The non-Jarawa use cane for making furniture and constructing houses. They procure cane on payment of royalty. The demand for cane is increasing day by day. The sports goods industry at Meerut and Jalandhar are interested in getting *Calamus andamanicus* (mota beth) cane species to manufacture cricket bats, hockey sticks and other sports equipment. Annually about 200 tons of canes are harvested from this area by various agencies, viz., government, businessmen, free grantees and right holders (Basu 1993). In the South and Middle Andaman Islands, the cane is extracted in most cases from the 'Jarawa Reserve'. Besides cane, the seeds of canes are collected by the non-Jarawa on behalf of the businessmen. These seeds find various uses in the mainland markets at Kolkata and Chennai. At times, the collection of these cane seeds is so much so that it hinders the natural regeneration of cane.

Dhup and Gum

White dhup and red dhup yield a very useful resin called rock dammar. It is collected both by the Forest Department and the Non-Jarawa. Nabbe (*Lannea coromandelica*) yields a mucilaginous gum from wounds or cracks in the bark. Gum is used as an adhesive.

Tans and Dyes

In order to make tans and dyes, the bark of the mangrove trees (*Bruguiera spp.* and *Rhizophora*) is used by the non-Jarawa. The bark of mangrove is rich in tannin but it contains an excessive quantity of colouring matter. Forest Department issues licences to the local people for the collection of raw materials for tans and dyes. So far, no systematic attempt has been made to extract mangrove bark for tannins.

Honey and Wax

The non-Jarawa collect these materials. It is collected mainly for personal consumption. So far, no effort has been made to collect honey on a commercial basis because the availability of honey is too small for any commercial exploitation.

CHARCOAL

A small quantity of charcoal is made by the Forest Department and sold to the non-Jarawa, and mainly the owners of the blacksmith shops buy it. The wood for preparing the charcoal is derived from the forest. The non-Jarawa are also issued licenses on payment of royalty for the extraction of firewood and its conversion into charcoal.

COMMERCIAL WOODS

The dense tropical rain forests of the Andaman Islands have high species diversity. Various species are commercially important and find a ready market. The commercially important wood are extracted by the Forest Department, though after 1997 it has been stopped. However, there is illegal extraction of timber woods also. The commercially important woods can be put into five categories according to end uses, i.e. ornamental timber, plywood, matchwood, general utility timber and packing case wood (Table 3.7). The above mentioned categories of timbers are in much demand in the markets of both the mainland and Andaman and Nicobar Islands.

ANIMAL RESOURCES

The animal resources procured by the non-Jarawa people comprise both terrestrial and aquatic animal resources. Among the animal resources, pigs, deer, monitor lizards and birds are the important food resources. Though the hunting of these animals is prohibited under the forest law, the rural people are found to be involved in hunting these animals. These resources are mainly procured from the 'Jarawa Reserve'. Among the aquatic resources, fish, molluscs, shells, crabs, lobsters, prawn, sea cucumbers, turtles and turtle eggs are the important resources collected by the non-Jarawa. These are vital food resources for the Jarawa as well. The people settled on the periphery of the 'Jarawa Reserve' procure these resources mainly from the Jarawa territory.

TABLE 3.7: TIMBER TYPES

Category	Species
(a) Ornamental timber	Padauk (*Pterocarpus dalbergioides*)
	Silvergrey (*Terminalia bialata*)
	Chooi (*Sageraea ellipitica*)
	Marble wood (*Diospyros marmorata*)
	Satin wood (*Chloroxylon swietenia*)
(b) Ply wood	Gurjan (*Dipterocarpus Spp.*)
	Badam (*Terminalia procera*)
	White Chuglam (*Terminalia bialata*)
	Lalchini (*Amoora wallichii*)
	Red Dhup (*Parishia insignis*)
(c) Match wood	Papita (*Pterocymbium tinctorium*)
	Didu (*Bombax insigne*)
	White Dhup (*Canarium euphyllum*)
	Lambapathi (*Sideroxylon longepetiolatum*)
(d) General utility timber	Pyinma (*Lagerstroemia hypoleuca*)
	Koko (*Albizzia lebbek*)
	Black Chuglam (*Terminalia manii*)
	Hill Mohwa (*Madhuca butyracea*)
	Red Bombwe (*Planchonia andamanica*)
	Jhingam (*Panjanelia longifolia*)
	Thingam (*Hopea odorata*)
	Yewgi (*Adenanthera pavonina*)
	Nabbe (*Lannea coromandelica*)
	Thinkla (*Nauclea gageana*)
	Gangaw (*Mesua ferrea*)
	Mau (*Duabanga sonneratioides*)
(e) Packing case wood	Softwood logs of the match woods, except *Pterocymbium tinctorium.*

Source: Field Investigation, 1998-2004.

CONFLICT FOR RESOURCES

The above discussion shows that many of the resources used by the Jarawa and the non-Jarawa are common to both of them. During the pre-1997 period, the extraction of resources by the non-Jarawa from the Jarawa territory was one of the reasons for hostility between the Jarawa and the non-Jarawa. However, it was very much restricted. But in the post-1997 phase (i.e. in the post hostility phase) when the Jarawa have become friendly to the non-Jarawa, the resource base of the Jarawa is being extensively used by the non-Jarawa. Now, it has created a situation where the two groups of people are using the same set of resources and that too from the same ecosystem. The point worth mentioning is that both groups have different technology and purpose for resource extraction. The technology used by the non-Jarawa is better in comparison to simple technology used by the Jarawa. The non-Jarawa use more efficient hunting technologies, like firearms, traps and sawing machines. Definitely, the non-Jarawa have an advantage. In case of the Jarawa, the purpose of resource extraction is to satisfy their bare minimum needs, while for the non-Jarawa it is for personal as well as commercial purposes. If the present trend of resource extraction by the non-Jarawa continues unhindered, it will soon put the resources of the 'Jarawa Reserve' under stress.

CHAPTER 4

Adaptation of the Jarawa to the Andaman Environment

Human adaptation to the environment is a process involving technology and strategy employed by man for harnessing the biophysical resources of an ecosystem not only for his sustenance and survival but also for future growth. Instead of being static, human adaptation is dynamic which includes the adjustment of activities to changing environment. The growth of human adaptation is spiral in form (Husain 2002). Hunting and gathering is considered the most ancient adaptation of humanity to its environment.

The term 'ancient' has been used in relation to time as well as technology. In relation to time, the term 'ancient' refers to the initial human response to its environment, while in terms of 'technology' it refers to simple technology employed for harnessing resources. It is surprising to find that there are still some human groups in the world who practise hunting and gathering. Therefore, it is interesting to know how hunting and gathering are still being practised as a means of subsistence in modern times. In order to answer this question, in-depth studies have been conducted by many social scientists about the subsistence mode of economy of the hunter-gatherers. In these studies, attention has been given to the availability and seasonality of resources that influence the items hunted and gathered, the technology and strategy used in the procurement of resources and the movement pattern of the hunting and gathering bands (Lee 1968, Yellen 1971, Sahlins 1972, Harris 1985, Farb and Armelagos 1980, Keene 1981, Winterhalder and Smith 1981 and others). These studies have tried to develop predictive models of the subsistence economy of hunter-gatherers based on rigorous analysis of the ecological context in which they live and survive today, like 'input-output analysis' and 'optimum foraging behaviour'. The 'input-output analysis' is done to find out how much effort in terms of time a hunter-gatherer group makes towards the satisfactory collection of resources in foraging activity and how far the human adaptation itself is successful, whereas the 'optimum foraging analysis', is tried to find out how far the hunting behaviour of a human group conforms to a hunter-gatherer group.

FORAGING TECHNOLOGY AND STRATEGY

For hunting, fishing and gathering, the Jarawa use simple implements, technology and strategy. The implements used by the Jarawa are few like bows, arrows, knives, dao and small fishing nets. There is only one type of bow used by them. The average length of the bow used by the Jarawa is about one metre. As per earlier reports, they had bows of more than one metre in length (*cf.* Sreenathan 2001, 41). But now such long bows are not used by them. The Jarawa have different types of arrows for different purposes. Iron for the arrowhead is supplied either by the local administration, or the Jarawa collect it from the neighbouring settlements of the non-Jarawa. The tempering of iron is unknown to them. The shaping of iron into an arrowhead is done with the help of a hammer and chisel (Plate 4.1). There are five types of arrows (Plate 3.11 and 3.12) used by the Jarawa depending on the nature of use:

(i) *Thoochalotuvopaattoov*—used in pig hunting
(ii) *Toomeedituvopattoov*—used for hunting monitor lizard
(iii) *Thaahoodintaavpaattoov*—used for killing humans
(iv) *Thaahoodintaavpaattoov*—used in fising and
(v) *Taaheteyaalpaattoov*—arrow with a detachable head, used for hunting wild pig and turtle.

Apart from the bow and arrow, there are other items also which are made and used by the Jarawa. The knife (*tuvoodu)* is made from iron/aluminium which they procure either from the settlement of the non-Jarawa or get from the AAJVS. The knife is used for polishing the shaft of the bows and arrows, making sparks for fire and for

Source: Anthropological Survey of India.

Plate 4.1: Making of an iron arrowhead

making a design on the bow and bucket. Besides, they also use machetes (*tottichale*) which are supplied by the local administration. These are of three types, viz., sickle tipped, straight tipped and flat-tipped. It is generally used for cutting vegetation.

For fishing, women use fishing nets (*pootho*) which is conical in shape and made from plant fibre (Plate 4.2). But nowadays nylon string is also used for this purpose. The fishing net is used in both individual and group fishing. For gathering and storage purposes, dug-out wooden buckets (*uuhu*) and baskets (*taaiku*) are used (for detail see Chapter 3).

The foraging pursuit of the Jarawa is a collective response to the environment of the Andaman Islands to harness the resources spread over space and time. The Jarawa set up their camps at locations, which give them access to a wider resource base. To harness the resources of their territory, they move from one place to another which involves meticulous planning and execution. The resources are harnessed by employing simple technology and strategy. The

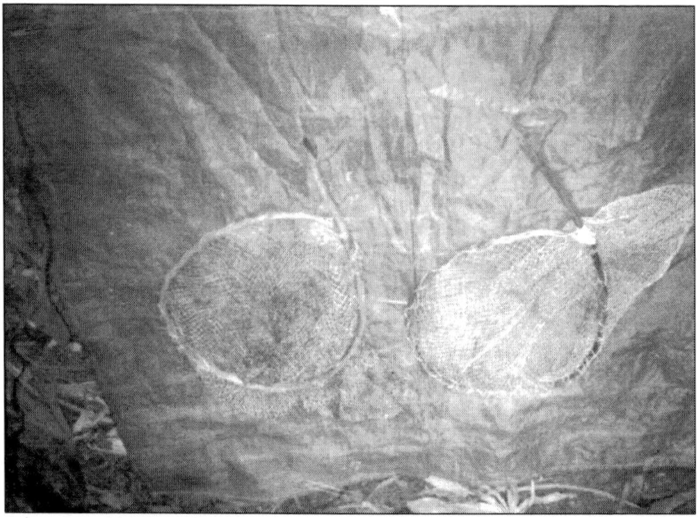

Source: Anthropological Survey of India.

Plate 4.2: Conical fishing nets of the Jarawa

foraging strategy of the Jarawa can be explained in relation to (i) location of the camps, (ii) movement pattern, (iii) foraging methods, (iv) search image, (v) role specialisation, and (vi) sharing.

LOCATION OF CAMPS

The Jarawa, like other hunter-gatherers of the world, construct huts (camps) from forest products. The huts are called *chadda.* In the process of food collection, the camps play an important role as the foraging area begins from outside the camp. During the course of the study, about 69 camps of different types and at different locations were visited. Out of 69 camps, mentioned above, 40 were located along or near the coast while 29 were in the forest (Appendix I). A few of them have been shown in Figure 4.1. The huts can be placed in three categories – permanent, semi-permanent and temporary camps (Sarkar 1990, 12-15) which are in descending order as per the size of the camps. The functions of the first two camps, i.e. permanent and semi-permanent are almost similar, hence they serve as the 'base camp' (Plate 4.3). They are large and

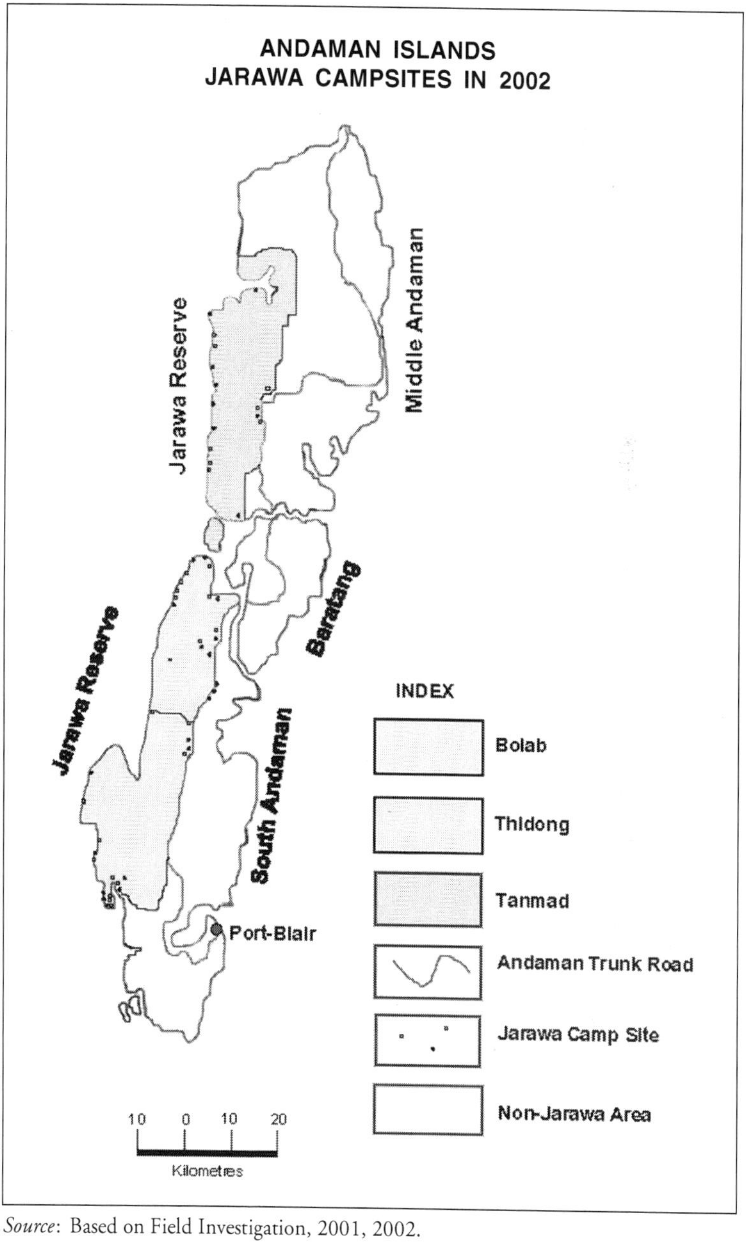

Source: Based on Field Investigation, 2001, 2002.

Figure 4.1: Andaman Islands: Jarawa Campsites in 2002

Source: Anthropological Survey of India.

Plate 4.3: A permanent hut (camp) of the Jarawa

remain occupied for a longer period of one to three months. The third type is a lean-to type hut where they spend a day or two in the course of their foraging movement (Plate 4.4). The base camps of the Jarawa are not randomly distributed over space. Instead, the

Source: Anthropological Survey of India.

Plate 4.4: A temporary hut (camp) of the Jarawa

location of a camp at a place is governed by a combination of three factors, viz., (i) ecological edges, (ii) proximity to potable water, along with easy availability of one of the edible resources and (iii) seasons.

ECOLOGICAL EDGES

A well-known facet of ecosystems is the edges – the boundaries or transitions from one ecosystem to another – which often exhibit a high level of species richness or biodiversity. Ecological edges facilitate the exploitation of a wide variety of micro-sites and habitat interfaces situated within a major ecosystem. Human societies situated on the ecological edges are likely to benefit from the increased biodiversity in terms of their access to the resources of two or more ecosystems (Odum 1971, Turner et al. 2003).

The cognisance of territory into five broad zones by the Jarawa is, in fact, the division of space into five broad physiographic zones (Figure 3.2, Chapter 3). Each of these zones has a different assemblage of resources. Spatially most species, even those that are widespread in terms of their overall range, are restricted in their living requirements to particular ecological habitats or niches (Winterhalder 1983). It is these characteristics of ecological edges which make them suitable places for the location of camps (Brothers 1993, Meiners and Steward 1999). By locating their camps on the ecological edges, the Jarawa get access to the resources of two or more ecological zones having high resource diversity.

The locations of the camps along the waterways and the roads are very common among the Jarawa. But the use of waterways for transportation is not a deciding factor for the location of the camps because the Jarawa do not have a well developed water transportation system like that of their counterparts (Sentinelese, Onges, Great Andamanese) who make out-rigger canoes. The Jarawa do not make canoes. Instead, the Jarawa make a very rudimentary raft (Plates 4.5, 4.6), which they use to cross the small creeks. Camping sites of the Jarawa are found at points along streams, inlets, creeks and shorelines. It gives them access to resources of two or more than two ecological zones. For example, the location

Source: Anthropological Survey of India.

Plate 4.5: A rudimentary raft of the Jarawa

Source: Anthropological Survey of India.

Plate 4.6: A Sentinelese in his out-rigger canoe

of campsites near a creek or coast provides easy accessibility to inter-tidal zone (renowned for the richness and productivity of its food resources) towards the seaward side, and the wetlands, creeks, marshes, as well as forest of various types on the landward side. Thus, they get access to diverse range of resources available in different ecological zones, which, in turn, widen their resource base. In the post-hostility phase (after 1997), the proximity to the road has emerged as another important factor for the location of the camp. It provides them easy access to the vehicular traffic plying on the Andaman Trunk Road. By using the vehicular traffic, they are reducing the travel cost in terms of time and exploit the resources of a larger area along the road. This phenomenon is more pronounced in the Thidong and Tanmad areas as compared to the Boiab area.

AVAILABILITY OF WATER AND EDIBLE RESOURCES

The setting up of the camps at ecological edges is governed by the proximity to potable water, and availability of one of the edible resources in plenty, particularly the aquatic resources. When the camp has an inland location, the edible resources available in plenty are the bivalve shell followed by fish. These resources are found in the nearby creek or stream, and in the case of a coastal location, the edible resources available in abundance are different species of molluscs and fish.

SEASONS

Seasons play a decisive role in the location of the camps along the coast and in the forest. At any given point of time, the Jarawa have between two to three permanent camps in any territory. During the rainy season (south-west monsoon) from May to September, the permanent campsites along the western coast are avoided as the south-west monsoon winds thrash the western coast harshly. Consequently, the sea remains turbulent and rough on the western side of the Islands. On the seaward side, the sheltered bay and creeks are ideal sites for the location of the camps. Inside the forest, raised grounds are selected as campsites.

With the onset of the cool winter season from November to February, both seaward and landward locations are preferred for setting up the camps. The underlying strategy is to harness the abundantly available seasonal resources, particularly honey, followed by turtle eggs. While the former is available in the forest, the latter is found along the coast on sandy beaches. During the dry summer period, the camps are usually located a bit away from the coast, well inside the forest, to gather honey and jackfruit. As such the ideal location for setting up the camp is generally inside the forest so that both the resources could be exploited.

MOVEMENT PATTERN

There are a number of factors that condition the way hunter-gatherers position themselves over space and make movements. Movement strategies are organisational responses to the structural properties of the natural and social environment (Binford 1980). The logistical component of a settlement system, in which task specific groups range out from residential locations for purpose of obtaining food, raw materials or information, is related to the organisation of production of society as well as to the distribution of critical resources in the environment (Kelly 1995). There are two types of movement – residential and logistical (Binford 1980, Kelly 1995). In the case of residential movement, the entire group, producers and dependents, move from one place to another in their territory (Plate 4.7). It involves the change from one base camp to another. Logistical movement, on the other hand, is the movement to and from a base camp by an individual or task oriented group for obtaining matter, energy, or information. The logistical movement also includes the movement between base camps and temporary camps.

The logistical trips of the Jarawa consist of either daily forays or expeditions of a few days. During all three phases of primary data collection for the present study, it was observed that the Jarawa were always on the move from one place to another in search of

Source: Anthropological Survey of India.

Plate 4.7: Residential movement of a group of Jarawas (shfting of permanent camp)

food resources. Concentration and dispersion or fusion and fission of families in a group were constant features. Based on the frequency of the movements and distance covered, the Jarawa may be divided into three groups. The most mobile group is that of unmarried boys who have been initiated into the hunter-hood through the *lepa* ceremony. Even within their territory, they move frequently from one camp to another. In fact, they help spread information from one group to another. The least mobile group comprises unmarried girls and widows. They never venture out of their territory alone and generally move along with the family units. In the family groups, widowers and boys of adolescent age stand in between the above two groups.

The fieldwork of three months in three different seasons has given a glimpse of the movement patterns of the Jarawa. It reveals that the movements of the Jarawa oscillate between the coasts and forests. The underlying strategy behind such movements is to exploit the resources of both areas and have access to a broad resource base. The one day trip of the Jarawa is within a radius of 10 km. Initially, the resources that are at a lesser distance from the camp are exploited. With the thinning of resources in the vicinity, they travel longer distances to exploit distant resources. However, in the case of pig hunting, the strategy of exploitation of resources in a sequential manner (i.e. first the nearest resources) is not applicable. Further, when the movement requires covering of more than 10 km of an area, then they either stay overnight in the forest or organise foraging expeditions ranging from a few days to two weeks.

At any given point of time, the Jarawa have between two to three permanent camps in an area. All the logistic movements are made from any of these campsites. The movement pattern of the Jarawa is governed by the seasons also. During the summer season when the wild jackfruits and seeds of *Cucas rumphii* are available in plenty, the movement of the Jarawa is oriented towards the collection of these resources. Since the former is available in the forest while the latter is found in the creek, the movement of the Jarawa oscillates between creek and forest. During the dry season, less numbers of logistical movements are made compared to other seasons. The reason for this is attributed to the fact that the gathering and processing of jackfruits require them to stay at a place for about 4 to 5 days at a stretch when they are away from the base camp.

During the rainy season, when the sea is rough due to the southwest monsoon, it is virtually impossible to exploit the marine resources on the western coast. Therefore, the permanent campsites are not located along the western coast. Instead, they are located inside the forests away from the western coast, where they do most of the pig hunting. As pig is a mobile prey, the Jarawa have to undertake a number of logistical trips for hunting it. As a result, the numbers of foraging expeditions of more than 5 days at a stretch are more in the rainy season. In the fieldwork, it was observed that during the rainy season, eight foraging expeditions were performed in one month (August-September 2002) from the Ulia base camp.

During the cool-dry season, the movements of the Jarawa oscillate between the sea coast and forests. It is because the sea remains usually calm during this season. Interestingly, it is also the season when turtles lay eggs on sandy beaches, and honey is available in the forests. Hence, the movements of the Jarawa are oriented towards the exploitation of these resources. During this season, the stay of a family at a base camp is comparatively longer, ranging from a minimum of 4 days to a maximum of 15 days.

The role of information in this system of concentration and dispersion is important. Everyone knows the location of each group and which group is to move where within a territory. This kind of information system serves as a means of ensuring subsistence security and reduces the chance of many groups converging at the same place for the resources. Monitoring and information among groups and individuals are crucial in decision making about movement.

FORAGING METHODS

Foraging methods, besides tools and technology, are an important aspect of human adaptation. It usually maximises returns in less time with minimum efforts. In the course of deriving resources, particularly the animal resources, the Jarawa employ a particular set or sets of foraging methods. It involves the interplay of three variables, viz., (i) selections of food resources, particularly prey animals, (ii) methods employed in the collection of plant and animal resources, and (iii) search image.

SELECTION OF FOOD RESOURCES

By now, 221 species of plants and animals have been documented as the food articles of the Jarawa. Of the total known species, 136 are plants and 85 animals. Despite the wide edible resource base, the Jarawa are found to be highly selective about food. They tend to eat only the most palatable and abundantly available food items and bypass the less desirable foods. However, the exception is the flesh of game animals (wild pig, monitor lizard, turtle) which is the most desired and sought after food item though not available in abundance. For harvesting the resources, both plants and animals, various factors are taken into consideration, which are discussed below.

METHODS EMPLOYED IN THE COLLECTION OF ANIMAL AND PLANT RESOURCES

Hunting, fishing and gathering are three means of getting animal resources. They require the application of a specific method for satisfactory gains in terms of resources. The meticulous execution of the method undoubtedly enhances the chances of getting satisfactory gains. Jarawa use the following methods in relation to hunting, fishing and gathering.

HUNTING

The game animals of the Jarawa include wild pigs, monitor lizards and turtles. During hunting the Jarawa use any of these three methods to get the prey.

1. *Ambushing*: In this case, the hunter is stationary. He does not pursue the prey. Rather he waits for the prey to approach a pre-selected site and as soon as the prey is within the shooting range, he shoots the arrow. It is applied in the case of all game animals.
2. *Besetting*: It is opposite to ambushing. Here the hunter roams in search of a stationary prey at their resting or nesting places. This method is also applicable in case of all the game animals.
3. *Following the moving prey*: In this case, both hunter and prey are mobile. Here the hunter actively seeks, tracks, stalks and pursues the prey. This method is applicable only in the case of hunting pigs and monitor lizards.

Further, the first two methods of hunting are used when the hunter is individually pursuing the prey, while the third method is used in both individual and group hunting. The kind of game animal determines whether it will be individual hunting or group hunting. In the case of turtle and monitor lizard, it is individual hunting, whereas pig is hunted both individually and in groups. It is to be noted that the Jarawa engage in group hunting only in the case of wild pigs. Both individual and group hunting begin in the morning and end by the early evening. Generally, hunting is not practised at the night.

FISHING

Fishing provides an excellent opportunity for the examination of foraging methods and techniques employed by the Jarawa. This is precisely because the prey is small, quick and has the capacity of escaping away in the water from the predator. Traditionally, the fishing sites are the coastal areas, creeks, swamps and dammed-off channels where a creek or stream has parted around an island. In fact, fishing is carried out generally during low tide. The male folk does fishing with bows and arrows while the female folk does with a hand nets and pointed wooden sticks and iron rods. Fishing by putting poison in the water is unknown to the Jarawa. Fishing is done both individually and in a group (Plate 4.8 and 4.9). Group fishing has an obvious advantage over individual fishing. In the case of individual fishing, the success rate is less compared to the group fishing. It is so because if a fish escapes an individual's arrow or spear jab or hand-net, it returns only after a time lag of a few minutes.

Group fishing is generally carried out in dammed off channels, creeks and marshy areas during the low tide. Though both men and women take part in fishing, there is a preponderance of women in this activity. In group fishing, the females form a semi-circle and drive the fish into a corner by moving forward. Once the fish

Source: Anthropological Survey of India.

Plate 4.8: Jarawa children fishing near the shore

Source: Anthropological Survey of India.

Plate 4.9: A male Jarawa fishing with bow and arrow in the reef area

have been cornered, they put the hand net at the escape routes. It is followed by jabbing the fish with a pointed wooden stick or iron rod. Thus, some of the fish are jabbed while others, which try to escape, are trapped in the net. The success rate in terms of a catch is certainly very high in group fishing. However, in the case of both individual and group fishing, the probability that an individual fish will be encountered is directly related to the number of persons fishing in the area, the size of the area and size and number of fish.

Collection of Grub Larvae

The grub larvae are collected from the rotting trunk of trees. It has been observed that some trees are felled to create clear space for setting up a camp at a new site. This serves some purpose. Firstly, it allows the sunlight to reach the ground. Secondly, the felled trees soon begin to rot under the hot and humid conditions and in these rotting tree trunks, the grub larvae flourish. Thirdly, the clear space help accelerates the rate of the natural regeneration of species, particularly moist deciduous species. Thus, the distribution and abundance of the grub larvae to some extent is influenced by human intervention also.

Harvesting of Tubers

Tubers (*Dioscorea* sp.) are one of the plant resources harvested by the Jarawa. It is one of the food items which meets their carbohydrate needs. To ensure the long term adequacy of the tubers, the plants are not killed when harvested. When tubers are dug up, roots at the base of the tuber are normally left. From these roots grow new vines and tubers.

SEARCH IMAGE

Many of the species sought as prey by the Jarawa are located in or obtained from particular physiographic zones or in some cases from particular places. For example, wild pigs are most often sought in the forested piedmont zone and extensive back swamps. Bivalve shells are available in high quantities in streams that drain the back swamps. The larvae of some species of beetle are collected from the rotting trunks of trees. Besides, many of the strategies used are best suited to a particular species or sets of ecologically similar species, as in the case of fish. Some tactics used for hunting pigs, monitor lizards, and turtles are, in fact, incompatible with other prey animals. Thus, it is apparent that strategies employed in search image are not only location-specific but in some cases prey specific as well.

As a consequence, the search image, during a single episode of hunting, is usually narrow. People seek a particular species or set of species within a particular environment using a particular strategy. While searching for one category of prey, the Jarawa seldom divert their attention to another. It means one kind of prey at a time. Again, this behaviour presumably enhances the effectiveness with which the targeted category of prey is pursued.

ROLE SPECIALISATION

Role specialisation in hunting may be quantitative, with some individuals or groups of individuals taking more game than the others. It is mainly due to differences in the strategy they follow or the categories of prey animals they pursue. It has been found that there is a division of labour in the Jarawa society for every type of work or activity. Though the females do not hunt wild pigs, they do gather small animals like snails, molluscs, etc. Women do most of the fishing and collection of bivalve shells. In fact, most of the gathering is done by the womenfolk. Though men also take part in the gathering, it is comparatively much less. It is interesting to note that the female gatherers bring in the bulk of the edible resources, i.e. honey, roots, tubers, grub larvae, etc. (Table 4.2 and 4.4). Thus, a combination of food from both animal and plant sources provide the necessary balanced diet comprising of protein and carbohydrate. Much of the qualitative difference in terms of food collection between males and females is because the females do not use bows and arrows while collecting animal food. Several reasons are responsible for this difference, some of which seem to be rooted in biological differences between the male and female.

1. Most of the Jarawa women in their prime age are apt to be either pregnant or nursing mothers. In either case, their ability to travel long distances on foot, something that is unavoidable in hunting, is significantly restricted.
2. There is a higher risk involved in hunting than in other tasks of food gathering usually performed by the Jarawa women. To place women at such a high risk would mean placing children also in actual or potential risk.

Among males, the amount of meat collected individually in hunting varies greatly. The performance of a male is not examined in terms of either age or marital status. Some men get a lot of meat and some get very little. The variations in individual performance in hunting appear to be related to differences in hunting skills and chances of getting prey.

SHARING

Sharing the resources of the habitat is a norm in the hunting and gathering human groups, and the Jarawa are no exception. The first application of this norm is seen in the distribution of territorial groups of the Jarawa at the spatial level where the natural resources of a particular territory can be accessed only by that group which inhabits it. It means all the members or sub-groups of a particular territory have the right to access the natural resources of the territory they are inhabiting. As discussed earlier (Chapter 3), there are three territorial groups among the Jarawa and each one of them has its well-defined territory from where they gather their resources. Secondly, the edible resources collected by an individual or a family or a group are brought to the campsite. The campsite is the place that acts as the centre of daily activities. It is the place where the sharing of the collected resources actually occurs. The edible resources gathered and brought to the camps are shared systematically among the constituent members or families. While the meat of the game animals is shared among the constituent families of a camp, sharing of other resources is at the intra-family level. In the Jarawa society, a relatively regular supply of protein to all the members is ensured through sharing of meat of the wild pig, monitor lizard and turtle. Though sharing of meat is the norm, there is a lack of sufficient quantitative information about this practice for attempting further analysis. The meats of the game animals are routinely distributed from a communal hearth; each household is given a portion of the meat, while family units generally consume small animals and plant foods separately. Usually, the hunter's family gets the larger share while other constituent families get the comparatively small but equal share of the meat.

One can easily understand why sharing is considered necessary if the game is hunted collectively, and how the survival of every member of the group is related to it. The individual hunters find it in their interest to share what they cannot consume entirely. For the individual hunter, food sharing is a way of storing food for the future; his generosity gives him a claim in future on the surplus of other hunters. As the flesh of pig is the most preferred of all food items, the Jarawa always share this item as a part of survival strategy. The visitors (i.e. Jarawa from other territories) are common to the Jarawa, and they are offered meat available with the host. The Jarawa never consider the visitors as a burden as the latter also participate in food collection and share their collection with other members of the group, when they are staying with the host. The meat of the hunted game animals are distributed across the group of families, however, the amount of meat an individual hunter contributes to the common pool varies greatly. Given the type of hunting system, this is inevitable because hunting skills vary from person to person. There is little likelihood that they would achieve similar returns. To sustain sharing in the face of unequal contributions calls for mechanisms that would level the effects of varying individual performance so that the group can benefit from the overall performance. In the Jarawa community, there are no sanctions associated with performance, particularly poor performance in hunting. Consequently, the varying individual performance is not associated with any reward or penalty.

FORAGING STATUS

The Jarawa are a group that lives solely by hunting and gathering. To illustrate their hunting and gathering (foraging) status, first, it is important to know how much time is expended towards a satisfactory collection of resources. Second, it is equally important to find out how far the hunting behaviour of the Jarawa conforms to the hunting behaviour of a hunter-gatherer group. Lastly, based on the two above mentioned conditions an attempt has been made to explain the dynamics of the interrelationship among three factors, i.e. people, resource and work.

INPUT-OUTPUT ANALYSIS

The Jarawa have a simple, self-contained economy. The hunting and gathering pursuits of the Jarawa are based entirely on the extraction of resources from nature. The accumulation of food is minimal. Domestication of plants and animals is absent. The relation between the collection and consumption of food is immediate in terms of space and time. In the Jarawa society, every able-bodied person above the age of 14 is an economically active member of the society, supporting himself or herself and the dependent members as well. There is no dependent population except the children. Surprisingly, no handicapped person, who is unable to support himself/herself or is dependent on the other members of the band, is found in the adult age groups. In other words, the person with a crippling disability is not supported by the Jarawa. Consequently, he/she dies very soon. There is a generalised reciprocity in terms of sharing of resources. The flesh of the game animals is shared routinely among the constituent families of a group, while the other foraged items are shared only within a family. It, therefore, presents a suitable case for the application of the input-output analysis.

Having taken cognisance of the above mentioned points, the 'input-output analysis' has been applied to the data collected on the subsistence effort of the Jarawa. The subsistence effort is a compilation of all days of work carried out by a member of a group within a specified period. It has been described in terms of the number of days per week per hunter.

The formula used for 'input-output analysis' is taken from Lee (1969), which is as follows:

S = W/C
where S = the Index of Subsistence Effort,
where W = the number of man-days of work, and
where C = number of man-days of consumption.

In a self-sufficient human group, the magnitude of 'S' (Index of Subsistence Effort), refers to the efforts made for the collection of resources to feed the group.

Summary of the diary at the Alaoethala base camp in the Thidong area for the period from 12 December 2001 to 8 January 2002 is presented in Table 4.1. It is the season of honey gathering, turtle eggs collection and hunting. The average group size varies from 15.1 to 40.4 persons. Of the total population at the campsite, 52 per cent (475 persons) are active population while the remaining 48 per cent (443) are dependent. The work week varies between 3.8 and 4.0 days a week, with the average being 3.9 days a week. It means they have 3 to 3.2 days per week for leisure, socialising and other activities.

The 'Index of Subsistence Effort' (S) for four weeks is 0.30. The value of 'S' indicates 30 days of work per hundred days of

TABLE 4.1: SUMMARY OF SUBSISTENCE EFFORTS AT ALAOETHALA BASE CAMP (FROM 12 DECEMBER 2001 TO 8 JANUARY 2002)

Week	Mean group size	Adult	Chil-dren	Man-days of consum-ption	Man-days of work	Man-days of hunting	Meat out-put (kg)	Male involved in hunting %	Work week	Index of Subsist-ence
I week (12-18)	40.4 (31-42)	128	155	283	074	27	83	33	4.0	0.26
II week (19-25)	51.8 (42-57)	193	170	363	108	29	69	25	3.9	0.30
III week (26-01)	23.7 (10-26)	089	077	166	050	13	23	25	3.9	0.30
IV week (02-08)	15.1 (10-16)	065	041	106	035	11	34	24	3.8	0.33
4 Weeks Total	131.0	475	443	918	267	80	209	107	15.67	1.19
4 Weeks Average	32.75	118.75	110.75	229.5	66.75	20	52.25	26.75	3.9	0.30

Source: Field Investigation, December 2001- January 2002.

man-days consumption, or each day's work provided food for the worker and 2.3 dependent persons. The week wise analysis of Table 4.1 reveals that the 'S' was 0.26 in the first week, which increased to 0.30 in the second and third weeks. In the fourth week, it increased further to 0.33. This increase in the value of 'S' was due to the onset of the season for collection of honey and turtle eggs, which began from the second week of December 2001. Then the subsistence effort of the group was directed towards the collection of honey and turtle eggs. Interestingly, it was observed that a decline in the success rate of wild pig hunting due to long stay of the Jarawa at the same place was offset by success in the monitor lizard hunting. Of the total adult male population, subsistence effort of only 27 per cent was directed towards hunting, while the rest of the males were involved in gathering activities. The hunting accounted for 30 per cent of the total man-days of work while 70 per cent of the man-days of work was oriented towards fishing and gathering activities.

Table 4.2 shows the collection of total food items at the Alaoethala base camp from 12 December 2001 to 8 January 2002. The analysis shows that about 679 kg of different food articles were collected by 475 Jarawa in 28 days. The flesh of wild pig and monitor lizards constituted about 30.78 per cent (209 kg) of the total resources collected. It was followed by honey and tuber. Each one of these constituted about 27.25 per cent (185 kg) of the total collected

TABLE 4.2: PROCUREMENT OF FOOD ARTICLES (FROM 12 DECEMBER 2001 TO 8 JANUARY 2002)

Food Article	Quantity (kg)
Meat	209
Honey	185
Tubers	185
Molluscs	65
Fish	25
Turtle eggs	10
Total	679

Source: Field Investigation, 2002.

resources. These were followed by the fish and turtle eggs. It may be noted that it was the season for the collection of turtle eggs and honey and only major resources were taken into account for analysis.

Table 4.3 is the summary of the work diary at the Ulia base camp in the Tanmad area for the period from 12 August 2002 to 8 September 2002. It is the period of rainy season when pig hunting along with the collection of seeds of *Cycas rumphii* is a major subsistence activity. The group size varied from 23.3 to 47.6 persons. The work weeks varied between 3.4 to 3.9 days a week, with the average being 3.7 days a week. It implies that they had 3.1 to 3.6 days for leisure, socialising and other activities.

The average value of 'S' for four weeks was 0.29 (29 work days per 100 consumption days). The value S = 0.29 indicates 29 man-days of work per hundred man-days of consumption, or each day's work provided food for the worker and two and a half (2.4) other people. A week-wise analysis of subsistence index shows, it was high in the first week, i.e. 0.32, while in the following three weeks it remained between 0.27 and 0.29. The reason for the high value of 'S' in the first week was due to greater effort made for hunting. In the subsequent weeks, less effort was made for hunting owing to less availability of pigs. It is evident from the column 'man-days of hunting' that only 32 man-days (40 per cent) of work was expended for hunting in the last three weeks compared to 48 man-days (60 per cent) of work in the first week. Of the total adult males, about 31.5 per cent adult males were involved in hunting. The hunting accounted for nearly one-third (32 per cent) of the total man-days of work while approximately two-thirds of efforts in terms of man-days were oriented towards fishing and gathering.

At the Ulia base camp, there were about 466 Jarawa who collected 685 kg of food in 28 days (Table 4.4.). Among the collected food items, the flesh of wild pig (223 kg) was the main item, followed by *Cycus rumphii* (177 kg), tubers (173 kg), fish (55 kg), molluscs (52 kg) and honey (5 kg). It may be noted that it was the rainy season when pig hunting and collection of seeds of *Cycas rumphii* were major activities. Of the total collected food items, the pig accounted for 32.56 per cent followed by *Cycas rumphii*

TABLE 4.3: SUMMARY OF SUBSISTENCE EFFORTS AT ULIA BASE CAMP (FROM 12 AUGUST 2002 TO 8 SEPTEMBER 2002)

Week	Mean group size	Adult	Children	Man-days of consumption	Man-days of work	Man-days of hunting	Meat output (kg)	Male involved in hunting %	Work week	Index of Subsistence
I week (12-18)	47.6 (16-73)	190	143	333	107	48	150	54	3.9	0.32
II week (19-25)	23.3 (16-33)	082	081	163	044	05	014	13	3.7	0.27
III week (26-01)	24.6 (16-33)	089	083	172	048	15	032	36	3.8	0.29
IV week (02-08)	27.0 (23-30)	105	084	189	051	12	027	23	3.4	0.27
4 Weeks Total =	122.5	466	391	857	250	80	223	126	14.8	1.15
4 Weeks Average =	30.6	116.5	97.75	214.25	62.5	20	55.75	31.5	03.7	0.29

Source: Field Investigation, August and September 2002.

TABLE 4.4: PROCUREMENT OF FOOD ARTICLES
(FROM 12 AUGUST 2002 TO 8 SEPTEMBER 2002)

Food Article	Quantity
Meat	223
Honey	005
Tubers	173
Molluscs	052
Fish	055
Cycus Ramphii	177
Total	685

Source: Field Investigation, 2002.

25.84 per cent, tubers 25.26 per cent and fish and molluscs approximately 8 per cent each.

When both the Tables (4.1 and 4.3) are taken together, the 'input-output analysis' shows that the average value of 'Index of Subsistence Effort' for the Jarawa varied between 0.29 and 0.30, the average being 0.295. It meant 29.5 days of work per hundred man-days of consumption, or each day's work provided food for the worker and 2.38 other members of the band. The average work input varied between 3.7 to 3.9 days a week. It meant they still had between 3.1 to 3.3 days in a week left for socialising and other leisure activities. Of the total adult male population, approximately 29 per cent were involved in hunting. It accounted for 30 per cent of the total man-days of work. It may be generalised that nearly one-third of the subsistence effort of the Jarawa was oriented towards hunting and the remaining two-thirds for fishing and gathering. This result, in turn, supports the earlier statement that despite their preference for the meat of game animals, the fish and molluscs are the keystone resources for the Jarawa.

From the above analysis, it can be deduced that the Jarawa work for only a limited time, the average being between 3.7 and 3.9 days in a week and the rest of the time is spent in socialising and other leisure related activities. Secondly, in the subsistence efforts of the Jarawa, fishing and gathering account for nearly two-thirds of their total subsistence effort while hunting accounts for nearly one-third of it.

FORAGING BEHAVIOUR OF THE JARAWA

Foraging behaviour of many human groups of the world has raised important questions, which have been investigated by a number of social scientists (e.g., Lee 1968, 1979, Sahlins 1972, 1976, Harris 1985, Farb and Armelagos, 1980). Models derived from optimal foraging theory are being used increasingly to evaluate human foraging behaviour (Winterhalder 1981, Hawkes, et al. 1982, Smith, 1983, Hill and Hurtado, 1989). These models have provided useful insights into human subsistence patterns, particularly of the hunter-gatherers concerning their hunting behaviour.

The conventional optimal foraging models make three constraint assumptions (Stephens and Krebs 1986: 10-11), viz., (i) the exclusivity of the acts of search and exploitation of resources, (ii) complete information – the forager behaves as if he or she is aware of the rules of the model, and (iii) prey items are encountered sequentially and as a Poisson process. Of these three central assumptions, the final one – sequential Poisson encounters – is unique in that it can be quantitatively verified. The validity of this assumption has been examined utilising the data collected on the hunting behaviour of the Jarawa. Because of the importance of the assumption and the relative ease with which it can be verified, it is viewed as an important and necessary first step in any optimal foraging analysis. If the hunting encounters do not conform to a Poisson process, then any results generated by an optimal foraging model needs to be questioned.

The first necessary analytical step is to derive an encounter distribution for each hunter. This step is accomplished by dividing each hunter's time, spent searching for prey, into equal units of one hour within which the number of prey encountered is counted. The choice of a particular time unit, such as the one-hour unit used here, is an arbitrary matter within certain constraints keeping in mind that the time unit must be neither so short that the distribution decomposes into its component Bernoulli (binary) distributions, nor so long that there are too few units of observations in the sample. The one-hour time unit is convenient, readily interpretable, and meets the constraints.

The next step is to compare the observed distribution with an expected Poisson distribution characterised by the same mean. The Poisson distribution itself is a distribution of discrete, independent, and rare events. It is represented by the following equation:

$$f(x) = \frac{\mu^x(e^{-\mu})}{x!}$$

where μ = mean of the distribution,
x = number of events per unit time, and
e = base of natural log.

Along with the more familiar normal distribution, the Poisson distribution is a type of probability distribution. It is utilised in optimal foraging models because it describes discrete events (such as encounters with prey items in a given time) that do not occur frequently. Further, in order to generate confidence in the results, a Chi-square goodness-of-fit test has been done to compare observed distributions with expected Poisson distributions having the same mean. Though the value in some of the categories is less than five (5), yet in order to generate further confidence in the results Chi-square goodness-of-fit test has been used following Zelenznik and Bennet (1991). The distributions have also been compared graphically.

Table 4.5 shows 55 observations. It demonstrates that the mean (2.0727) and variance (2.4761) of this distribution approximate each other though not equivalent. There is a greater similarity between the observed and expected distributions. However, there is a period with no encounters and an under-representation of the two categories. Despite these discrepancies, the Chi-square value of 3.533 is associated with a 'p' value of approximately 0.8317 for 7 degrees of freedom, which is well above the standard alpha value of 0.05. It means the $p > 0.05$. Therefore, it can be concluded that these distributions are insignificant. Graphically also, these distributions appear similar (Figure 4.2).

Table 4.6 has 47 observations. Here also, one finds that the mean (2.021) and the variance (2.108) approximate each other. The observed and expected distributions are quite similar as well with a total Chi-square value of 2.199418 and an associated 'p'

TABLE 4.5: OBSERVED AND EXPECTED FREQUENCY DISTRIBUTIONS

Encounter per Hour	Observed Frequency	Probability	Expected Frequency	Chi-square
0	9	0.126162	6.923015	0.62312
1	14	0.261499	14.34952	0.008513
2	12	0.271008	14.87132	0.554387
3	10	0.187242	10.27473	0.007346
4	6	0.097025	5.324177	0.085786
5	2	0.040221	2.207113	0.019435
6	2	0.013895	0.762457	2.008654
7	0	0.004114	0.225766	0.225766
Sum	55	1.001168	54.9381	3.533008

p value = 0.832, Mean = 2.0727, Variance = 2.4761
Source: Field Investigation, 2002.

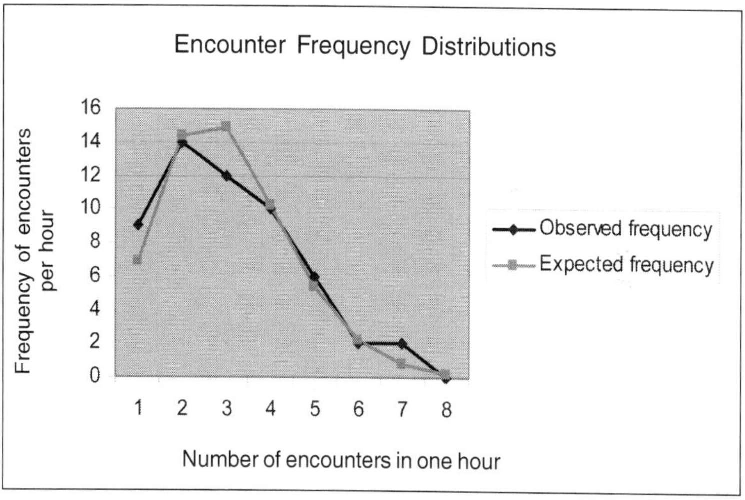

Figure 4.2: Encounter Frequency Distributions

value of approximately 0.948 for 7 degrees of freedom. The 'p' value is greater and well above the standard alpha value of 0.05. It means the $p > 0.05$. These distributions, therefore, are also insignificant. Graphically, these distributions appear similar as well (Figure 4.3). Once again, here also, there is a period with no encounters and an under-representation of the two categories.

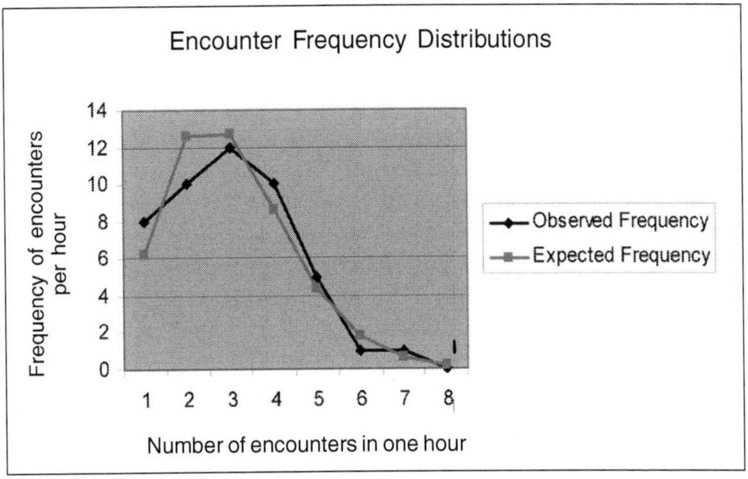

Figure 4.3: Encounter Frequency Distributions

TABLE 4.6: OBSERVED AND EXPECTED FREQUENCY DISTRIBUTIONS

Encounter per Hour	Observed Frequency	Probability	Expected Frequency	Chi-Square
0	8	0.132327	6.219363	0.509806
1	10	0.267469	12.57105	0.525837
2	12	0.270315	12.70479	0.039098
3	10	0.182127	8.559968	0.242255
4	5	0.092032	4.325517	0.105173
5	1	0.037205	1.748613	0.320495
6	1	0.012533	0.589072	0.286657
7	0	0.003619	0.170097	0.170097
Sum	47	0.997627	46.88848	2.199418

p value = 0.948, Mean = 2.021, Variance = 2.108
Source: Field Investigation, 2002.

Finally, in Table 4.7 the data sets of two seasons (Tables 4.5 and 4.6) are combined into a single distribution. The similarity between the observed and expected distributions has further increased. The mean (2.049) and variance (2.285) approximate each other, and the total Chi-square value is 4.810616 with an

TABLE 4.7: TOTAL OBSERVED AND EXPECTED FREQUENCY DISTRIBUTIONS

Encounter per Hour	Observed Frequency	Probability	Expected Frequency	Chi-Square
0	17	0.129	13.158	1.121824
1	24	0.264321	26.960742	0.325139
2	24	0.270797	27.62128018	0.474767
3	20	0.184954	18.86533436	0.068246
4	11	0.094743	9.663767527	0.184764
5	3	0.038826	3.960211933	0.232818
6	3	0.013259	1.352412375	2.007189
7	0	0.003881	0.395870422	0.39587
Sum	102	0.999781	101.9776188	4.810616

p value = 0.683, Mean = 2.049, Variance = 2.285

associated 'p' value of 0.683 for 7 degrees of freedom. Here also, the 'p' value is greater and well above the standard alpha value of 0.05. It means the $p > 0.05$. These distributions, therefore, are insignificant. Graphically also, a similar distribution has been achieved (Figure 4.4).

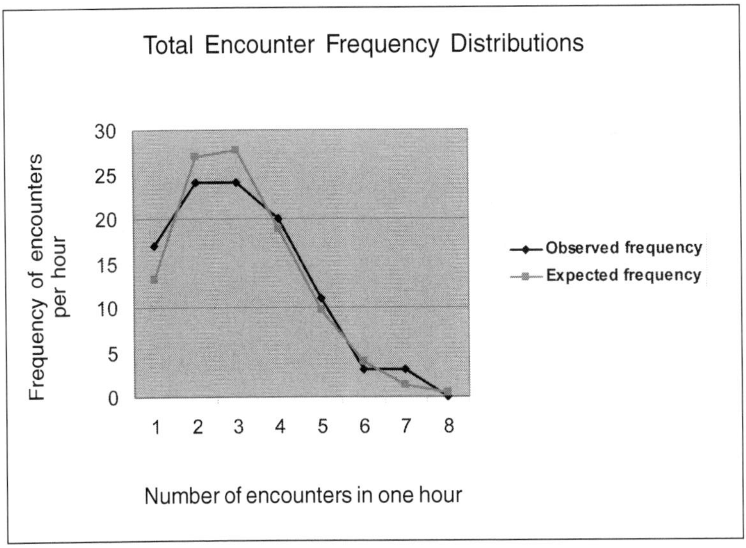

Figure 4.4: Total Encounter Frequency Distributions

From the above analysis, it can be concluded that all three distributions are remarkably similar and closely resemble a Poisson distribution. It means the prey items are encountered sequentially as a Poisson process. The results also have a very important implication in a sense that it shows that the Jarawa are still a hunting and gathering community as their foraging behaviour conforms to it. Further, as noted above, the Poisson distribution is a probability distribution of discrete, independent and rare events. Its occurrence here suggests that in terms of encountering animals, the Jarawa do not consciously manipulate their environment in order to make prey encounters uniform, or if they attempt to, they are not successful at it. This distribution of encounters reflects the interaction between moving foragers and the distribution of prey animals in an environment. If prey animals were highly aggregated or the Jarawa hunters were able to manipulate their encounters, one would expect a bimodal or unimodal non-Poisson distribution, respectively. This simple analysis is a critical step in the analysis of the hunting behaviour of the Jarawa based on 'optimal foraging theory'.

PEOPLE, RESOURCE AND WORK

In foraging activities, foraging efficiency is related to a satisfactory collection of resources. The satisfactory collection of resources, in turn, ensures adequate consumption of required calories. These calories provide the maintenance energy required for the survival of an individual and replacing of oneself with one's offspring (Winterhalder 1993). If the net acquisition rate of edible resources is greater than the maintenance rate then the forager produces extra energy that is available for individual reproduction above replacement resulting in population growth; if it is less, then individuals do not meet their maintenance need and eventually, the population begins declining due to malnutrition. It is, therefore, important to find out whether the resources collected by the Jarawa meet their calorie requirement or not.

As discussed earlier, the edible items of the Jarawa consist of both terrestrial and aquatic resources. The nutritional study conducted by the Department of Health, Port Blair and Indian Institute of

Public Hygiene and Health (2002) has put major edible items of the Jarawa diet under two categories, i.e. (i) pig dominant diet, and (ii) other diets (Tables 4.8 and 4.9).

The pig dominant diet of the Jarawa comprises pig meat, pig fat, honey, tubers, fruits and fruit seeds (Table 4.8). On average, an individual consumes about 925 gm of food (2432 KCal), of which animal foods comprise 54.05 per cent (500 gm) and plant foods 44.95 per cent (425 gm). However, in terms of calorific value of the edible items, the Jarawa derive 71.96 per cent (1750 KCal) from the animal foods and 28.04 per cent (682 KCal) from the plant foods. It means animal foods are the major source of energy for the Jarawa.

Other diets of Jarawa consists of pig fat, honey, fish, molluscs, turtle eggs, tubers, fruits and seeds (Table 4.9). In this case, the percentage contribution of plant foods is more than animal foods. Of the total diet, the plant foods constitute about 54.5 per cent (625 gm) and animal food 45.4 per cent (529 gm) in terms of weight. However, in terms of the total calorific value of the resources, the 58.87 per cent of the calorie (1489.7 KCal) is derived from the animal foods and 41.13 per cent calorie (1041 KCal) from plant foods. Thus, the above analysis suggests that in the case of other diets also, the animal foods constitute the major part of the Jarawa diet in terms of calorific value.

The analyses of Tables 4.8 and 4.9 also support the fact that the net acquisition of resources in case of the Jarawa is satisfactory because on average an adult Jarawa gets approximately 2,500 KCal

TABLE 4.8: PIG DOMINANT DIET

Food Article	Amount	KCal
Wild pig meat	350	400
Wild pig fat	150	1,350
Honey	150	478
Tubers	150	105
Fruits & seeds	125	99
Total	925	2,432

Source: Department of Health and Indian Institute of Public Hygiene and Health, 2002.

TABLE 4.9: OTHER DIETS

Food Article	Amount (gm)	KCal
Wild pig fat	120	1,080.0
Fish	250	252.5
Mollusc	100	97.0
Turtle eggs	50	60.2
Honey	250	767
Tubers	250	175.0
Fruits & seeds	125	99.0
Total	1,145	2,530.7

Source: Department of Health and Indian Institute of Public Hygiene and Health, 2002.
Note: Time period of data from 12 December 2001 to 8 January 2002, 12 April 2002 to 9 May 2002 and 12 August 2002 to 8 September 2002.

from the major resources alone. If the minor resources are also included, then it will well be around 2,800 KCal. It means the net acquisition rate of resources in case of the Jarawa is above the maintenance requirement and thus, theirs is a growing population. The ratio of surviving children per couple is more than two or around three, which is a sign of a growing population (Sarkar and Sahani 2002).

The present area of the 'Jarawa Reserve' is 1,028 sq km and the total population of the Jarawa is 534. Thus there exists an approximate population density of 0.52 people per sq km. For a hunting and gathering community, it is a satisfactory condition as each person has approximately 2 sq km of area for foraging. However, an increase in the area of the Jarawa territory from 765 to 1,028 sq km in 2004 has not added to the actual resource area of the Jarawa. Under this situation, the man-land ratio come to 1:1.43 (each person has 1.43 sq km area). Besides, if the population growth of the Jarawa continues at the same rate, then the carrying capacity of the land will soon be reached. It will certainly not be a good situation for the Jarawa.

The study by Kumar and Biswas (2002) says that during the first four to five days of their camping at a certain place, the Jarawa do not put in more than three to four hours a day for hunting and gathering activities. Thereafter, the foraging time starts increasing as resource density begins to decrease. After about ten to twelve days of their stay at one place, the time spent in the collection of resources goes up to about five hours per day. In such a situation, they desert the place and move to another area. The movement of the Jarawa is related to the resource density of the area. Once they realise that the resources of a place have been exploited to the extent where returns are not enough, they leave the place allowing a fallow period for the replenishment of resources, which ranges from two to three months in case of the inland/forest locations depending on the regeneration rate of resources. The fallow period is much less, i.e. about a month in case of the coastal sites. The analysis, thus, shows that after a few days of hunting and gathering, the law of diminishing return sets in.

The results of the 'input-output analysis' show that on average the work input of an adult Jarawa varies between 3.7 to 3.9 days a week. It is considered a healthy condition for a hunter-gatherer group that devotes a great deal of time on leisure-related activities and socialising (Winterhalder 1993). There are certain reasons, why the Jarawa and some other groups of people in similar situation work only for a limited period or days. The reasons are as follows:

1. The Jarawa have a non-accumulative foraging based economy.
2. Sharing is an effective means of reducing the uncertainty of food quest, particularly during the lean period. Thus sharing is a powerful disincentive for individuals who might be inclined towards extra work. Winterhalder (1990, 1-40), in his studies on hunter-gatherers, says sharing of collected resources reduces the demands on individuals to increase foraging hours.
3. Foraging time/days are related to the satisfactory collection of resources and opportunity costs. The foraging days in case of the Jarawa are between 3.7 to 3.9 days a week. It means foraging days are kept within a limit so that time becomes available for alternative activities. Riches (1982, 214-16) has argued that the time allocation decision of hunter-gatherers is affected by cultural factors because they place a high value on leisure and other non-subsistence pursuits.

Thus, the foregoing analysis reveals that Jarawa of Andaman Islands are one of the few remaining hunter-gatherers of the world whose subsistence economy approximates the classical hunting and gathering economy of the foragers and they have successfully adapted themselves to the island environment.

CHAPTER 5

Contact, Conflict and Adaptation

For centuries, many of the human groups living in the environment of dense/deep forests, mountain interiors, deserts and isolated islands remained unknown, fully or partially, to the rest of the world. Over a period of time, contacts have been established with many of them, but some exceptions exist. The Jarawa are, probably, the most recent group of hunter-gatherers with whom the friendly contact has been established. Whether it is isolation or contact of a human group with others, it has its advantages and disadvantages. The disadvantages are more if a human group happens to be small in size and its members practise the hunting and gathering mode of subsistence activities with simple tools and technology. This is true for most of the indigenous human groups of the world, including the Jarawa.

The indigenous human groups in most parts of the world have been subjected to various types of threats, sometimes even endangering their very existence. They are vulnerable to the situation of being pushed out of their resources as well as livelihood. The smaller the size of the population of the group, the greater the risk of exclusion that looms from resources and livelihood options. Therefore, small indigenous populations appear extremely vulnerable in the event of a direct or indirect threat from various forces, particularly encroachment of their territory by others, invasion of modern culture, etc., as an aftermath of the contacts. Such examples are not rare where vibrant human populations, consequent upon the intervention of forces of modern culture, including the spread of communication networks and market mechanisms, were altogether obliterated or eliminated or assimilated. For example, the Tasmanian aborigines, who once dwelt on the island with mighty strides, could not withstand the pressure let loose by the expansion of

European empires on their land (Danda 1993). Several among the tribes of Australia, America and Canada failed to adjust to the new situation owing to the arrival of waves of the white immigrants to their territories and in the process were ultimately eliminated. The examples of the Great Andamanese and the Onge of the Andaman Islands make almost close parallels in this respect. Though they have not been eliminated, their population has decreased alarmingly.

It is important to note that in the present context, even apparently conducive programmes of welfare states or those introduced through activities of the other agencies do not appear to be wholly beneficial to the indigenous populations. In fact, there appears something rather paradoxical in this context. While the intentions of welfare states or governments need not be doubted, despite serious endeavours on their part, the net results of welfare programmes have not largely been very rewarding. In fact, the outcomes have often been quite baffling to the governments or the welfare agencies. The overall impact of such a situation has mostly been frightening. Owing to exposure to such a situation, the small groups often face cultural disintegration, if not biological extinction. Thus, small populations have become pathetically vulnerable almost everywhere. Besides, they are declining in number all over the world. Of late, the Jarawa have been undergoing a similar situation and experiences as witnessed by the Great Andamanese and the Onge. An effort has been made in the following discussion to analyse the history of contacts, causative factors behind it, its impact on the Jarawa, and adaptation of the Jarawa to the changing situation. Both friendly and unfriendly contacts have been discussed and the unfriendly contact is termed as 'conflict'.

CONTACTS AND CONFLICTS

Contacts of the Jarawa with the other people have not followed a uniform and linear pattern. In fact, contacts between the Jarawa and the non-Jarawa have a chequered history. There have been definite phases of contacts characterised by specific nature, extent, characteristics, forces and impacts.

THE PRE-COLONIAL PERIOD

The Andaman Islands have found a place in the accounts of sailors, travellers and traders for long, much before the colonial control over these Islands. For example, the Island of Buzacat, as described by Claudius Ptolemy in the second century AD, was probably the Andaman Islands. While the Chinese mentioned it in their accounts of the seventh century, the Arabs in the ninth century and the Europeans in the thirteen century (Mathur 1968: 7). The central theme in almost all these references was the cruel nature and the demonic appearance of the cannibal inhabitants of the Islands. The Arabs wrote that '. . . the people on this coast eat human flesh quite raw . . . their countenance and eyes frightful, their feet are very large . . .' (cf. Portman 1899: 51). Marco Polo's account was no less interesting, 'The people are . . . no better than wild beasts and I assure you all the men of this Island of Angamanian have heads like dogs, and teeth and eyes likewise; in fact, in the face, they are just like big mastiff dogs . . . they are a most cruel generation, and eat everybody that they can catch, if not of their own race' (cf. Portman 1899: 52). Traders and travellers from distant places might have been misinformed about the physical appearance and nature of the inhabitants of the Andaman Islands, but there was no such confusion in the neighbouring countries of Southeast Asia. In reality, the Andaman Islands were not as isolated as the travellers have described them. Pirates from the neighbouring Southeast Asian countries often used the shores and creeks of these Islands as harbours. They plundered ships sailing through the sea and sometimes they even ventured into the surrounding and interior of these Islands to collect edible birds' nests, shark fins and tortoise shells. The most prized catch for them was the Andaman Islanders who were sold as slaves in different parts of Southeast Asia (Portman 1899, 11-19).

THE COLONIAL PERIOD (1789 TO 1947)

During the colonial period, a number of events that shaped the history of the Islands took place and brought about a great variety of changes in the human population, cultural fabric and environment of the Andaman and Nicobar Islands. Of course, this definitely looks a very long period spanning over almost 160 years, but there were some lulls and gaps. For example, between 1796 and 1858 there was a gap of approximately half a century, i.e. the time gap between the first and second penal settlement when there were no reported contacts. Contacts during the colonial period can be divided into two distinct phases, i.e. first penal settlement and second penal settlement, each representing its own period, nature of contacts and different happenings.

The 'first penal settlement' was established by the British in September 1789 in the Andaman Islands. A documented account of contacts with the Negrito populations of the Andaman and Nicobar Islands is available only since the first penal settlement (Majumdar 1975: 52). When the British set their foot on the Andaman Islands in 1789, the behaviour of the Andaman Islanders was baffling for them during the brief phase of colonisation. While the tribesmen on the northern side of the Port Cornwallis (Port-Blair of the present day) were very hostile, those inhabiting the southern side were quite friendly. To the British, both the groups were the same while in reality, they were confronting two different tribes, the hostile Aka-Bea, a group of the Great Andamanese in the north, and the friendly Jarawa in the south. Lt. Colebrook and Archibald Blair were the first to encounter the Jarawa and described them to be indifferent (Portman 1889: 76). There was practically no major confrontation even with the different groups of the Great Andamanese. Nevertheless, it was the first major contact of the Negrito tribes with the alien people or non-Islanders. However, the British vacated the Islands in May 1796 on many counts, the most important was that they were prone to tropical diseases, particularly malaria.

The 'second penal settlement' in the Andaman Islands was established in March 1858 after the acceptance of 'the Report of a Committee' formed to give its suggestion, regarding reoccupying the Andaman and Nicobar Islands and establish a penal settlement by the British Government. It was done immediately after the First Indian War for Independence in 1857. Interestingly, there were penal settlements already existing in this part of the world, which had been established by the British. The first in the order was Benkulen in Sumatra followed by Singapore, Penang and some places in Myanmar (erstwhile Burma) (Majumdar 1975: 48-9). By establishing a penal settlement in the Andaman Islands, the British government was faced with two urgent problems that required immediate attention. The first was the general policy to be adopted towards the aborigines and the second was the creation of suitable machinery of administration for the Islands. Considering the aborigines as primitive and cruel, the Court of Directors formulated a policy of behaviour towards the aborigines. The British officials were told '. . . all possible precautions may be taken to protect the aboriginal inhabitants of the Andaman Islands from the collision with convicts, which, it is not too probable will be provoked on both sides and which once commenced are so likely to end in the extermination of the weaker race. . .' (cf. Mathur 1968: 69). However, the British failed to adhere to the said policy. In the following discussion, the history of contacts and their impacts on Negrito groups have been elucidated.

THE GREAT ANDAMANESE

The Great Andamanese originally had ten sub-groups which were distributed from south to north in the Andaman Islands. The present day Great Andamanese include members of three groups namely the Aka-Chari, Aka-Jeru and the Aka-Bea-da. Besides these three, they had other seven groups, viz., the Aka-Kora, Aka-Bo, Aka-Kede, Aka-Kol, Okka-Juwai, Aka-Puikwar and the Aka-Bele. Each group had occupied a certain area of the island. Leaving aside the Aka-Bea, the average extent of territory occupied by a tribe was about 264 sq km (Figure 5.1). Of the ten tribes, the largest in terms of area was probably the Aka-Kede, having over 300 sq km of territory, while the smallest was probably the Aka-Chari having a territory of less than 160 sq km (Radcliffe-Brown 1922: 25). Within their territory, these small subgroups were nomadic in order to make the best use of natural resources available there. The relationships among these groups were not friendly. On the contrary, there existed tribal warfare among these different groups.

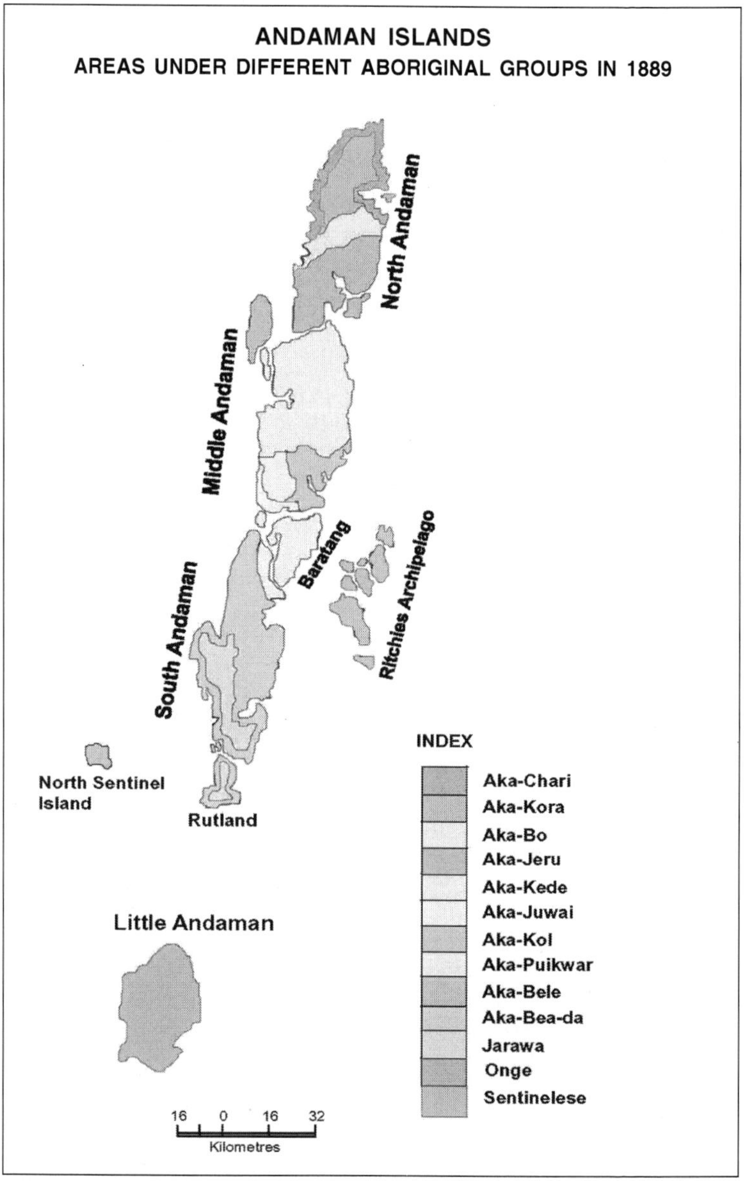

Source: P. Lal 1976: 51.

Figure 5.1: Andaman Islands: Areas Under Different Aboriginal (Negrito) Groups in 1889

As expected, skirmishes of different types started taking place immediately after the establishment of the penal settlement. Hitherto the tribal groups were in a sullen mood of anger and discontent at the intrusion of the outsiders into their habitat and this feeling found vent in occasional clashes and skirmishes. As punitive measures, several expeditions were sent to teach a lesson to them. Government communication admitted that the settlement officials preferred to ignore the path of conciliation and selected to play the role of assailants (Portman 1899: 271-3). It was evident from the suggestion of the Superintendent of Port-Blair, Mr. P. Walker, who had sent a proposal to the Secretary for State to the British Government in India that the Great Andamanese should be driven out by the military guards from the southernmost part of the Great Andaman Island and the area should be cordoned off by military in order to prevent the entry of the aborigines. But the Government did not accept the proposal of Mr. Walker.

However, the cruel and vindictive policy of the British officials posted in the area generated among the aborigines a definite spirit of hostility against the British and a grim determination to drive them out from their habitat. It found expression in a series of attacks by them in quick succession during the months of April and May 1859. But the bows and arrows were no answer to the firearms of the British. The first organised attack by the Great Andamanese was made on 6 April 1859. It was followed by another attack on 14 April 1859, in which about 1500 aborigines participated (Majumdar 1975: 82-3). It was a revelation to the whole spectrum of contacts of the aborigines with the British and the latter's relation with and attitude towards the aborigines. In the said attack, the Great Andamanese vented their wrath on gang men but were quite friendly with convicts who had iron rings around their ankles as distinctive marks. According to Portman, the Great Andamanese told him that they objected to the clearing of the forests. Important among them was the conflict of 17 May 1859, also known as the 'Battle of Aberdeen'. In this skirmish, many Great Andamanese were killed (cf. Majumdar 1975: 82-3). Portman (1899: 279, 288) writes 'Far from being a ludicrous skirmish, it was the most desperate and determined attack by the aborigines ever made on the settlement. The policy of Mr. Walker must be held responsible for these unfortunate episodes'. After the retirement of Mr. Walker in 1859, his successor adopted a friendlier attitude towards the aborigines and consequently a gradual change in the attitude of the aborigine towards the settlers was noticeable.

In 1863, E.H. Man at Port-Blair established the 'Andaman Home'. Rev. Corbyn, a priest, was entrusted with the task of civilising the Great Andamanese. 'Here they were provided free rations, lodgings and medical attendance' (Radcliffe-Brown 1922: 10). The Great Andamanese were free to come and stay as long as they wanted and then could go back with gifts from the British administration. Nevertheless, the Portman report (1899) reveals the yearning of the Great Andamanese to go back and live the traditional way of life in the forests always remained strong among them. In the later years, the situation improved gradually and by the end of 1860s almost all the subgroups of the Great Andamanese had been slowly and gradually tamed following the policy of carrot and stick. The Aka-Bea-da was the first to be completely befriended followed by other groups of the Great Andamanese. But an obvious fallout of the contact situation was the sudden decline in their population from a strong 3,500 in 1858 to 50 in 1951 and 19 in 1961 (Tables 5.1 and 5.2). In the post-Independence period, they were living in a despicable conditions in and around Port Blair. Finally, the Andaman and Nicobar Administration settled them at the Strait Island in 1974 (Chakraborty 1990). Presently their population is 75 (AAJVS 2019). Now they are no longer full time hunter-gatherers. Presently, a few of them are working in different departments of the Andaman and Nicobar Administration also.

THE ONGE

The Onge are another Negrito tribe who inhabit the Little Andaman Island. Like other Negritoes, they also resented any intrusion into their territory. They put up resistance within the limitation of their weaponry based on simple tools, technology and their physical strength, which lasted for several years. References are found of

TABLE 5.1: DECADAL POPULATION OF NEGRITO GROUPS IN THE ANDAMAN ISLANDS (UPTO 1951)

Tribe	Estimated Population					
	1858	1901	1911	1921	1931	1951
Aka-Chari	100	39	36	17	9	
Aka-Kora	500	96	71	48	24	
Aka-Jeru	200	48	62	18	6	23*
Aka-Bo	700	218	180	101	46	
Aka-Kede	500	59	34	6	2	
Okka-Juwai	300	48	9	5	–	
Aka-Kol	100	11	2	–	–	
Aka-Puikwar	300	50	36	9	1	
Aka-Bea-da	500	37	10	1	–	
Aka-Bele	300	19	15	4	2	
Onge	700	672	631	346	250	150
Jarawa	600	585	231	231	120	50

Source: Mathur 1968: 128-9.

*It is the combined population of the Great Andamanese groups.

TABLE 5.2: DECADAL POPULATION OF NEGRITO GROUPS IN THE ANDAMAN ISLANDS (AFTER 1960)

Tribe	Population						
	1961	1971	1981	1991	2001	2011	2019
Great Andamanese	19	24	27	45	43	57	75
Onge	129	112	93	95	96	101	121
Jarawa	500*	275*	200*	280*	265	380	534
Sentinelese	50**	82**	100**	100**	39**	50**	50**

Sources: Census of India, 1961; 1971; 1981; 1991; 2001; 2011; AAJVS Records, 2019.

* Population of the Jarawa was estimated till 2001. First time in 2001-2, a head count of the Jarawa population was done.

** Population of the Sentinelese is estimated.

many unsuccessful attempts between 1867 and 1874 by the British to bring the Onge in the fold of friendship. The goodwill efforts of M.V. Portman, Officer-in-Charge of relations with the Negrito groups from 1879 to 1900, bore fruits in 1886 when he succeeded in establishing friendly contacts with the Onge. Within a span of twenty years since their friendly contact with outsiders in 1886, the Onge had completely been befriended (Sarkar 1993: 171). This change in their outlook from hostility to friendliness towards outsiders proved a turning point because thereafter, they never picked up bows and arrows to defend themselves and their territory. The British did not colonise the Island of Little Andaman as they had done in South, Middle and North Andaman Islands, nor were the Onge put in any kind of 'homes' to civilise them. In the post-Independence period, Little Andaman Island was opened for the rehabilitation of the refugees in 1967 (Pandit and Chattopadhyay 1993: 171). It dealt a major blow to the Onge as it not only reduced the size of their territory but also curtailed their resource base. To compensate for the loss of space (niche) and resources, they were settled in 1974 at two places in the Little Andaman Island, namely the South Bay and Dugong Creek. After tsunami, which struck the Andaman Islands on 26 December 2004, the Onge of the South Bay were also settled at the Dugong Creek. Today they are no longer solely dependent on hunting, fishing and gathering. At the new place of settlement, the Andman Administration regularly provides them with the articles of daily use including food items. Like the Great Andamanese group, the Onge population has also declined from 700 in 1858 to 150 in 1951 and 97 in 2002 (Tables 5.1 and 5.2). Presetly, the total population of the Onge is 121 (AAJVS 2019).

THE SENTINELESE

The Negrito hunter-gatherers of the North Sentinel Island are known as the Sentinelese. They have been described as the world's most isolated population and hence the least known. As such, there has been a mystique about their lifestyle, culture and society. The British in the absence of any urgent need for land and forest resources of this small Island (area 50 sq km) off the west coast of the South Andaman did not make any efforts to befriend them. Only a few visits were made from 1867 onwards by the British but no close contact was established. In the post-Independence period from 1967 onwards, occasional expeditions were sent to the North Sentinel Island, but the Sentinelese did not like it. On a few occasions, they even shot arrows at the visiting party, though nobody was hurt. The situation improved with time and a breakthrough was achieved in February 1991 when the Sentinelese accepted the gifts from the hands of the members of the contact team who were awaiting ashore (Pandit and Chattopadhyay 1993, 176). Thereafter, a few of them even boarded the lifeboat and then disembarked on their own. Despite the initial success, there still exists an ambience of hostility between the Sentinelese and the outsiders. Occasional expeditions are still being sent by the local Administration into their area to establish friendly contacts with them, but of no avail (Justin 2016, 659-79). Presently, the Andaman and Nicobar Administration is following the policy of non-interference with respect to the Sentinelese (Sasikumar 2019, 37-44).

THE JARAWA

While all ten groups of the Great Andamanese and the Onge tribes had come under the influence of the British within the few years of the establishment of the second penal settlement at Port-Blair in 1858, the Jarawa, however, did not accept the friendly overtures of the British. The Jarawa suffered violence because of the punitive expeditions sent by the British Administration against them for their disinclination to be friendly with the new settlers and their unwillingness to submit to new arrangements. The Jarawa continued with their defensive posture until the second half of 1997 and then they became friendly with the non-Jarawa. The history of the contacts of the Jarawa with non-Jarawa during the British period has been discussed in three broad time periods: (i) contacts from 1858 to 1900, (ii) contacts from 1901 to 1939 and (iii) contacts during the Japanese occupation between 1942 and 1945. The details of the contacts during the aforementioned time periods have been discussed below.

Contacts from 1858 to 1900

As mentioned earlier, during the period of the first penal settlement, the Jarawa behaved in a nonchalant manner with the colonisers in contrast to the Aka-Bea-da tribe. During the initial years of the 'second penal settlement', the Jarawa remained inoffensive. The British learnt about the hostility of the Jarawa around 1863 when Topsy, the Great Andamanese girl staying at the 'Andaman Home', told the Reverend H. Corbyn, in-charge of the 'Home' that there were tribes in the south like the Jarawa who were hostile not only to the Andamanese but also to the British and warned him not to proceed to their settlement (Majumdar 1975: 87). However, he failed to understand the reasons behind their hostility. In the annual report for the year 1872-3, General Steward wrote that the Jarawa '. . . seem to be peacefully disposed of, whereas the Little Andaman Islanders habitually kill or attempt to kill, everyone that lands on their shores . . .' (cf. Portman 1899: 716). The Jarawa attacked the settlement for the first time in 1872. However, the situation took a turn for the worse in the following years and hostility with Jarawa scaled up, and hardly a year passed without violent skirmishes between the Jarawa and the non-Jarawa (Census of India 1931, 14). There appeared to be the following reasons for the Jarawa turning hostile against the non-Negrito population:

1. The Jarawa resented the partiality shown by the settlers to them in treatment compared to the other tribes of the Great Andamanese group.
2. The clearing of the forests near the Port Blair made them angry, as they regarded forests as a part of their homeland.
3. In the later years, several expeditions were sent against them. It resulted in the killing of many Jarawas, which further worsened the situation.
4. To add fuel to the fire, the Great Andamanese were used to catch and befriend the Jarawa ignoring the fact that the Great Andamanese, particularly the Aka-Bea-da, were traditionally at enmity with the Jarawa. The objective was to catch the Jarawa, bring them to Port Blair, keep them in 'Home' as had been done in case of the Great Andamanese, give them gifts and then send them back. The underlying idea was that it would help establish friendly relations with the Jarawa as this method had contributed partially to the overall efforts of establishing friendly contact with the Great Andamanese and the Onge. Even this

method did not bear fruit. For example, the British Administration succeeded in capturing one Jarawa man with the help of the Great Andamanese in March 1885 and he was kept in Mr. Portman's house. However, the Jarawa kept begging the Great Andamanese to kill him by throttling or cutting his throat and rejected all overtures of friendship (Portman 1899: 60).

By sending armed personnel into their territories, people with friendly disposition were pushed to abject hatred, and the British Government refused to learn any lessons from it. By the end of the nineteenth century, the situation had worsened further. The British Administration was thinking of invading the Jarawa territory and catching them alive with the help of armed police and convicts. Astonishingly, some British officials even wanted complete extermination of the Jarawa.

Contacts from 1901 to 1939

After the retirement of Mr. Portman in 1900, the conciliatory policy that was followed till 1900 for the Jarawa was abandoned. As a result, the hostility on both sides aggravated. At this time the Jarawa were even resisting the establishment of any settlement in their territory with all their might. In turn, the settlers and British authority were attacking the Jarawa frequently. The turnaround from a policy of protecting the tribes from a collision with the settlers and thus saving the indigenous people from extermination was complete when in 1905 a 'Bush Police Force' was formed with friendly Great Andamanese as members and Burmese Jamadar in-charge of it. The job of the 'Bush Police Force' was to hunt the Jarawa and the runaway convicts (Mathur 1968: 114-15). In one such expedition by Captain West in 1925, as many as 37 Jarawa were claimed to have been shot dead (Census of India 1931: 16). With each passing year, the number of punitive expeditions sent inside the Jarawa territory increased. Consequently, the feeling of hostility in the Jarawa against the outsiders was further fuelled. Later at some point of time, it was felt that the most effective way to conciliate the Jarawa was to capture them in large numbers, tame them and then send them back as messengers of peace. One such expedition, organised in 1939 by McCarthy Commandant, Civil and Military Police, was considered to be successful as they could capture one young Jarawa woman with three of her children (Census of India 1961: 104). However, in the following years, such expeditions could not be carried out because of the Japanese occupation of these islands during the Second World War.

Contacts during the Japanese Occupation (1942-1945)

The Andaman and Nicobar Islands were under Japanese occupation from March 1942 to October 1945. The Japanese were interested in fortifying the entire coast but the Jarawa made their work difficult on the west coast of the Andaman. Consequently, the Jarawa areas were reported to have been machine gunned from the air because two Japanese soldiers had allegedly been killed at the hands of the Jarawa (Sarkar 1993: 104). Though nothing is known about the causalities the Jarawa suffered in that attack, it did increase their hatred towards the outsiders.

THE POST-INDEPENDENCE PERIOD: CONTACT MISSIONS AND THE JARAWA

After the Independence, under the new policy of the Indian Government, the legacy of large scale and organised state violence and the policy of punitive expedition towards the Jarawa was given up entirely. The Jarawa were declared a 'Scheduled Tribe' along with five other tribes of the Andaman and Nicobar Islands. Their territory was declared a reserved territory under the 'Government of India Forest Act', and the 'Tribal Regulation of the Andaman and Nicobar Islands'. Further, to befriend the Jarawa, intermittent gift giving operations were started.

In mid-1968, three Jarawa were caught by the villagers of the Kadamtala in Middle Andaman when they had come to pick up some metal implements from the village. They were taken to Port Blair, kept for a month and then sent back to Kadamtala for release. After this incidence, the gift dropping operations in the Jarawa area were increased and systematised. On 18 February 1974, a gift dropping party, under the supervision of Shiv Prasad Singh, Head Constable, Bush Police Force, was accosted by a group of unarmed Jarawa with a friendly gesture. This was followed by vigorous efforts to renew contact with the Jarawa in the area. On 5 and 10 April 1974, Mr. Bakhtawar Singh, Officer-in-Charge, Bush Police, and other members of the contact team were able to meet the Jarawa at Lakra Lungta on the west coast of the Middle Andaman (Pandit and Chattopadhyay 1993: 173). This was followed by frequent contact missions organised by the Andaman Administration. Between 1974 and 1996 scores of visits were paid to the Jarawa area. The contact parties used to visit the western coast of the Middle Andaman Island in small vessels and make contact with the Jarawa on the shore. Such visits were conducted on every full moon day and the visitors used to be officials of the local government, doctors and anthropologists. The underlying idea was that the Jarawa would be able to understand the regularity of such visits if they were visited on each full moon day, keeping in mind that natural cyclic phenomenon would presumably be intelligible enough to the Jarawa. It was also recommended that the visitors should be medically screened to prevent any possible spread of communicable diseases among the Jarawa (Awaradi 1990: 132). During the contact missions, the Jarawa were gifted with huge quantities of bananas, coconuts, and pieces of red cloth.

The contact missions did succeed in creating some positive impact on the Jarawa. After some time, the Jarawa started coming forward on their own to greet the members of the contact team. However, the nascent friendship and amity were interrupted time and again by continuing conflicts with the settlers (Mukhopadhyay 2002: 24-9). In this way, one comes across the ambiguous behaviour of the Jarawa, i.e. both friendliness and hostility towards the non-Jarawa after 1974. While on one side the Jarawa were hostile to the settlers, forest labourers working in and around the 'Jarawa Reserve' and vehicles passing through the 'Jarawa Reserve', on the other, they displayed friendly gestures to the members of the contact team. It clearly explains the fact that the Jarawa did not like encroachment on their territory and sharing of natural resources by others as it was a question of life and death for them. Nevertheless, the Jarawa were friendly with members of the contact team as the Jarawa found them to be not encroaching and destroying their ecological niches. However, after 1990 the Jarawa have also demonstrated more friendly behaviour towards their non-Jarawa neighbours.

ENMEI EPISODE AND FRIENDLINESS OF THE JARAWA

In April 1996, an interesting incident happened. A Jarawa boy named Enmei with a broken leg was captured and admitted to the Primary Health Centre at Kadamtala and then referred to G.B. Pant Hospital, Port Blair, where he received treatment for about six months. Following this incident, the contact situation took a decisive turn. After being released from the hospital, Enmei was sent back to Kadamtala from where he was released in the Jarawa territory. The underlying approach of the administration behind this act was that he would carry back to his Jarawa people the message of goodwill and friendship. Unexpectedly, a few months later, one day in October 1997, a group of unarmed Jarawa appeared at Uttara Jetty, Middle Andaman. This event was a watershed in the history of the relationships of the Jarawa with the non-Jarawa as it marked an end to the phase of hostility and the beginning of friendly relations between the Jarawa and the non-Jarawa. After that eventful day, the Jarawa started visiting the settlement areas frequently. On the subsequent visits, they started plucking bananas from the plantations of the settlers and soon it became a regular phenomenon. The Primary Health Centre was the other place, which they visited quite often. It was a welcome change as hardly any incident of conflict between the Jarawa and the villagers was reported thereafter (Kumar and Biswas 2002: 58-70; Mukhopadhyaya et al. 2002).

IMPACT OF CONTACTS AND CONFLICTS

Every contact, whether friendly or hostile, between two human groups has its impact on both the groups. The contacts have their own origin, nature and development. In the background of the above mentioned contacts, it would be worthwhile to understand the impact of contact and conflict on the Jarawa and their habitat. The impact of contact and conflict has been seen through two time periods, i.e. pre and post Independence periods.

IMPACT DURING THE BRITISH PERIOD (1858-1947)

The major impact of contact during the British period was in the form of territorial displacement and redefining of boundaries. Both the social and geographical boundaries amongst the Andaman Islanders have evolved through many factors such as language, customary law, spatial organisation and access to resources. Such variables are applicable to most societies in the world. The tribes of the Andaman Islands largely distinguished themselves by their own territory and dialect. Maintenance of exclusive territories by these groups gave them the benefits of extraction of resources from specific areas and social cohesiveness of small groups, and at the same time created a situation of diversity of cultures. Previous studies on Andamanese culture and social organisation described the Andamanese tribes based on their spatial organisation as people were divided into groups. The area used and occupied by a particular Andamanese group was delineated by specific names pertaining to and corroborative of both natural features and accounts that were associated with the area (Man 1883: 30-40).

For a long time, different Negrito groups of the Andaman Islands were hostile to one another and their territories were well demarcated and protected. During 1889, the North Andaman Island was inhabited predominantly by four major tribes, i.e., the Aka-Chari occupying the coastal areas of the North Andaman Island and the Aka-Kora living mostly in the interior of the Island while the Aka-Bo and the Aka-Jeru inhabited the central and southern part of the Island respectively (Figure 5.1). By 1901, there was remarkable shrinkage of the Aka-Jeru territory and a conspicuous spread of the territory of the coastal Aka-Chari (Figure 5.2). It means the coastal tribe dominated their counterpart in tribal warfare. By 1961 there was a complete disappearance of the Aka-Kora and the Aka-Bo from the North Andaman Island (Mathur 1968: 105) (Figure 5.3).

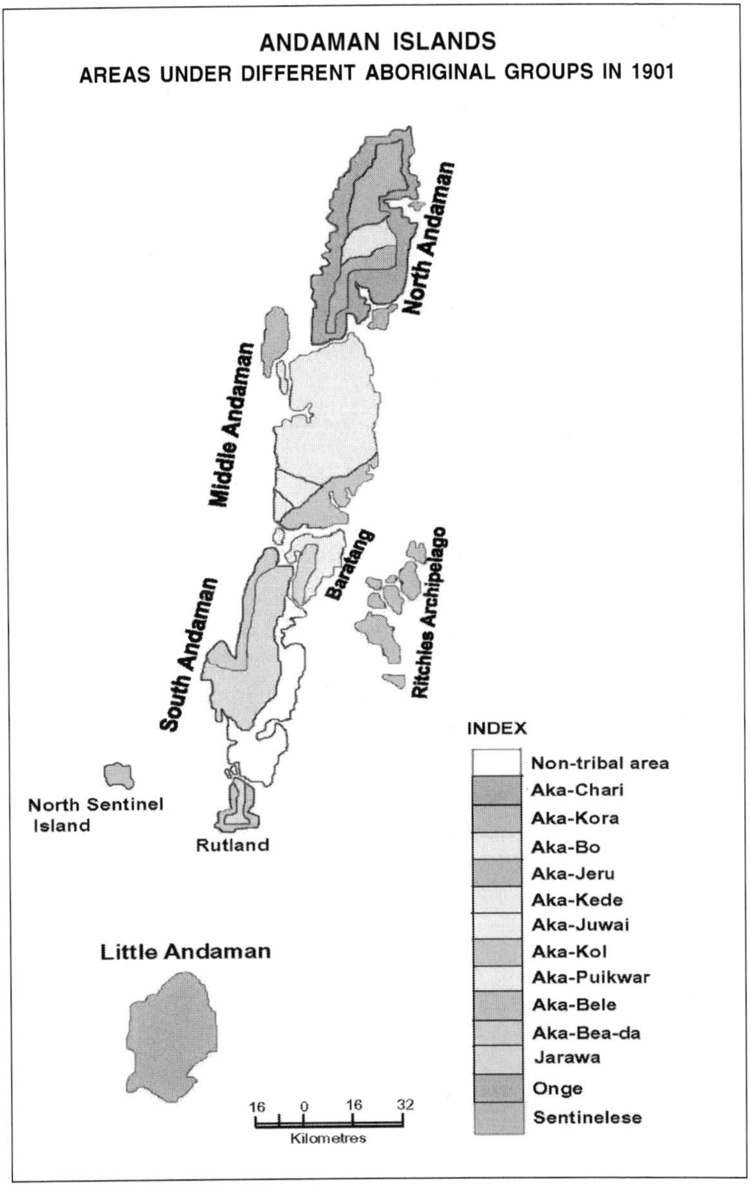

Source: P. Lal 1976: 51.

Figure 5.2: Andaman Islands: Areas Under Different Aboriginal (Negrito) Groups in 1901

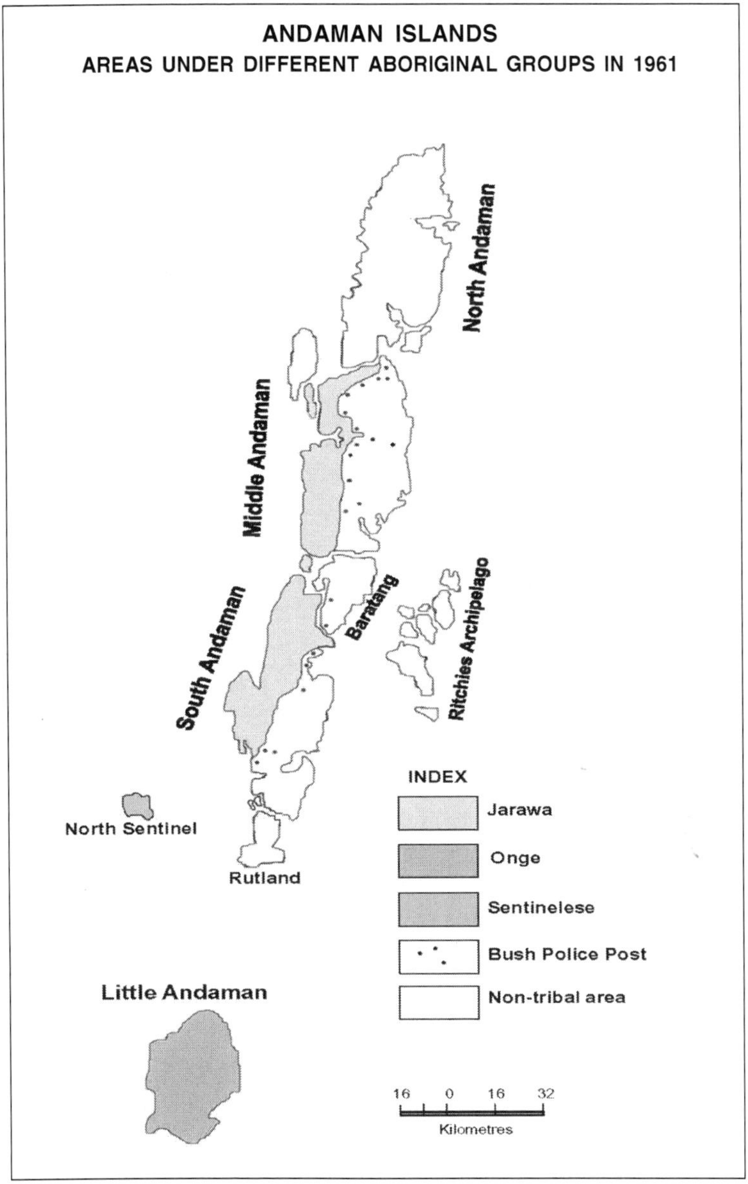

Source: P. Lal 1976: 51.

Figure 5.3: Andaman Islands: Areas Under Different Aboriginal (Negrito) Groups in 1961

In the Middle Andaman Island, during 1889, there were four main tribal groups (Figure 5.1). These were the Aka-Kede occupying more than half of the Middle Andaman Island, the Aka-Kol settled along the south-eastern coast, the Okka-Juwai occupied the south-western interior, and the Aka-Puikwar the southern coastal area of the Middle Andaman Island. By 1901, the Aka-Kede had pushed their territory southward by dominating the other tribes (Figure 5.2). Consequently, the Aka-Kol were pushed further south and south-west dominating the other two tribes, i.e. the Aka-Puikwar and the Okka-Juwai. Later on, all suffered the same fate as those of the North Andaman groups and in the process completely vanished, and sometime around 1930, the area came under the control of the Jarawa (Figure 5.3 and Table 5.1).

Further south, the Baratang Island and a part of the South Andaman Island were inhabited by the Aka-Puikwar tribe during 1889 (Figure 5.1). In 1901, the Jarawa from the south invaded their territory and pushed them out of the South Andaman Island and occupied a part of the Baratang Island also (Figure 5.2). In the following decades, the whole of the Aka-Puikwar had vanished. Later, the British pushed the Jarawa out of Baratang Island. (Mathur 1968: 123).

The South Andaman and Rutland Islands were inhabited by three major tribes in 1889 (Figure 5.1). The Aka-Bea-da had occupied the major areas of South Andaman Island; the Jarawa were in the interior and the Aka-Puikwar in a small territory along the north-eastern coast. The Aka-Bele tribe inhabited the Richie archipelago. Table 5.1 shows a progressive decline of all these tribes except the Jarawa in 1901 that had moved from south to north. By the 1930s, the Jarawa had established themselves over major parts of the South and Middle Andaman Islands.

Most of the sub-groups of the Great Andamanese had vanished by 1951. Of the ten groups of the Great Andamanese, only three were surviving and had a total population of 19 only in 1961 (Table. 5.4). They were namely the Aka-Chari, the Aka-Jeru and the Aka-Bea-da. They had no control over their formal territories (Figure 5.3). Having been reduced in number and without any territory of their own, they were living in miserable conditions in and around Port Blair. Finally, they were settled at Strait Island in 1970 (Sarkar 1993: 7).

By 1951, the Jarawa had completely vacated the Richie Island and were occupying the western part of the South and Middle Andaman as these Islands were vacant (Figuare 5.3). The situation remained the same in the following decades (Figure 5.4). The Onge, who were once the sole inhabitants of the Little Andaman, were settled in 1974 at two places, namely, Dugong Creek and South Bay and since then the situation has remained more or less the same (Figure 5.4). After the tsunami of 2004, the South Bay group was resettled at Dugong Creek. The Little Andaman also witnessed rehabilitation of refugees from the erstwhile East Pakistan (Kumar 2002, 131). The Sentinelese are the only human group whose territory and most probably the population have remained more or less intact owing to the absence of any contact with the non-Sentinelese.

As discussed earlier, because of the growing hostility with the Jarawa, the British Government started the 'Bush Police Force' in 1905 to contain the Jarawa and protect the settlers and convicts. As such, several outposts of the 'Bush Police Force' were established on the periphery of the Jarawa territory. Many of these outposts continued to exist even in the post-Independence period (Figure 5.3). After 1997, when the Jarawa became friendly with the non-Jarawa, the name of the 'Bush Police Force' was changed and now it is known as the 'Jarawa Protection Force'. Only a few outposts of the 'Jarawa Protection Force' exist at present. From the above discussion, it can be inferred that the population size of the Negrito groups declined to a great extent for which the following reasons may be considered responsible:

1. War was one of the major factors. The British used to conduct punitive expeditions against the warring tribes. Though some information is available on the number of persons (of expedition party) killed in such wars, it was never known how many of the tribesmen were wounded and afterwards, succumbed to their injuries. However, it certainly disrupted their sex and age structure and that negatively impacted their overall population
2. War was followed by the spread of diseases among the Islanders

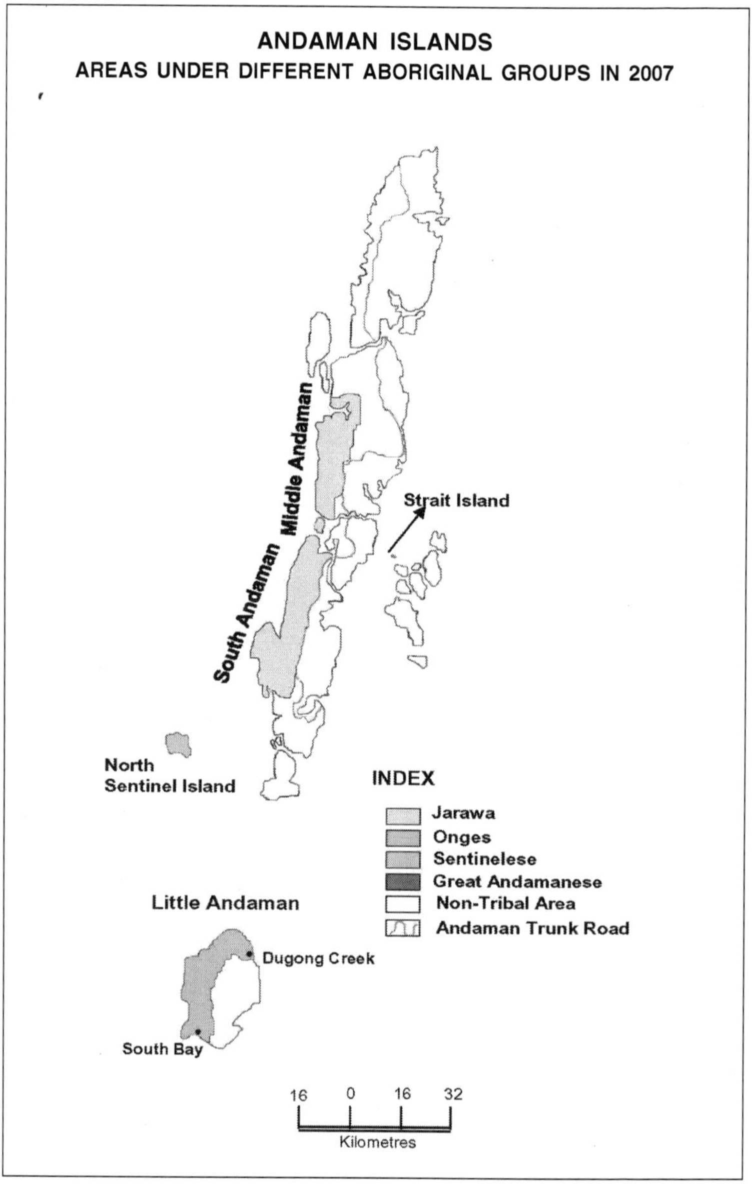

Source: Andaman Adim Janjati Vikas Samiti.

Figure 5.4: Andaman Islands: Areas Under Different Aboriginal (Negrito) Groups in 2007

in the aftermath of trying to 'tame' them. The physical contact with the outsiders led to the emergence of many diseases, like syphilis, measles, influenza and smallpox, which proved fatal for the Great Andamanese group and the Onge. In 1870, the tribes of South Andaman Island contracted syphilis that soon spread to other tribes and took the form of an epidemic. Similarly, in March 1877 an epidemic of measles spread among the Andamanese, killing many of them (Sen 1962: 86). In 1897, measles and smallpox killed almost half of the total population of the South Andaman Island (Sarkar 1993: 18). The measles proved fatal for the Onge also as it struck disastrously on a number of occasions (Cipriani 1966: 46). The Jarawa were not reported to haved suffered from any such diseases as they were not in the friendly fold or in regular contact with the non-Jarawa groups.

3. A large number of tribesmen of the Great Andamanese group and the Jarawa died due to traditional tribal warfare going on among them.
4. Many tribesmen, particularly the Jarawa, were killed in the Japanese bombardment of the tribal areas during the Japanese occupation of the Andaman Islands between 1942 and 1945.

IMPACT DURING THE POST-INDEPENDENCE PERIOD

The independence of India ushered in a new era for all the tribal groups of the country including the Jarawa. Initiation of a number of developmental activities, rehabilitation of the refugees from the erstwhile East Bengal (now Bangladesh), redefining of the Jarawa territory, construction of the 'Andaman Trunk Road' (ATR), etc., were crucial events that had a telling impact on the Jarawa and their territory. Development of the events was in the following manner.

REFUGEE REHABILITATION

Between 1949 and 1959, altogether 68 villages of the refugees consisting of 2328 families having a total population of 10,018 persons were rehabilitated in the South and Middle Andaman Islands (Tables 5.3 and 5.4). It was an open case of invasion of

TABLE 5.3: YEAR-WISE ACHIEVEMENT OF THE REHABILITATION PROGRAMME IN SOUTH ANDAMAN

Years	Number of villages established	Number of families rehabilitated	Population settled (in persons)	Area allotted for paddy cultivation (in acres)
1949	6	202	830	1,530
1950	10	265	1,165	1,765
1951	4	114	554	0,625
1952	8	123	595	0,789
1953	NA	NA	NA	NA
1954	3	97	400	0,575
1955	5	130	620	0,735
Total	36	931	4,164	6,019

NA= Data Not Available. *Source*: Chakraborty and Dinda 2002, 46.

TABLE 5.4: YEAR-WISE ACHIEVEMENT OF THE REHABILITATION PROGRAMME IN MIDDLE ANDAMAN

Years	Number of villages established	Number of families rehabilitated	Population settled (in persons)	Area allotted for paddy cultivation (in acres)
1953	3	198	812	1,439
1954	12	438	1,810	1,905
1955	7	264	1,157	0,725
1956	8	400	1,729	1,884
1957	NA	NA	NA	NA
1958	1	88	807	400
1959	1	09	039	45
Total	32	1,397	5,854	7,398

NA= Data Not Available. *Source*: Chakraborty and Dinda 2002, 47.

the Jarawa territory. During that time the forest cover in the Andaman Islands was wider and thicker and it was very difficult to get any large patch of cleared land. Hence the patches of forests were cleared in different parts of the South, Middle and

North Andaman Islands to rehabilitate the refugees. It was also estimated that approximately 5,000 refugee families could be rehabilitated in those areas (Sen 1962, 92).

In course of the rehabilitation programme, the refugees were taken in batches to the Andaman Islands. Initially, some parts of the South Andaman Island were selected for rehabilitation because of the readily available cleared land, nearness to the administrative headquarters at Port Blair and communication facilities. The first batch of 202 families was rehabilitated in March 1949 (Table 5.3). Each of the rehabilitated families was provided with certain facilities. They were given an ex gratia grant of Rs. 1,050, a recoverable loan of Rs. 1,730 and a total of 10 acres of land, five acres each of paddy land and hilly land (Sen 1962, 103-4). In addition to this land, each family was given five acres of land as homestead and for other uses. During a span of seven years from 1949 to 1955, altogether 931 families were rehabilitated in various villages of the South Andaman like Homfregunj, Herbertabad, Guptapara, Wimberlygunj and Shoal Bay.

A similar process of encroachment on the Jarawa territory was repeated in the Middle Andaman Island during the second phase of rehabilitation. In the Middle Andaman alone, between 1953 and 1956 as many as 1300 families were rehabilitated (Table 5.4). The peak years of the rehabilitation activities were 1954 and 1956. Within a period of seven years, about 1397 families were rehabilitated in six batches in different parts of the Rangat valley, stretching from Betapur to Uttara. Here, each family was provided with Rs. 2,000 as a loan in addition to the usual allotment of 10 acres of land. This area had certain special features like good soil, abundant rain, and perennial sources of freshwater, which attracted more settlers. As a result, the population in this part of the Island registered phenomenal growth.

Administratively, elaborate arrangements were made to protect the villages, forest camps and persons working in the Reserve or the adjoining areas. The 'Bush Police Force' was no more a group of game trackers and hunters. By 1961, it was manned by 35 Jamadars, 311 Constables and 1 Inspector from 44 camps along the periphery of the Reserve. In addition, the Forest Department also maintained 150 constables. Both forces were armed (Census of India 1961: 104). Besides giving protection to the non-Jarawa, one of the aims of the 'Bush Police' was to keep a watch on the movement of the Jarawa.

Under the resettlement plan, about 13,417 hectares of forest lands were cleared for rehabilitation alone. All these resulted in the shrinkage of the Jarawa territory. Besides, the unfortunate part of the rehabilitation plan was that the refugees were settled near sources of fresh water, which effectively barred the Jarawa access to this vital resource. The intrusion on their habitat and the resultant loss of territory and life sustaining resources because of the establishment of refugee settlements must have made the Jarawa more and more hostile towards the non-Jarawa. Therefore, the Jarawa resisted rehabilitation. There were 76 encounters with the settlers between 1946 and 1961 in which 15 settlers and a number of Jarawa were killed (Census of India 1961).

DEFORESTATION AND COMMERCIAL FORESTRY OPERATIONS

The development of the 'Andaman Trunk Road' (ATR) through the South Andaman and Middle Andaman Islands also caused large scale deforestation in the areas inhabited by the Jarawa. A notification issued by the Chief Commissioner of the Islands in 1957 had virtually declared the whole of the northern part of South Andaman Island as a 'Tribal Reserve'. Later the same authority amended the notification in 1979 and excluded the areas east of the ATR from the 'Tribal Reserve' and opened the area to logging and for the construction of the road (Mukhopadhyay 2002: 41).

The eastern portion of the forest along the trunk road beyond Jirkatang was felled in suitable areas and regenerated with teak *padauk, didu* and other timber wood species. Forestry operations also led to setting up of temporary camps at Pochang, Poona Nallah and Puttatang. This must have caused great distress to the Jarawa as it disturbed their foraging area. Forestry operations were finally stalled after March 1996 when about 60 to 70 Jarawas ambushed workers of the Forest Department from three sides, killing two and injuring three of them (Department of Police 1997). Now the Putatang camp has been abandoned.

SHRINKAGE OF THE JARAWA TERRITORY

The historical events in the Indian sub-continent following the termination of colonisation led to the opening up of the Andaman Islands for the rehabilitation and resettlement of refugee population. It had far reaching consequences for the surviving Negrito populations of the Andaman Islands, particularly the Jarawa and the Onge, as their territories were chosen by the Government for rehabilitation. However, in order to facilitate the rehabilitation and protect the Jarawa area, a regulation for the protection of aboriginal tribes of the Andaman and Nicobar was notified in 1956. Exercising this power in April 1957, the Chief Commissioner declared certain areas as reserved for the 'aboriginal people'. Consequently, the 'Jarawa Reserve' boundary was described but never delimited and demarcated on the ground. A subsequent notification was issued in 1979, which modified the boundary of the 'reserved areas' in South and Middle Andaman (Mukhopadhyay 2002: 40-1). Under the notification a large part of the 'Jarawa Reserve' was de-notified, particularly the area east of the Andaman trunk road, thus causing a reduction in the Jarawa territory. This exposed the denotified area of the Jarawa territory to logging, plantation and construction of road, leading to erosion of their resource base in terms of thinning and reduction of resources in the areas close to the forestry operation.

At the time of the Independence of India, the Jarawa territory extended over the northern part of South Andaman and the entire Middle Andaman Islands with a total area of approximately 2,950 sq km. Besides, the forest areas of Baratang Island were also well within the functional resource region of the Jarawa. However, in the post-Independence period, the opening of the Islands for resettlement and rehabilitation of the refugee population, and modifications in the boundary of the Jarawa territory in subsequent Gazette notifications resulted in a huge reduction of the Jarawa territory from 2,950 sq km to 765 sq km. This shrinkage entailed a substantial curtailment of the life sustaining resource base of the Jarawa. Besides, in those notifications, the 'Jarawa Reserve' was defined only on paper. As a result, it always remained vague on the ground. In addition, there was no buffer area between the 'Jarawa Reserve' and the settlement areas of the non-Jarawa. Subsequently, it resulted in the illegal extraction of resources and encroachment in the 'Jarawa Reserve'. In 2004 the boundary of the 'Jarawa Reserve' has been redrawn and now it extends over 1028 sq km (Gazette Notification 2004). But the actual resource base of the Jarawa has remained the same.

ILLEGAL EXTRACTION OF RESOURCES FROM THE JARAWA TERRITORY

As discussed earlier, the Andaman Islands were opened for the resettlement and rehabilitation of the refugees from erstwhile East Pakistan. In the initial days of rehabilitation, the settlers were primarily involved in agricultural activities. Besides, some of them also worked as agricultural labourers for a secondary source of income. A few of them worked as wage labourers in the Forest Department. Those immigrants who reached the Andaman Islands on their own and were not allotted any land by the authorities, started carpentry work with wood and cane, in addition to working as wage labourers in various works.

With an increase in population over the decades (Table 5.5), the tendency to exploit both forests and aquatic resources increased. In the beginning, only jobless and landless persons entered the forest in search of some livelihood. Later, people who had land or other means of livelihood also started exploiting the natural resources on a regular basis. Even the cultivators, whenever they were free, entered deep into the forest for either hunting or collecting non-timber forest products. In this way, people were involved in illegally extracting valuable timber and collecting various non-timber forest products like resin, honey and fruits. Besides,

TABLE 5.5: POPULATION GROWTH IN CENSUS YEARS

Area	South Andaman*					
Year	1951	1961	1971	1981	1991	2001
Population	16,844	30,644	86,530	1,02,394	1,62,781	2,08,471
Area	**Middle Andaman****					
Year	1951	1961	1971	1981	1991	2001
Population	5,392	11,082	23,686	55,239	46,820	66,789

Source: Census of India 2001, 2001, 91; 81; 61.

* South Andaman includes the population of Port Blair also.

** Middle Andaman includes the population of North Andaman also.

they were also involved in the hunting wild boars and deer (Chakraborty and Dinda 2002: 48-50). However, all these activities were restrained and under control because the hostile relationship with the Jarawa acted as a deterrent.

However, in the post-hostility phase, i.e. after 1997, the situation changed. With the absence of hostility, the illegal exploitation of resources from the Jarawa territory has increased manifold. Based on fieldwork and discussion with a large number of people, it has been found that poaching activities are quite high in the Jarawa territory. Such activities include the illegal extraction of minor forest products, fishing and hunting, which have been discussed below.

Extraction of Timber and Minor Forest Produce

For some villagers, illegal extraction of timber from the forests for making furniture has become a ready means of earning. Even foreign poachers are found to extract good quality timber, particularly *padauk* and black marble woods, from the 'Jarawa Reserve', for this area is rich in such resources. To accomplish their illegal task, they first befriend the Jarawa by offering them some edible items so that they do not resist them. However, the illegal extraction of timber is not very high.

To meet the day-to-day requirements of minor forest products, the villagers extract the required materials from the forests. These minor forest products include fuelwood, wooden poles, leaves for thatching and cane as a building material and for making furniture. Besides the villagers, some businessmen engage people to collect forest produce, like certain fruits and seeds, which have commercial value. Such extraction might turn out to be harmful in the long run as indiscriminate plucking and picking of fruits would interfere with the natural regeneration of the forests. It is done by misusing the forest permit which is given to the villagers for collecting minor forest produce from the forests outside the 'Jarawa Reserve'. But the forest or vegetation outside the Reserve is so degraded that the villagers are tempted to sneak into the Jarawa territory, where the vegetation is abundant, to meet their needs.

Fishing and Hunting

A study by Chakraborty and Dinda (2002: 47-50) shows that persons from both landowning and landless households earn part of their livelihood from fishing or trading in aquatic items, like fish, crab, sea cucumber, lobster and prawn. Now, their favourite hunting grounds are the coastal waters and creeks of the 'Jarawa Reserve'. The presence of many fishing canoes in the creeks and along the western coast of the 'Jarawa Reserve' was noticed during the course of the fieldwork. It indicates the extent of illegal fishing in the Jarawa area. Interviews with the villagers revealed that most of them are ignorant about the extension of the Reserve by 200 m in the sea. Earlier fishermen used to stay away from the shoreline to save themselves from Jarawa arrows. Now they lay nets pretty closer to the shore, sometimes they even seek help of the Jarawa while fishing. 'The Jarawa Report' of the Anthropological Survey of India (An.S.I. 2002) also mentions illegal fishing, hunting and extraction of timber and non-timber forest products from the Jarawa area. Further, it cites one case where five persons were arrested along with three dinghies along the western coast of the Reserve with the catch of shark, turtles, ray fish, flat fish, king shells and other marine animals (Table 5.6).

TABLE 5.6: ANIMALS FOUND IN POACHERS' NET

Species	Total number	Live	Dead
Shark	3	2	1
Golden turtle	3	–	3
Green turtle	1	1	–
Ray fish	16	4	12
Flat fish	2	–	2
King shell	2	2	–
Miscellaneous	17	5	12

Source: An.S.I, 2002.

Similarly, hunting wild pigs and deer during the hostility phase was very limited and used to be mainly for domestic consumption. However, post-1997, poaching of these game animals has become another way of income generation for the neighbours of the Jarawa.

Data were collected on fish and pig catch for 10 days each in the years 1999, 2002 and 2004 near Dhani Nala in the Kadamtala area (Figures 5.5 and 5.6). The objective was to find out whether there was any impact of poaching on the resources, particularly of

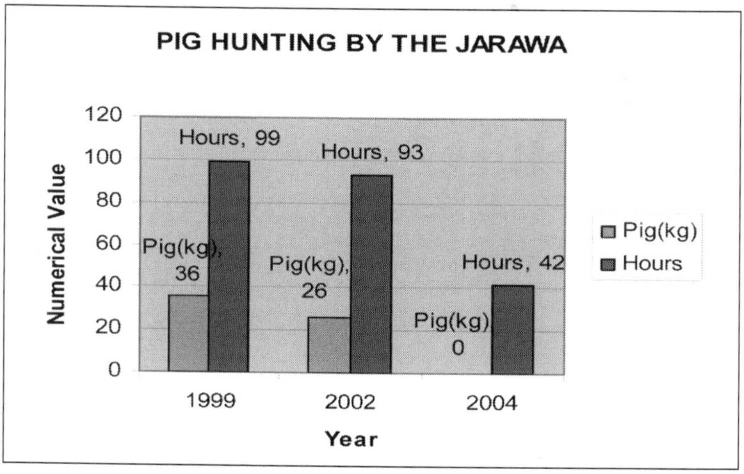

Source: Based on Field Investigation, 2002.

Figure 5.5: Pig Hunting by the Jarawa

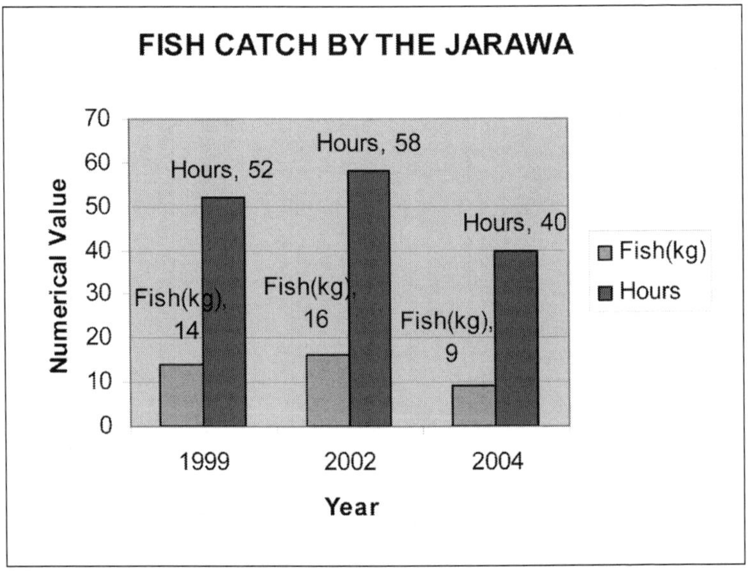

Source: Based on Field Investigation, 2002.

Figure 5.6: Fish Catch by the Jarawa

the pig and fish population in those areas of the Jarawa territory which are close to the villages of the settlers (non-Jarawa). Dhani Nala was one such place which was close to Kadamtala and frequented by both the Jarawa and the settlers.

Figure 5.5 reveals that the Jarawa hunted pigs weighing in total around 36 kg by spending 99 hours in 10 days in 1999. However, pig hunting registered a decline in 2002. Despite spending 93 hours in 10 days, they could hunt pigs which in total weighed about 26 kg only. However, in 2004 they could not hunt any pigs even after spending 42 hours. Though it would be incorrect to deduce from the above analysis that there are no pigs available now in that area for pig is a mobile prey, it certainly reveals the fact that pig density has decreased owing to poaching in that area. Poachers do not take care of the regeneration cycle, but the Jarawa do. However, in the case of fishing, no significant change was observed in the total fish catch between 1999 and 2002 (Figure 5.6). But in 2004, a marginal decline in the total fish catch was observed as the Jarawa could catch only 9 kg of fish after spending 40 hours. It shows that fishing grounds of the Jarawa, which are nearer to settlements of the non-Jarawa, have begun to exhibit the sign of over exploitation owing to fishing by the villagers.

The above findings on the poaching are also corroborated by the survey of five small hotels at Kadamtala, which reveal that the meat of wild boar and deer is invariably available in a couple of these hotels. Though the deer is not a game animal for the Jarawa, the pig is. More importantly, if the poaching continues to grow at the same rate, it will soon surpass the rate of natural replenishment, and that would be detrimental to the Jarawa. It is because the Jarawa are a foraging group. A foraging economy coupled with simple technology requires a very high resource density to get a satisfactory collection of resources in a limited time. This, in turn, gives them sufficient time for social and leisure activities. Now with the shield of hostility gone, the poaching inside the Jarawa territory has increased. As a result, the Jarawa are competing with poachers for the natural resources (both terrestrial and aquatic). The poachers, on the other hand, have superior technology compared to the Jarawa. Such competition, if not controlled or curbed, may soon turn out to be fatal for the Jarawa for two reasons:

1. The Jarawa do not have access to any other set of resources except those available in the 'Jarawa Reserve'. So any scarcity or degradation of these resources on which the Jarawa are dependent would cause immense hardship to them.
2. The Jarawa have a non-accumulative (except the seeds of wild jackfruit and *Cycas rumphii*) subsistence economy. Accumulation or storage of food resources is minimal. They collect only that much of resources from nature which is essential for their sustenance by practising hunting and gathering. The poachers, on the other hand, are equipped with superior technology. They indulge in extracting as many resources as possible. Besides, they follow a carpet approach in which they do not discriminate between adult and young animals in the course of poaching. Presently, the Jarawa and the poachers compete over the same set of resources with their respective technologies. In such a

situation, the latter has the advantage over the former in terms of technology.

From the above analysis, it is apparent that many of the resources used by the Jarawa and non-Jarawa are common to both. It was one of the reasons for hostility between Jarawa and non-Jarawa in the past (i.e. before 1997) and a matter of concern in the present (i.e. after 1997). In the post-hostility phase, the Jarawa have to share in a big way their resource base with the non-Jarawa. It is more so in the case of animal resources. Now, it has created a situation where the two groups of people are using the same set of resources and that too from the same ecosystem. Such exploitation of the resources of the 'Jarawa Reserve' by the non-Jarawa is disadvantageous to the Jarawa, as it may cause diminishing of the resources in the Jarawa territory, and finally hardship for the Jarawa.

ENCROACHMENT

In the absence of a clearly delimited and demarcated boundary of the 'Jarawa Reserve', it is very difficult to discern the boundary of the 'Jarawa Reserve' on the ground. As a result, it is difficult to ascertain the extent of encroachment in the reserved area. However, it has been found that encroachment has taken place on two types of land—(i) the fringe area of 'Jarawa Reserve', and (ii) those parts of the forest which are not in the 'Jarawa Reserve'. There are the following three types of encroachers:

1. One group is of those people who were refugees from the erstwhile East Bengal or East Pakistan and were settled by the Government of India under the refugee resettlement and rehabilitation scheme. Over a period of time as their population grew, the need for extra land was felt which found expression in terms of the expansion of their land into the adjacent territory. The areas of many of the refugee villages are contiguous to the 'Jarawa Reserve' or reserved forest. Few such villages are Colinpur, Manpur and Ferargunj in the South Andaman and Kadamtala, Shantanu, and Phooltala in the Middle Andaman. Instead of

clear-felling, the people have thinned the forests, and have planted coconut, areca nut, banana, etc., in the encroached lands. Consequently, there is vegetation fragmentation, which is very high near the settlements of the non-Jarawa (Figures 5.7, 5.8 and 5.9).

2. The second category is of those people who had been brought here as labourers and later found jobs in the Forest Department and 'Bush Police Force'. Since most of the time they were posted in or around Jarawa areas, they constructed huts in the forest in the absence of any other proper residential facilities. Some of these settlements are at Jirkatang-2, Jirkatang-7, Putatang, Beach Dera, Putatang, Bamboo Tikri, Sippi Tikri, Kesri Dera, etc.
3. In the third category are those people who moved into these Islands on their own, cleared the forests and settled down. In fact, it is mainly a post-1970 phenomenon when the communication between these Islands and the mainland became more regular on account of the introduction of more ships.

The thinning of the forest and the degradation of the resources outside the 'Jarawa Reserve' are also harmful to the Jarawa because forests adjacent to the Jarawa area function as a buffer and reduce the pressure on the Jarawa area. Unfortunately, the forests outside the Jarawa area are almost denuded. They have fewer resources to offer. The above mentioned fact is also supported by the satellite imageries, which clearly show that the fragmentation of the forest is considerably high near the settlements of the non-Jarawa (Figures 5.7, 5.8 and 5.9).

DETRIMENTAL EFFECTS OF THE ANDAMAN TRUNK ROAD (ATR)

The induction of new settlements brought with it the need for the development of road for transportation and communication between Port Blair and the settlements. The easiest method of surface communication would have been by ships and boats, as in the first decade of settlement the sea transport was the main means

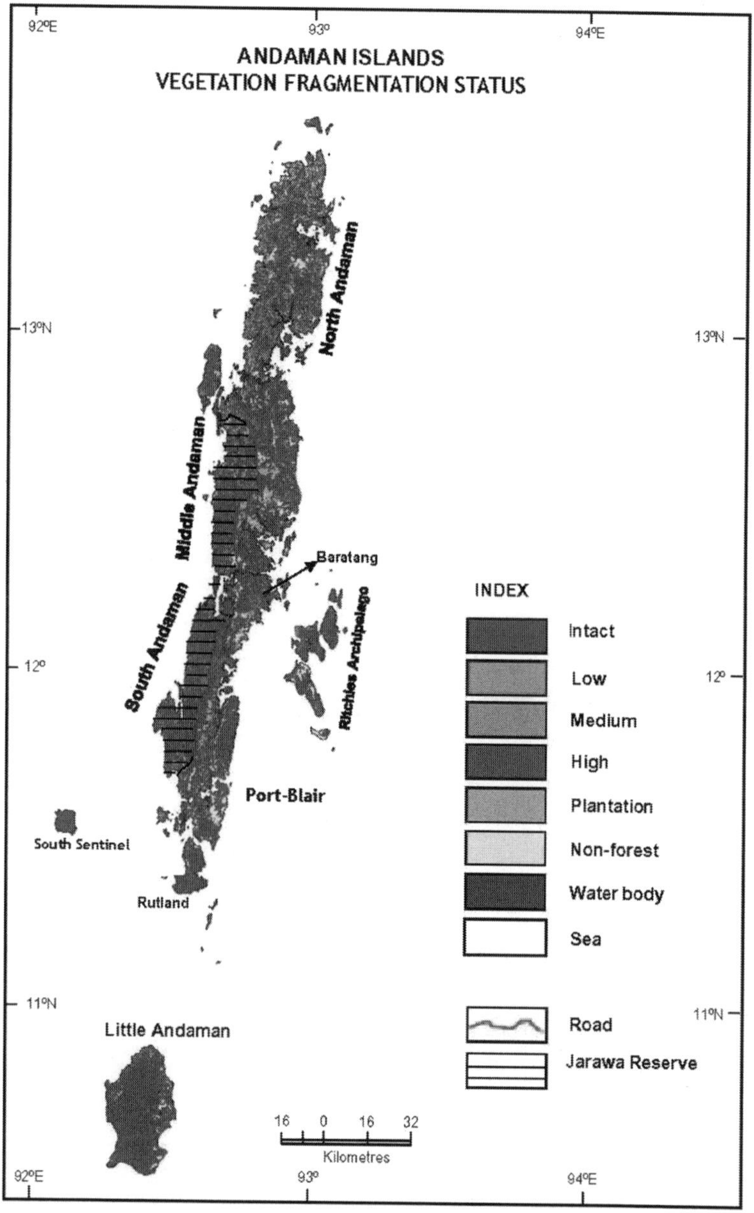

Source: Indian Institute of Remote Sensing, Dehradun, 2006.

Figure 5.7: Andaman Islands: Vegetation Fragmentation Status

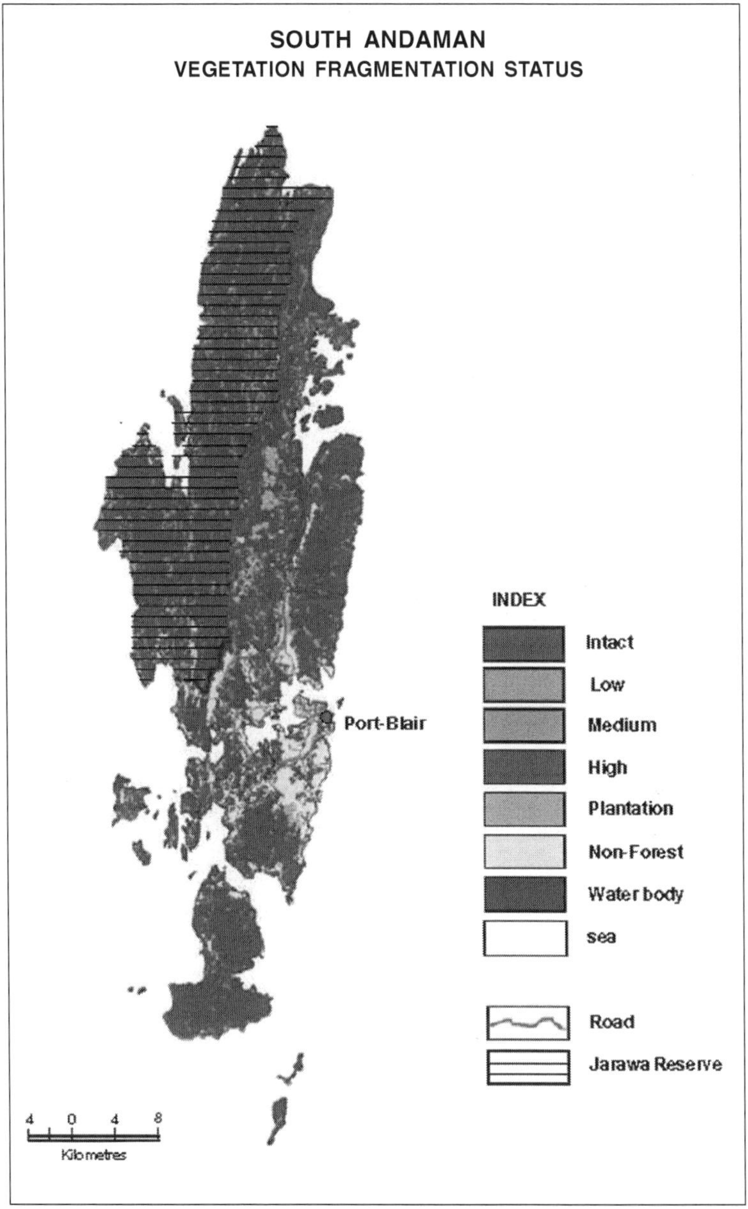

Source: Indian Institute of Remote Sensing, Dehradun, 2006.

Figure 5.8: South Andaman: Vegetation Fragmentation Status

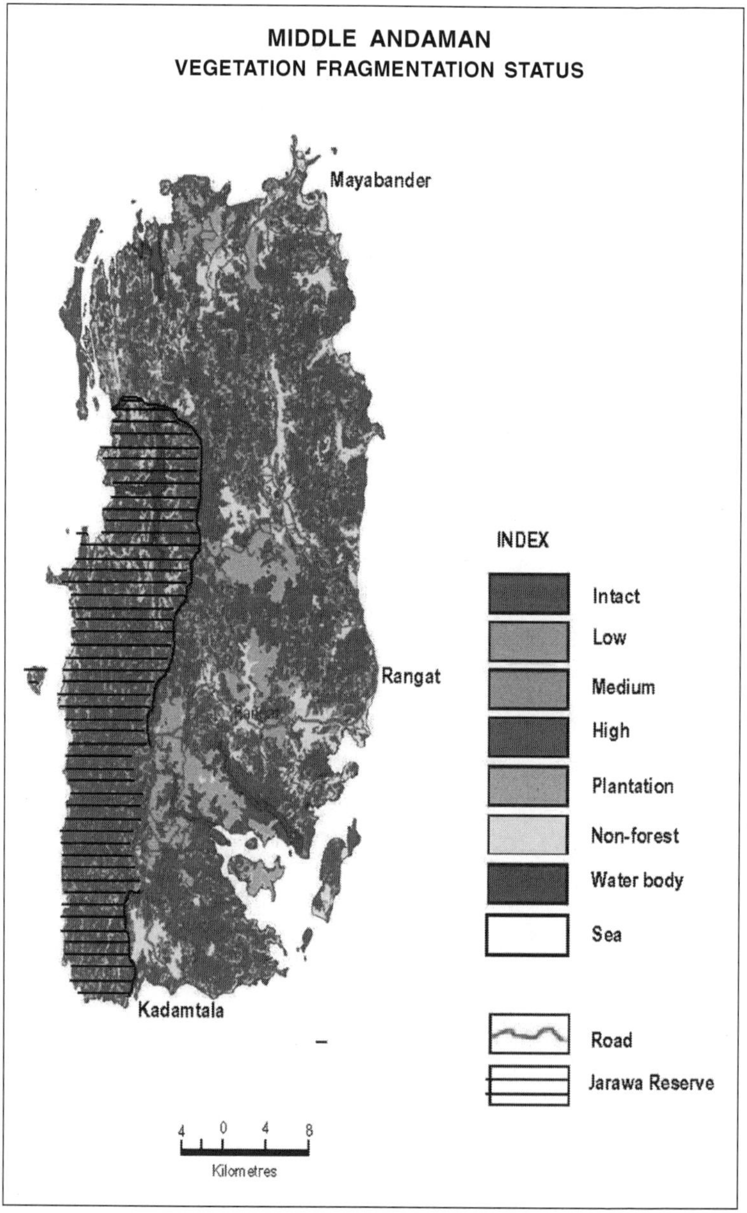

Source: Indian Institute of Remote Sensing, Dehradun, 2006.

Figure 5.9: Middle Andaman: Vegetation Fragmentation Status

of transport between Port Blair and the settlements. However, the settlers had a continental mindset, distinctly different from that of a true islander. They were gripped by the natural fear and mistrust of sea transport. To them, the road was a preferred means of transportation. Even more, the administration and decision makers in the Independent era were also mainlanders with continental mindsets and preferences.

A grandiose project was conceptualised and soon the survey work for the proposed 343 km long ATR started in the 1970s. The road became fully operational in 1989, which now connects the four major Islands, namely South Andaman, Baratang, Middle Andaman and North Andaman, from Chiriyatapu in South Andaman to Diglipur in North Andaman. When the road construction started, the Jarawas actively opposed it as it was passing through their territory and disturbing their way of life (Acharya 2002: 170). Besides, the Jarawa were also traumatised by the large scale tree felling and use of noisy heavy machinery for construction of the road, which probably drove their game species away and scared them. The Jarawa regularly raided the labourers' camps, drove wedges in the water pipes to obstruct the flow of water and made log barriers. On the other hand, the armed police protected the construction crews. According to a report in the local press, the construction agency used to surround the camps with live electric wire, a sort of improvised electric fence, which claimed many lives (cf. Acharya 2002: 167-9). Many incidents of conflicts had taken place on the road since the 1970s and continued until 1997 when the situation changed. The number of Jarawas killed during the road construction will never be known, be it by electrocution, bullets or other means. Attacks on labourers, 'Bush Police', trucks and buses by the Jarawa were merely a form of resistance against the intrusion into their lives and territory. Apart from it, the road led to many encroachments *en route* and later facilitated forestry operations also. The ATR had marginalised the Jarawa like never before, admits the Master Plan for the Tribal Development (Awaradi 1990).

The Andaman and Nicobar Islands experience rain for about eight months in a year, as such the maintenance cost of the road is very high. Every year 20 per cent of the total length of the road is taken for repair. Such repair work alone requires 38 metric tons of bitumen and 88 metric cords of firewood (approximately 249.04 cubic metres). The use of firewood for the 50 km stretch of road that is repaired every year is estimated to be 12,452 cubic metres. The said firewood is extracted from the 'Jarawa Reserve'. Thus, the very existence of the road appears to be posing a threat to the forest too (Acharya 2002, 168).

In the post-hostility phase when the Jarawa first started coming out on road, there were certain risks involved in terms of road accidents. The Jarawa did know how to behave on the road in the presence of moving traffic. On the other hand, the drivers using the trunk road were not sure what to do when confronted with some Jarawas who were either standing in the middle of the road or trying to stop the vehicles. During the initial two to three years, few road accidents did occur and in one of the accidents in 1999, a Jarawa boy even lost his right hand (AAJVS 1999). Over a period of time, the Jarawa have learnt ways to avoid accidents caused by the vehicles plying on the road. Now the risk of accidents has decreased to a great extent but it still persists, particularly where children are concerned.

Andaman and Nicobar Islands have been one of the preferred locations for the Indian tourists, but before 1997, the tourist flow to the islands was not very high. In the wake of the Jarawa becoming friendly, the tour and travel operators have used this new situation as an opportunity. The tourists are promised to be taken through the 'Jarawa Reserve' with all possibilities of seeing and meeting the *Homo sapiens* who are still in the 'Stone Age'. Consequently, it has found expression in terms of sudden spurt in the number of vehicles plying on the ATR, which passes through the 'Jarawa Reserve'. It is directly related to the sudden increase in the number of tourists visiting the Andaman and Nicobar Islands. In the year 1996, a total of 3,695 buses and 5,802 other vehicles crossed the Jirkatang Check post either way. By applying the IRC norms for calculation of the volume of traffic, one finds that the road was used by only 515 persons daily or a total of 1,87,895 persons in the entire year (Acharya 2002, 169). By 2004, there was a 150 per cent increase in the traffic volume with more than 1500 persons crossing the 'Jarawa Reserve' every day. A large section of them are tourists desirous of seeing the Jarawa. The movement of so many vehicles across the 'Jarawa Reserve' disturbs the tranquillity of their habitat, scares away their prey and poses a danger of accidents to the Jarawa.

The commuters and tourists who travel along the ATR meet the Jarawa at different points in the South and Middle Andaman Islands. They feel pity for the Jarawa and consider them hungry when they find the Jarawa to be asking for food. But asking for food on the part of the Jarawa is not due to the fact that they are hungry or there is a shortage of resources in their territory. It is rather an induced habit. The genesis of this habit is related to earlier practice and act of giving gift articles by the Andaman Administration.

During the contact mission in the hostility phase, it was a practice to give gift articles to the Jarawa whenever and wherever the contact party was able to contact them. In fact, this practice remained in vogue for a few years even after the cessation of hostility in 1997. Besides, during the initial years of the post-hostility phase, most of the passengers of the vehicles passing through the Jarawa territory used to give gift items to the Jarawa. Now, this practice of giving the gift has been banned by the Administration. Still, whenever a Jarawa confronts a passing vehicle, he or she asks for food or other articles. This behaviour of the Jarawa is being interpreted as 'begging' and it is correlated with food scarcity in their habitat. However, there is no paucity of food resources in the 'Jarawa Reserve', except in some of the border areas adjacent to the villages. Many of the commuters are found to be carrying edible items like bananas, biscuits, etc., for the Jarawa. Sometimes, they are found to dispense fried and spicy food items among the Jarawa. However, the oily and spicy food articles pose health hazards to the Jarawa, as they are not accustomed to such food. Moreover, no one knows how far these items are hygienic and safe for eating.

SPREAD OF DISEASES

It has been observed throughout the world that whenever a hunting and gathering group is exposed to the outsiders, they suffer from some health problems. It is believed that this is primarily because of their long isolation from other human groups, and thus certain pathogens or disease-causing organisms do not reach them. As a result, such communities never develop immunity in their body against all such pathogens. Once a contact is established, the pathogens get a chance to enter their bodies that can offer little or no resistance. Diseases that are very common among sedentary populations can be fatal for hunting and gathering communities. The same pattern has been repeated time and again in different parts of the world. For example, in the Andaman Islands, the Great Andamanese suffered from epidemics caused by diseases like measles and pneumonia, which were largely responsible for the rapid population decline of the Great Andamanese and to some extent of the Onge (Cipriani 1966).

The analysis of data on diseases among the Jarawa since 1998 shows outbreaks of many diseases like community acquired pneumonia in 1998, measles in 1999, malaria in 2000-1 and mumps (Table 5.7). Except for malaria and mumps, the other two diseases are highly contagious. These diseases were probably absent among the Jarawa before their friendly relations and free mixing with the non-Jarawa people. The outbreak of measles among the Jarawa in

TABLE 5.7: DISEASES DETECTED AMONG THE JARAWA BETWEEN 1998 AND 2001

Year	Name of Disease	Male	Female	Total
As per records available between 1998 and 2001	Community-acquired Pneumonia	27	22	49
	Measles with its complication	45	50	95
	Mumps	18	9	27
	Malaria	37	28	65

Source: Directorate of Health Services, 2002.

1999 needs special mention. When there was an outbreak of measles in 1999, the Jarawa of the Tanmad and the Thidong areas were quick to seek medical help and, therefore, timely medical aid was provided that could save them. However, this was not the case with the Jarawa of Boiab area, as they were still hesitant to seek any medical help. Therefore, it could not be confirmed how many of them suffering from measles, died of it. However, through the field investigation, it could be ascertained that at that time approximately 25 to 30 Jarawas of Boiab died due to measles or secondary infection caused by measles.

Among other diseases, which have witnessed a sudden increase are anaemia, skin diseases, and respiratory tract infection. Besides these diseases, hepatomegaly, spleenomegaly, and hepatitis B are the new diseases detected among them (Table 5.8). In the past, the Jarawa were not reported to be suffering from any infectious skin diseases, but after 1997 manifold increase in skin diseases has been recorded. The causative factors behind the sudden spread of the skin diseases are attributed to the mingling of the Jarawa with the non-Jarawa and the giving of used clothes by the latter to the former. Moreover, the consumption of alien food items prepared with oil, salts and spices is causing high blood pressure among many of the Jarawas.

The laboratory investigation of 120 Jarawa's blood samples with ELISA method for HBsAg has revealed some startling facts about the presence of deadly diseases among the Jarawa. About 49.10 per cent of the Jarawa were found to be HBsAg positive (Table 5.8). It is also known as hepatitis B. Fortunately, all of them are healthy carriers of HBsAg. However, there is a danger of contracting HBsAg by some of the non-Jarawas who quite frequently come in contact with Jarawa for various purposes. Similarly, the laboratory investigation of the blood sample of 231 Jarawas reveals that about 27.7 per cent of them were suffering from hepatomegaley while 13.8 per cent from spleenomagaly. Though these diseases are not as dangerous as the HBsAg, they are caused due to chronic infection. The diseases detected among the Jarawa can be put under the following four broad categories:

TABLE 5.8: TYPES OF DISEASES AND NUMBER OF AFFECTED JARAWAS

Diseases	Sample size	Number of persons affected			Per-centage	Remarks
		Male	Female	Total		
Anaemia (WHO criteria)	120	–	–	33	27.5	Nutritional
Chronic Energy Deficiency	96	11	4	15	15.6	Nutritional
Malaria	120	2	0	2	1.6	P. falciparum
Skin infection	231	50	41	91	39.3	Fungal & bacterial
Respiratory tract infection	231	15	11	26	11.2	Infective
Hepatomegaly	231	–	–	64	27.7	Chronic infection
Spleenomegaly	231	–	–	32	13.8	Chronic infection
Hepatitis B carrier stage	120	35	24	59	49.1	Viral

Source: Directorate of Health Services 2002.

1. Nutritional diseases: anaemia and chronic energy deficiency.
2. Infectious diseases: pneumonia, measles, respiratory tract infection and fungal infection of the skin.
3. Endemic: HbsAg (Hepatitis B).
4. Other diseases: hepatomegaly and spleenomegaly.

Nevertheless, the acceptance of the new way of life by the Jarawa has made them understand the importance of taking timely medical aid from the nearby health centres or from the medical personnel who pay visits to their territory. It has resulted in a reduction in morbidity and mortality among them.

USE OF TOBACCO AND BETEL LEAF (*PAAN*)

The friendly relationship between the Jarawa and the non-Jarawa has brought in its wake some of the vices and one of them is addiction to tobacco and *paan*. Until 2000, the Jarawa were never seen chewing tobacco and *paan*. Now many of the male Jarawas have become addicted to tobacco and *paan*. They have picked up this habit from the villagers, drivers and police personnel who are in regular contact with them. If the situation is compared with the Onge, the Great Andamanese and the Shompen, it is found that the Jarawa, like their counterparts, have also fallen prey to these intoxicants, though partially, after becoming friendly with the non-tribal people. In fact, presently the Great Andamanese and the Onge are exposed to liquor also, which is fortunately not the case with the Jarawa yet. However, their addiction to intoxicants may soon prove to be an Achilles heel for them. The burning examples are the Onge of Little Andaman and the Shompen of the Great Nicobar Islands who part with many of their valuable resources like honey, resin, etc., to get a small amount of the intoxicants.

JARAWA ADAPTATION TO THE CHANGING ENVIRONMENT

The historical development of contact between the Jarawa and non-Jarawa is marked by a number of incidences, like the British policy towards the Jarawa during the colonial period, post-Independence policy towards the Jarawa, settling of the refugee population in the Andaman Islands and the resultant enmity of the Jarawa towards them, the reduction and erosion of the resources base of the Jarawa due to numerous factors, impact of contact and conflict on the Jarawa, etc. Against this backdrop, it is worthwhile to understand how the Jarawa have adapted themselves to the changed environment/situation. It is also significant to know how far the Jarawa have been successful in retaining their traditional hunting and gathering way of life, culture, and growth (in terms of number and health). Therefore, the following lines are devoted to the adaptation of the Jarawa to the changing environment.

STAYING CLOSE TO ATR

It is well known that the Jarawa usually set up their huts at the transition of two ecological zones, but staying close to the road was never an option in the ambience of hostility. However, in recent times some of the huts of the Jarawa have been set up close to the road, particularly in the Thidong area. Staying close to the road gives them certain benefits. As already mentioned, the daily movement of the Jarawa from the base camp is generally in a radius of five to six km. However, while camping close to the road, they make use of the vehicles plying on the road to cover longer distances in search of edible and non-edible resources. Thus, in less time they are able to reach distant places. Besides, the Jarawa also make use of the vehicles while shifting their camp from one place to another. Of course, the road, besides facilitating faster movement, also offers other attractions like foreign food and lots of fun and amusement.

USE OF BOAT

In the post-hostility phase, particularly after 2000, it has been observed that when the Jarawa camp near the Jetly or the villages of the settlers and they require to shift their camp to a place along the coast, they make use of the boat (motorised canoe). To avail of the boat, they approach either police personnel or the staff of the AAJVS, who are posted at that place and make them aware of their need. At times, they also ask the fishermen to help them shift their camps by taking them in their motorised canoe. Thus, the Jarawa are making use of both water and road transport to their advantage to cover longer distances in less time and with much ease.

IRON IMPLEMENTS FOR MAKING TOOLS

Iron is of prime importance to the Jarawa. It is one article along with other metal items that are not naturally available in their territory. Earlier (during hostility phase) the Jarawa used to obtain these articles from the jetty, shipwreck and the settlements of the non-Jarawa. The recent development, however, has assured them of a regular supply of iron. These days they are getting a regular supply of iron both as raw material and as iron tools from the AAJVS. Now the Jarawa can be seen working with the hammer, chisel, file, and makeshift anvil made of huge pieces of iron rails or thick iron sheets for making hunting and fishing implements. While some years back, they used to protect each piece of iron very jealously, now they do not mind gifting or bartering an arrow or a knife for some other articles.

ACCEPTANCE OF NEW TECHNOLOGY

Instances of acceptance of new technology by the Jarawa for their subsistence activity have not come to notice. It may be due to the fact that they continue to forage the way they were doing earlier. It is true that the Jarawa have observed and gathered information about some foraging techniques of the non-Jarawa, like the use of snare to catch pigs or use of line and hook for fishing. However, they still do not use snares for the purpose of hunting, though the children sometimes playfully fix up snares collected from the forest. In case of the other two Negrito tribes of the Andaman Islands, namely the Onge and the Great Andamanese, it has been found that they have learnt the hunting and fishing techniques of the outsiders and are using them successfully. However, the new techniques are yet to be accepted and adopted by the Jarawa. It may take some more time for them to accept new technology because they are still able to fulfill their needs with the help of their own traditional tools and techniques.

CHANGE IN RAW MATERIAL

Earlier, the Jarawa used to make use of bark fibre as thread while making their fishing nets, baskets and a few other articles. Now they also use nylon threads for making these items. However, there are certain articles, where only bark fibre is used, like tying arrowheads with the shaft.

FOOD

Nowadays, the Jarawa procure many non-traditional food items from the non-Jarawa. Earlier they did not consume these items. Before 1997, bananas and coconuts were the main non-traditional food items that used to be given to them as gifts by contact teams. However, after 1997, some more items have found their way into the Jarawa menu, though none of these items has yet become a part of their staple diet. The major non-traditional food items are rice, banana, coconut, biscuits, bread, paratha, vada, idli, etc. These items are procured from the tourists, drivers of tourist and other vehicles, shops located at the jetties, villagers and the policemen posted at the pickets near the huts of the Jarawa. This practice of procuring non-traditional food items influences their foraging behaviour also, particularly when they camp near ATR, for example, the Jarawa children and young boys invariably spend some part of the day on the road. Though it is done generally out of curiosity and to derive some entertainment, in the process they get some food items also which are given to them by the tourists passing through the Jarawa territory. Generally, the young Jarawa boys are more involved in it compared to the elderly persons.

COOKING AND STORING UTENSILS

The use of metal utensils was noticed among the Jarawa of Middle Andaman Island even in 1980s (Sarkar 1990). In the post-Independence phase, particularly after the settling of the refugee population at the fringe of the 'Jarawa Reserve' during the 1950s, the Jarawa used to procure metal utensils stealthily, mostly those made of aluminium and iron, from the settlements of the refugee population. Before coming up of the refugee settlements, the Jarawa had been collecting flotsam, bottles, pans, iron pieces, etc., for a long time from the coastal areas. Even now, one can see the huge amount of glass and plastic bottles accumulated along the western coast, carried there by the sea waves.

It has been observed that now the Jarawa depend more on the metal pans for cooking their food and less on their traditional pit ovens. Despite this, there are certain items that are broiled in an oven pit or roasted, like jackfruit, flesh of wild pig, etc. In the post-hostility period, the AAJVS is supplying metal utensils to the Jarawa for cooking and storing purposes. It is a welcome change.

ACCEPTANCE OF MEDICAL TREATMENT

Before 1997 when the Jarawa were still hostile, they used to seek first aid like bandages and ointments for the treatment of the injured parts and fungal infected areas of the skin from the members of the contact team. During those days, the Jarawa never accepted tablets, syrup, or any other oral medicines for their injuries or diseases. After 1997 when they became friendly with the non-Jarawa, the number of visits by the medical team to the habitat of the Jarawa and the number of the Jarawa being brought to the Primary Health Centre or Hospital at Port Blair for treatment increased manifold. It created further confidence in the Jarawa towards the non-Jarawa. Of late, it has been observed that the Jarawa have no hesitation in accepting any kind of medicine, either orally or externally. Changes have also been observed with respect to their behaviour in the hospital.

It has been observed that initially during 1998-99 (i.e. post-hostility time) when there was an outbreak of pneumonia and measles among the Jarawa, they were very much apprehensive about sending their fellow members, who were suffering from any of these diseases, alone to the health centre. Firstly, they always accompanied the patients to the hospital in large numbers. Secondly, they did not want to stay in the hospital for more than a day or two. With time, the Jarawa have developed more confidence in the non-Jarawa. Now, when a Jarawa patient is admitted to the hospital, he or she is rarely accompanied by more than two to three members of his/her community. Besides, they have also accepted the co-existence of other patients in the nearby wards, which they were earlier wary of. Further, in case they are required to stay in the hospital even for a week or so, the insistence to send them back to their habitat is not so strong.

These are positive changes, which will go a long way in providing modern medical coverage to the entire Jarawa population. It assumes more importance in light of the fact that in the post-hostility phase, the entire Jarawa community has suddenly been exposed to new diseases, which they are unable to treat through their traditional system of healing or ethnomedicine. Even more, it will also be helpful in the treatment of some of the endemic diseases that the Jarawa have been found to be the carrier, e.g. hepatitis B.

PREVENTIVE MEASURES FOR DISEASES

The acceptance of medical treatment has also paved the way for taking preventive measures to curb the spread of certain diseases. hepatitis B is the only endemic disease that could be detected among the Jarawa during the comprehensive health survey. Though the Jarawa are the healthy carrier of hepatitis B, it can be prevented by launching the immunisation programme among the Jarawa. It becomes more necessary in light of the fact that now the interaction between Jarawa and non-Jarawa has increased manifold and so has increased the risk of the non-Jarawa contracting hepatitis B.

The other new diseases detected among the Jarawa are community-acquired pneumonia, measles and malaria (*Plasmodium falsiparum*). Community-acquired pneumonia can be prevented by maintaining good sanitation and hygiene and avoiding overcrowding in the Jarawa hut. Besides, early detection and prompt treatment would also help cure the disease and its spread. The occurrence of measles can be prevented by immunising all children at 9-12 months of age with the measles vaccine. In recent times, the malaria cases have increased, including that of the fatalities. The occurrence of malaria among the Jarawa can be contained by detecting mosquito-breeding places and by introducing anti-larva measures around their habitat. However, as a precaution, mass administration of anti-malaria drugs should be avoided as the Jarawa may develop some other complications. Administration of anti-malarial drugs, including treatment of *Plasmodium falsiparum,* should be based on clinical tests and thorough medical checkups to avoid any side effects on the Jarawa as they are a small population. While popularising modern medical treatment among them, all possible care should be taken to keep the traditional medicinal knowledge of the Jarawa alive.

BEGINNING OF BARTER SYSTEM

In the Jarawa community, there exists a system of reciprocity within different groups as it happens in most of the hunting and gathering communities. However, with growing interaction between the Jarawa and the non-Jarawa, the demand for certain articles by both sides have surfaced. It, in turn, has led to the beginning of the barter system. The non-Jarawa, who are involved in it are the tourists, villagers, vehicle drivers and at times police personnel who are posted there. Earlier the Jarawa used to exchange resin and iron implements (particularly bows and arrows) in lieu of tobacco and paan. At times, they also exchanged these articles for colourful garments and some non-traditional edible items. Now many more items have entered in the barter system. The bartering items which are coming inward to the Jarawa are rice, biscuits, cooking oil, spices, tobacco, cloth, torch and battery, iron implements, metal utensils, safety pins, mirrors, plastic bottles, polythene sheet, nylon rope, plastic drum, soap, cosmetic articles, artificial jewellery, etc. The items which are flowing outward from the Jarawa area through exchange are deer meat, resin, mud crab, prawn, freshwater fish and other forest resources. In recent times, the factor of 'demand' has come into play. It is a significant development in the bartering system. Both sides put their demand for specific articles.

This kind of barter trade is disadvantageous to the Jarawa. For example, earlier the Jarawa were never found to part with iron implements because procuring iron was difficult and at times hazardous too. Now, with an assured supply of iron from the AAJVS, they easily give away their iron implements. To buy safe passage to the forests, the poachers offer tobacco, *paan,* and other articles to the Jarawa. Consequently, now the resource base of the Jarawa lie open to the poachers. But the Jarawa do not know the damages being caused to their habitat by such bartering due to their innocence and ignorance.

Thus, considering the baneful impacts of the bartering and taking lessons from the Onge of the Little Andaman and the Shompen of the Great Nicobar Islands, where they can part with almost any items in exchange for liquor and tobacco, it is necessary to ban any type of gift giving to and bartering with the Jarawa. Even more, efforts should be made to rid them of addiction to *paan* and tobacco. This will not only help maintain the health of the Jarawa but of their habitat as well.

DRESS AND ORNAMENTS

Traditionally, the Jarawa do not put on any clothes to cover their bodies. Instead, both males and females use various kinds of headbands, necklaces, armlets and waistbands made of shells, barks, leaves and flowers to adorn them. In addition, both males and females decorate their bodies and faces with white clay and red ochre. They also decorate their bodies with different types of seasonal flowers and tender leaves. They, however, were not found to use any clothes to cover their bodies. Despite knowing the use of cotton threads, extracted from the pieces of red cloth given to them as a gift, for making bands for the head, arm or waist, they never covered their bodies with clothes. However, in recent years, particularly after two to three years of their being friendly with the non-Jarawa, a number of Jarawas have been found to wear clothes. The clothes come from several sources, viz., hospitals, villagers, tourists and the Andaman Administration. Ornaments are another gift item that the Jarawa adore a lot. Almost all of them, including those who are not attracted to garments, enjoy wearing bead necklaces, plastic or metal bangles, rings and trinkets.

During the early years of friendly relationship, i.e. 1998-9, whenever the sick Jarawas were brought to Port Blair and admitted to the hospital, they were given clothes by either the hospital staff or the AAJVS officials. It was felt necessary because the Jarawa patients were visually exposed to the non-Jarawa present in the hospital. Later, when the Jarawa started visiting the villages, the villagers often presented them with used garments. Of late, many villagers have stopped giving clothes to them but some of the villagers continue with the practice of giving clothes to them. Besides villagers, the tourists also gift clothes, mostly used ones. The Jarawa generally carry all such used garments back to their huts. Nowadays, clothes are being provided by AAJVS.

It is the younger generation who is more interested in collecting and putting on such clothes (Plate 5.1). Among the young generation, the boys show more fascination for clothes. This is because the boys are fond of visiting the villages and public places like jetties and police stations frequently. Contrary to this, the older ones and the less frequent visitors possess fewer clothes, which they put on less frequently. The territory wise analysis shows that the Jarawa of the Thidong and Tanmad areas possess more clothes than those of Boiab because the contacts with outsiders are comparatively more prolonged and frequent in the case of the former than the latter. It also shows that the longer a person is in contact with outsiders, the more clothes he or she has in possession, and they use it more frequently than other Jarawas.

Covering the body with clothes is an induced cultural trait for the Jarawa. It is more pronounced among those who frequently meet the non-Jarawa. They have come to realise that they are expected by their neighbours to put on clothes when they

Source: Anthropological Survey of India.

Plate 5.1: Jarawa childen in clothes with gifted banana

meet them. They might have also learnt a bit about the positive preference for covering the body as prevalent among the non-Jarawa. However, for the Jarawa, wearing clothes is not a necessity. It is exemplified by the fact that when the Jarawa put up their camp inside the forest, away from the villages and road, they rarely use clothes.

Clothes have also brought in its wake health hazards. Most of the clothes given to them by the outsiders except by the Andaman Administration are used ones. As a result, when the Jarawa are wearing the clothes, they often contract skin diseases. Now, most of the Jarawa suffer from skin diseases, particularly ringworms. The situation worsens as the Jarawa have yet to learn to wash clothes. Another danger lies in the fact that they usually take a bath with clothes on their bodies and do not remove the wet clothes even after the bath. As a result, many of them get upper respiratory tract infections. Therefore, both the tourists and the villagers should be sensitised about the health hazards associated with their act of giving clothes to the Jarawa and should be prevented from gifting clothes to the Jarawa. Further, the Jarawa should also be slowly trained to wash their clothes with soap.

LANGUAGE

The Jarawa were a monolingual community until the other day. Their prolonged isolation from all other human groups did not warrant them to learn any other language. During the contact missions since 1974, they occasionally picked up a few words of Hindi, like *khana* (meaning food) from the visitors. With the end of the phase of hostility in late 1997, both the Jarawa and the non-Jarawa have started coming into more regular and prolonged contact with each other in comparison to previous years. In such interactions, participation by some of the Jarawas is more frequent compared to others. Similar is the case with the non-Jarawa also. A handful of the AAJVS workers, some policemen and paramedical staff meet the Jarawa more frequently, while the tourists, vehicle drivers and general villagers meet them only occasionally. Naturally, those Jarawas who are exposed to the outsiders more frequently, have a better opportunity of learning Hindi. Most of them are young boys of ten to twenty years of age. A few of them can speak Hindi better compared to others. Knowledge of Hindi also gives the Jarawa certain advantages while interacting with the non-Jarawa. For example, in a contact situation on the road, while the tourists cannot make out what the Jarawa children are discussing among them, the Hindi-knowing Jarawa children would be able to understand, at least partly, what the tourists or the drivers of their vehicles are talking about. Even a broken knowledge of Hindi puts them in a slightly advantageous position. The knowledge of Hindi on the part of the Jarawa has proved very useful in the case of medical treatment also as both the Jarawa and the medical attendant or doctor are able to communicate with each other. Thus, now the medical treatment of the Jarawa has become comparatively easier.

While some of the Jarawas are picking up Hindi, a few non-Jarawa people have also learnt the Jarawa language to various extents. The most proficient speakers of the Jarawa language are some of the AAJVS workers, who can converse very fluently with the Jarawa on subjects related to their needs and other daily life activities. However, the knowledge of the Jarawa language among other people like villagers, policemen and shopkeepers is very rudimentary.

KEEPING OF PETS

The Jarawa, like the Great Andamanese and the Onge, never kept dogs during the hostility phase. The reason for it is attributed to the fact that in a hostile environment keeping dogs would have been suicidal as the barking of dogs at their camps could have made it easy for their enemies to track them down. However, in the post-hostility phase, the presence of dogs at Jarawa camps was observed for the first time in mid-1999 in certain parts of the Middle Andaman Island (AAJVS 1999). They reportedly collected the puppies from villages of settlers as well as from forest camps. Initially, the puppies hardly served any practical purpose, but when these puppies grew up, they started accompanying the hunters to the forest on hunting expeditions.

Source: Anthropological Survey of India.

Plate 5.2: A Jarawa with his pet dogs

Relationship between the Jarawa and their dogs is noteworthy. Dogs have been accepted as members of the group (Plate 5.2). Food and living space are shared with them the way they share these two things with their children. However, recently they have developed some aversion towards dogs. It is primarily because of three reasons. Firstly, they have found that the dogs create more disturbance than convenience for them during hunting expeditions as the barking dogs scare away their prey. Secondly, the furs of the dogs soon become full of fleas, which, in turn, begin biting the masters of the dogs also. Thirdly, AAJVS workers have explained and convinced the Jarawa about the harmful effects of keeping dogs as many skin diseases are caused by dogs. Consequently, many dogs have been driven away from their camps, but there are still many dogs as pets with the Jarawa.

CHAPTER 6

Conclusion

I

Hunting and gathering constitute the oldest human mode of making a living, and the only one for which there is an uninterrupted record from origin of human beings to the present. Today there are a handful of hunter-gatherers who have persisted in a more or less direct tradition of descent from ancient hunter-gatherer populations who subsist exclusively through the hunting of wild animals, fishing and gathering of wild plants. The Jarawa of the Andaman Islands are one among them. Early ideas about hunter-gatherers were hampered by the fact that, by the time the professional ethnographers arrived on the scene in the twentieth century, most hunter-gatherers had been decimated and forced to change their way of subsistence. For those studying the remote past, the study on the Jarawa provides a chance to learn more about what life might have been like in the deep past. Conversely, the present work can help to test models that have been constructed to understand the links between various natural environments and the spectrum of human life. This can, in turn, help us to understand current or recent hunter-gatherers situations.

The present work pertains to studying the form and process of adaptation of the Jarawa to an Island ecosystem. It provides a nuanced understanding of the adaptive strategies of the Jarawa. Since the occupation of the Andaman Islands by the British till the present time, the Jarawa have been in contact with the non-Jarawa. The aspects of contact and conflict between both the groups and accruing changes among the Jarawa thereof have been analysed in the framework of impact. It also illustrates the fact that when a foraging group like the Jarawa are exposed to the technologically advanced group having a production based economy, what are the impacts on their resources base, health, population, habits and material culture. Equally significant is how primitive groups like the Jarawa are coping with the changed situation in the aftermath of their exposure to the outsiders in the post-hostility phase. The vulnerability of the Jarawa in the changed conditions, in terms of their survival as hunter-gatherers, is a matter of concern for all. Based on the discussion in the foregoing chapters, the following conclusion can be drawn.

The Jarawa of the Andaman Islands are one of the few remaining hunter-gatherers in the world whose subsistence economy is still in the elementary form. They subsist exclusively through hunting of wild animals, fishing and gathering of wild plants. In other words, it approximates the economy of the classical hunter-gatherers. Further, within the spectrum of hunter-gatherers, the Jarawa belong to the category of 'immediate return' foragers as they tend to consume most of the food resources immediately. The storing of food items is minimal. It, in turn, corroborates with their notion of the environment as 'giving environment'.

The insularity of the Andaman Islands' ecosystem and its typical resource base determine to a great extent the foraging pursuit of the Jarawa. The Jarawa pursue their hunting, fishing and gathering activities with an in-depth understanding and knowledge of the island ecosystem concerning availability, density, distribution and seasonality of resources along with their regeneration characteristics. The subsistence activities are accomplished with intelligently designed strategies related to the selection of sites for the location of camps, movement patterns, selection of prey, sharing of food resources, and proper use of different tools and technology to ensure satisfactory returns.

The implements used by the Jarawa in procuring resources are simple and few, comprising bows, arrows, fishing nets, digging sticks, baskets and buckets. Though the Jarawa have a broad resource base, they rely on a limited number of plants and animals to fulfill the bulk of their calorific requirements. They have a dietary preference for meat, fish and molluscs, but the pig is the most preferred among them. However, the 'keystone resources' are the molluscs and fish.

In the foraging strategy, the location of the campsites and movement patterns play an important role. In the location of the camps, the 'ecological edges' play a significant role as they exhibit a high level of species richness or bio-diversity. By locating camps 'on the edges', ecological or physiographical, the Jarawa benefit from the increased bio-diversity in terms of their access to the resources of two or more ecosystems. Mobility is another important aspect in their foraging strategy for dealing effectively with changes in the environment and with the seasonal variation of resources. They move from one campsite to another in search of food resources before they are depleted. Concentration and dispersion are an integral part of their mobility. They aggregate into a larger group and split up into smaller groups periodically. This pattern is influenced by fluctuations in the availability of resources and seasonal changes. However, the movement pattern of the Jarawa is not governed by ecological reasons alone. It is also influenced by social needs such as visiting relatives, teaming up for rituals, etc.

Like other hunting and gathering societies, sharing of gathered food resources is a norm in the Jarawa community. While the meat of the game animals is shared among the constituent families of a camp, sharing of other resources is at the intra-family level. For the individual hunter, food sharing is really a way of storing food for the future; his generosity gives him a claim in future on the surplus of other hunters. Thus, the sharing is also a strategy to facilitate access to food resources for all.

Contrary to the view held by the non-Jarawa that the Jarawa are leading a miserable life due to the paucity of food resources in their territory, the 'input-output analysis' reveals that there are still sufficient resources in their habitat to meet their needs. The sufficiency of resources should not be equated with abundance. The hunting behaviour of the Jarawa also conforms to the basic premise of the 'optimal foraging theory' by following a Poisson distribution curve. It shows that the Jarawa do not manipulate the frequency encounter of the game animal, and their hunting behaviour closely resembles the hunting behaviour of classical hunter-gatherers. They spend less number of man-days in a week on work and thus have plenty of time for leisure, ritual, social relations, and entertainment. It is one of the important preconditions for the happy survival of a foraging group. They are one of the few remaining human groups who, by all counts, fit into the framework of 'the original affluent society', of Marshall Sahlins (1972).

The Jarawa are not solitary in their habitation of the South and Middle Andaman Islands. The settlements of the non-Jarawa dot the boundary of the Jarawa territory. They had a hostile relationship with the non-Jarawa which came to an end in 1997 due to the goodwill efforts of the Andaman and Nicobar Administration. Hostility, however, was acting as a shield towards the protection of the resources of the Jarawa territory. Now the non-Jarawa have unhindered access to the Jarawa territory, though illegally. Presently, the Jarawa and the poachers compete over the same set of resources with their respective technologies. In such a situation, the latter has the advantage over the former in terms of technology. Consequently, it has begun impacting the resource density, particularly in the areas, close to the settlements of the non-Jarawa. There is no information available about the level of decline that has occurred regarding the availability of food resources, particularly the pigs and other marine resources, progressively over a period of time. Similarly, the specific areas facing the stress on resources are not accurately known.

The interaction of the Jarawa with the outside world is one of multifaceted inequality, which places them in an extremely weak position against the outsiders. People with vested interests coming in contact with the Jarawa include traders, contractors, labourers, villagers and petty shopkeepers. They manipulate the Jarawa by offering them certain edible and non-edible articles. Now the Jarawa are found to be addicted to the *paan*, *gutka* and tobacco, a habit learnt from their interaction with the outsiders. A few of the Jarawa are found to be taking alcohol also though occasionally. To make matters worse, a barter system has developed between the Jarawa and the non-Jarawa, particularly settlers. Now the non-Jarawa are getting access to the resources of the Jarawa area by providing them with rice, biscuits, cooking oil, spices, tobacco, cloth, torch, etc. This kind of barter trade is disadvantageous to the Jarawa. Considering the baneful impacts of bartering and taking lessons from the

Onge of the Little Andaman and the Shompen of the Great Nicobar Islands, where they may part with almost any items in exchange for liquor and tobacco, it is necessary to ban any type of gift giving and bartering with the Jarawa. Efforts need to be made to rid them of addiction to *paan* and tobacco.

ATR, which passes through the 'Jarawa Reserve', has witnessed a huge increase in tourist traffic, particularly in the post-tsunami period. This growth in traffic volume has emerged primarily on account of the voyeuristic instinct in a large section of visitors. The commercial interest in the island has fuelled this demand for making a fast buck. The ATR is changing the lifeways of the Jarawa significantly, like staying close to the ATR, making use of the vehicular traffic plying on the road, etc. It has also provided easy access to the poachers in the Jarawa area.

The ATR constitutes the single largest threat to the very survival of the Jarawa. It has created such an enormity of disastrous impact that the future of the Jarawa is in peril. The traffic on the road and the ease it has provided in approaching the Jarawa territory, as also the Jarawa themselves, has unleashed social and economic forces which have sucked the Jarawa completely into their orbit of exploitation. The gravity of the situation on ATR was also noted by the 'Shekhar Singh Committee' (2017) on the protection of environment in the Andaman Islands. It has recommended the closure of the ATR.

Ever since the cessation of the hostility, the Jarawa women have become extremely vulnerable to sexual exploitation. The danger of sexual exploitation is greater on ATR and in the areas where the campsites of the Jarawa are close to the villages of non-Jarawa. A note submitted to the 'Committee on Jarawa' (Saxena 2003) has also echoed it.

It has been observed that diseases that are very common among sedentary populations can be fatal for hunting and gathering communities. For example, in the Andaman Islands, the Great Andamanese suffered from epidemics caused by diseases like measles and pneumonia, which were largely responsible for the rapid population decline of the Great Andamanese and the Onge (Cipriani 1966). The Jarawa are no exception. The outbreak of measles among them in 1999 caused many deaths. Among other diseases, which have witnessed a sudden increase are anaemia, skin diseases, and respiratory tract infection. Besides these diseases, hepatomegaly, spleenomegaly, and hepatitis B are the new diseases detected among them. Nevertheless, the acceptance of the medical intervention on the part of the Jarawa is a welcome change in their behaviour. Medical intervention has helped to reduce morbidity and mortality among the Jarawa. Reduction in mortality has contributed significantly to the population growth of the Jarawa. The Jarawa population has grown from 265 in 2002 to 534 in 2019. If the population continues to grow at the same pace, it will soon reach the carrying capacity of the land. It is, therefore, required that initiatives should be taken to make the Jarawa learn horticulture.

The Jarawa are trying to adapt themselves to the changing situation as a part of their survival strategy like using the vehicles and boats plying on the roads and sea respectively to reduce the distance, accepting the medical treatment and learning many of the material traits of the non-Jarawa. But they have yet to learn the traits of production based economy, like horticulture and use of new techniques of resource acquisition. In the changed situation, learning these traits is necessary for their survival.

Thus, there are five major areas of concern which need immediate attention. These are, first, protection of their resource base from poaching; secondly, prevention of diseases; thirdly, de-addiction of the Jarawa; fourthly, helping them to learn traits of production based economy like horticulture; and finally, sensitisation of the villagers and personnel of AAJVS and police about the Jarawa.

II

For the protection and welfare of the Jarawa, Andaman and Nicobar Administration has taken a number of measures. Important among them are the Gazette notification of 'Policy on the Jarawa Tribe' 2004 and the 'Buffer Zone Notification' in 2007. The broad objectives of 'Jarawa Policy' are to protect the Jarawa from harmful effects of exposure and contact with the outside; to preserve the social organisation, mode of subsistence and cultural identity of the Jarawa community; to provide medical help to the Jarawa; to conserve ecology and environment of the 'Jarawa Reserve' and strengthen support systems to enable the Jarawa to pursue their traditional modes of subsistence and way of life, and to sensitise settler communities around the Jarawa habitat and personnel working for the protection and preservation of the Jarawa. The 'Buffer Zone Notification' is supplementary to the 'Jarawa Policy' as it discourages any kind of tourism and commercial activities in an area of 5 km radius around the 'Jarawa Reserve'. AAJVS, a wing of the Andaman and Nicobar Administration, is entrusted with the task of monitoring and implementing the measures for the protection and welfare of the Jarawa.

However, the present 'Jarawa Policy' has not looked into the aspect of population growth and its consequences, nor has it suggested any measures related to making the Jarawa learn the art of domestication of plants through horticulture. Nonetheless, the need of the hour is to implement the 'Jarawa Policy' in letter and spirit.

III

The present investigation on the human ecology of the Jarawa is a maiden study as no prior study has been conducted on the Jarawa's adaptation to the Island ecology, impact of contact and conflict and adaptation of the Jarawa to the changing situation. Though the aim of the present work was limited to fulfilment of the stated objectives, it has opened up many new areas of research, which are listed below that require a detailed scientific investigation:

1. The entire resource potential of the island ecosystem is yet to be identified and documented. Besides, a complete inventory of the resources used by the Jarawa is required to be prepared to find out the total number of resources available in the Island ecosystem and how many of these are used by the Jarawa.
2. It is also necessary to find out environmental constraints (like endemic diseases, natural hazards, wildlife menace, etc.) related to human adaptation and how many of these have been overcome by the Jarawa.

3. Regeneration rates of major and supplementary resources used by the Jarawa require to be investigated and have to be correlated with the movement pattern of the Jarawa, i.e. after how many days they occupy the abandoned campsites. It will throw light as to what extent the Jarawa are an eco-friendly group.
4. Except for a few, seasonality of all major and supplementary resources, particularly of marine life, is not fully known. Its investigation will also throw light on aspects related to the location of huts and movement patterns. Further, it will give information on the various types of food articles consumed by the Jarawa.
5. The net gathering rate of all the resources in terms of man-hours in a day needs to be calculated. This will reveal, on average, how many hours a day an economically active Jarawa works to eke out a livelihood. It, in turn, will help find out how close they are to the concept of 'original affluent society'.
6. Sharing, particularly the flesh of game animals like wild pigs, monitor lizards and turtles, is a part of the survival strategy of the Jarawa. The quantitative information about the inter-family distribution of meat is required to be calculated.
7. There is a need to map the ecological niches of the Jarawa territory, for it plays an important role in the demarcation of physiographic zones, location of the huts, movement patterns, and density of different plant and animal resources.
8. In a hunting and gathering society, the man-nature-spirit relationship needs to be investigated. A holistic study is necessary to find out the relationships among the three factors. There is very little information on the spiritual world of the Jarawa, which needs to be probed.

Undoubtedly, a detailed investigation of these points will help in understanding the intricacies of adaptation of the Jarawa to the Island environment.

APPENDIX

SETTLEMENT LOCATION OF THE JARAWA

BOIAB AREA

Name of Settlement	Location	Type of Camp
Jhaukona camp	11°42'58.6"N 92°34'31.2"E	Coastal, temporary settlement
Eno	11°43'04.6"N 92°33'13"E	Coastal, temporary settlement
Tatha-etha	11°42'28"N 92°34'38.1"E	Forest, temporary settlement
Tothi-duba	11°42'51.5"N 92°34'20.6"E	Forest, temporary settlement
Tinatho	11° 57'08.2"N 92°40'57.4"E	Forest, temporary settlement
Lapaitala (Jarawa Ring)	11°44'15.9"N 92°36'26.8"E	Forest, temporary settlement
Alugithale	11°59'34"N 92°42'0.2"E	Forest, temporary settlement
Ginaitala	11°44'58.0"N 92°36'52.7"E	Forest, temporary settlement
Thapiliem (Billy Nalla)	11°56'56.0"N 92°41'02.2"E	Forest, temporary settlement
Eanathilia	11°42'45.7"N 92°34'28.2"E	Coastal, temporary settlement
Gangapo	11°44'35.9"N 92°35'47.5"E	Forest, semi-permanent settlement
Pechleg	11°59'28.8"N 92°37'02.1"E	Coastal, semi-permanent settlement
Nono-uge	11°47'0.2"N 92°33'13.0"E	Coastal, semi-permanent settlement
We-shekup	11°46'13.8"N 92°32'49.0"E	Coastal, semi-permanent settlement
Wg-tha-waw	11°43'33.3"N 92°33'57.6"E	Coastal, temporary settlement

(Contd.)

APPENDIX (Contd.)

Name of Settlement	Location	Type of Camp
Totha-wikiji	11°48'56.7"N 92°333'34.6"E	Coastal, temporary settlement
Mutu-tuweya	11°54'18.2"N 92°32'9.3"E	Coastal, temporary settlement
Horpotale (Badabalu)	10°50'50"N 92°204'56"E	Coastal, temporary settlement
Y-enen chadda (Jhaukona)	11°42'58.2"N 92°34'32.6"E	Coastal, Semi-Permanent
Totale (Hathi-Tikri)	11°45'3.6"N 92°35'45"E	Forest, temporary settlement
Totahikichi (Port-Campbell)	11°52'31.2"N 92°29'43.3"E	Coastal, temporary settlement
Kinethala (Near JPF No.-2)	11°44'16"N 92°36'52.7"E	Forest, temporary settlement
Tinetha	11°57'82"N 92°40'57.4"E	Forest, temporary settlement
	THIDONG AREA	
Tahato	12°03'13.6"N 92°42'19.3"E	Forest, permanent settlement
Tuhi	12°07'29.2"N 92°43'09.3"E	Forest, permanent settlement
Tuterbeto	12°07'37.0"N 92°43'16.7"E	Forest, semi-permanent settlement
Mimun	12°2'33.5"N 92°42'19.6"E	Forest, temporary settlement
Inkamahe	12°11'59.8"N 92°39'37.4"E	Coastal, semi-permanent settlement
Othukunu (Hiran Tikri)	12°12'1.3"N 92°39'24.1"E	Coastal, semi-permanent settlement
Tanaoben	12°08'52.6"N 92°44'20.5"E	Coastal, semi-permanent settlement
Otathamele	12°9'23.1"N 92°44'50"E	Forest, temporary settlement
Moulahuchu	12°4'55.7"N 92°42'54.4"E	Forest, temporary settlement
Lebaitala	12°14'22.7"N 92°42'8.3"E	Coastal, semi-permanent

(Contd.)

APPENDIX (Contd.)

Name of Settlement	Location	Type of Camp
Thulug	12°14'32.4"N 92°41'58.0"E	Forest, temporary settlement
Thota-ulio	12°11'19.9"N 92°38'55.3"E	Forest, temporary settlement
Motebutu	12°10'29.1"N 92°38'45.1"E	Coastal, permanent settlement
Alo-ethala	12°06'55.2"N 92°42'51.1"E	Forest, temporary settlement
Huinaang (B.D. Nala)	12°02'18.3"N 92°42'17.9"E	Forest, temporary settlement
Ine-ethala (R.K. Nalla)	12°06'24"N 92°43'0.2"E	Forest, temporary settlement
Tutho-ela (R.K. Nalla)	12°07'37.1"N 92°43'16.7"E	Forest, temporary settlement
Ing-kathe-beda	12°08'25.6"N 92°38'21"E	Coastal, temporary settlement
Chaithemane	12°06'21.9"N 92°42'15.0"E	Forest, semi-permanent settlement
Thallang	12°05'51.3"N 92°41'33.4"E	Forest, semi-permanent settlement
	TANMAD AREA	
Daag-totembu	12°'18'22.11"N 92°43'28.7"E	Forest, semi-permanent settlement
Oleg (Near Lakralungta)	12°18'2.9"N 92°43'22.5"E	Coastal, semi-permanent settlement
Hochu	12°22'12.6"N 92°42'20.9"E	Coastal, semi-permanent settlement
Hiulele	12°22'52.6"N 92°42'17.9"E	Coastal, semi-permanent settlement
Uli	12°26'50.0"N 92°46'29.3"E	Coastal, semi-permanent settlement
Tanmad	12°11'43.9"N 92°43'0.06"E	Coastal, semi-permanent settlement
Dhani Nalla	12°27'42.1"N 92°44'54.0"E	Forest, semi-permanent settlement
Ullia	12°26'56.2"N 92°46'31.6"E	Forest, semi-permanent settlement

(Contd.)

APPENDIX (Contd.)

Name of Settlement	Location	Type of Camp
Elag-wae	12°45'11.5"N 92°17'50.1"E	Forest, temporary settlement
Elag-O	12°17'49.1"N 92°45'12.2"E	Coastal, temporary settlement
Southern part of Spike Is.	12°14'32.9"N 92°42'24.3"E	Coastal, temporary settlement
Tentul Tikri	12°14'43.6"N 92°41'51.4"E	Coastal, temporary settlement
Mohua Tikri	12°31'56.4"N 92°40'45.1"E	Coastal, semi-permanent settlement
Motieta (Foul Bay)	12°19'40.6"N 92°42'32.5"E	Coastal, semi-permanent settlement
Nalla	12°22'49.4"N 92°42'29.7"E	Coastal, temporary settlement
Fia-Fia	12°23'52.1"N 92°41'30.6"E	Coastal, temporary settlement
Hochabotha	12°26'16.2"N 92°41'30.4"E	Coastal, temporary settlement
Terobetale	12°27'26.5"N 92°41'28.5"E	Coastal, temporary settlement
Filetina buchu	12°28'24"N 92°41'29.6"E	Coastal, temporary settlement
Watabo	12°29'36.9"N 92°41'32.3"E	Coastal, temporary settlement
Iyo-no	12°30'56.9"N 92°41'23.2"E	Coastal, temporary settlement
Tinetal	12°32'7.1"N 92°41'26"E	Coastal, temporary settlement
Tinodo (Flat Is.)	12°35'13.7"N 92°41'38.6"E	Coastal, temporary settlement
Tatoianka (Flat Is.)	12°36'10.5"N 92°40'40.3"E	Coastal, temporary settlement
Inkobuduche	12°40'03.6"N 92°44'19.7"E	Coastal, temporary settlement
Phillip Nalla	12°24'26.4"N 92°44'9.5"E	Nalla, permanent settlement

Bibliography

Abdulai, H. 1962. 'Wild Pig in Andaman', *Journal of Bombay Natural History Society*, 59: 280-3.

Acharya, S. 2002. 'Andaman Trunk Road and the Jarawa Situation', in *Jarawa Contact: Ours with Them and Theirs with Us*, K. Mukhopadhyay, R,K. Bhattacharya and B.N. Sarkar, The Anthropological Survey of India, Kolkata, pp.166-73.

Ackerman, E.A. 1963. 'Where is a Research Frontier?' *Ann. Ass. Am. Geogr.*, 53, 429-40.

Adger, W.N. 2000. 'Social and Ecological Resilience: Are they Related?', *Progress in Human Geography*, 24: 347-64.

Adhikari, A.K. 1984. *Society and World View of the Birhor: A Nomadic Hunting Gathering Community of Orissa.* Anthropological Survey of India, Calcutta.

Andaman Adim Janjati Vikas Samiti. 1999. 'Records on Primitive Tribal Group of Andman' unpublished, Andman and Nicobar Administration, Port-Blair.

——. 2002. 'Records on Primitive Tribal Group of Andman', unpublished, Andman and Nicobar Administration, Port Blair.

——. 2007. 'Records on Primitive Tribal Group of Andman', unpublished, Andman and Nicobar Administration, Port Blair.

Andaman & Nicobar Administration. 2004. *Andaman and Nicobar Gazette: Extraordinary.* A & N Administration, Port Blair.

Anderson, K.M. 1996. 'Tending the Wilderness'. *Restoration and Management Notes*, 14(2): 154-66.

Anthropological Survey of India. 2002. 'Jarawa Report', unpublished, Kolkata.

Awaradi, S.A. 1990. *Master Plan (1991-2021) for Welfare of Primitive Tribes of Andaman Islands.* Andaman and Nicobar Administration, Port Blair.

Bahuchet, S. 1988. 'Food Supply Uncertainty among the Aka Pygmies (Lobaye, C.A.R.)', in *Coping with Uncertainty in Food Supply*, ed. I De Garine and G.A. Harrison, Oxford University Press, Oxford, pp. 118-49.

Bailey, R.C. and N.R. Peacock, 1988. 'Efe Pygmies of Northeast Zaire: Subsistence Strategies in the Ituri Forest', in *Coping with Uncertainties in Food Supply*, ed. I. De Garnie and G.A. Harrison, Clarendon, Oxford, pp. 88-117.

Bailey, R.C., G. Head, M. Jenike, B. Owen, R. Rechtman and E. Zechenter, 1989. 'Hunting and Gathering in Tropical Rain Forest: Is it Possible?' *American Anthropologist,* 91: 59-82.

Balikci, A. 1970. *The Netsilik Eskimo.* Natural History Press, Garden City, New York.

Barik, S.S., et al. 2008. 'Detailed mtDNA Genotypes Permit a Reassessment of the Settlement and Population Structure of the Andaman Islands. *Am. J. Phys. Anthropol.* 136: 19-27.

Barnard, A. 1992. *Hunters and Herders of Southern Africa.* Cambridge University Press, Cambridge.

Barnes, H.E. 1937. *An Intellectual and Cultural History of the Western World.* Random House, New York.

Barnes, H.E. and H. Becker, 1938. *Social Thought from Lore to Sciences.* D.C. Heath, Boston.

Barrows, H. H. 1923. 'Geography as Human Ecology'. *Ann. Ass. Am. Geogr.,* 13(1): 1-14.

Basu, B.K. 1990. *The Onges.* Seagull Books on behalf of the Anthropological Survey of India, Kolkata.

Basu, B.K. 1993. *Working Plan for the South Andaman Forest Division.* Department of Forest, Port Blair.

Bayliss-Smith, T.P. 1977. 'Human Ecology and Island Population: The Problems of Changes', in *Subsistence and Survival: Rural Ecology in the Pacific,* ed. T.P. Bayliss-Smith and Richard G. Feachem, Academic Press, London and New York, pp. 11-20.

Bellwood, P. 1985. *Prehistory of the Indo-Malaysian Archipelago.* Academic Press, New York.

Berkes, F. and C. Folke, 1994. 'Investing in Cultural Capital for the Sustainable Use of Natural Capital', in *Investing in Natural Capital: The Ecological Economics Approach to Sustainability,* A.M. Jansson, M. Hammer, C. Folke and R. Costamza, (eds.), Island Press, Washington, DC, pp. 128-49.

Berkes, F. and C. Folke, (eds.) 1998. *Linking Social and Ecological System: Management and Social Mechanisms for Building Resilience,* Cambridge University Press, Cambridge.

Bettinger, R.L. 1991. *Hunter-Gatherers: Archaeological and Evolutionary Theory.* Plenum, New York.

Bicchieri, M.G. (ed.) 1972. *Hunter and Gatherers Today.* New York: Holt, Rinehart and Wilson.

Binford, L.R. 1978. *Nunamiut Ethnoarchaeology.* Academy Press, London.

——. 1980. Willow Smoke and Dogs' Tails: Hunter-Gatherer Settlement Systems and Archaeological Site Functions'. *Journal of Anthropological Archaeology,* 1(1): 4-20.

Binford, S.R. and C.R. Binford (eds) 1968. *New Perspective in Archaeology.* Aldine, Chicago.

Bird-David, N. 1990. The Giving Environment: Another Perspective on the Economic System of Gatherer Hunters', in *Current Anthropology*, 31: 183-96.

——. 1992. 'Beyond the Hunting and Gathering Mode of Subsistence: Observations on the Nayaka and other Modern Hunter Gatherers. *Man*, 27(1): 19-44.

Boas, F. 1888. 'The Central Eskimo', in *Bureau of American Ethnology Annual Report 6*, Washington, DC.

Bodley, J.H. 1999. 'Hunter Gatherers and Colonial Encounter', in *The Cambridge Encyclopaedia of Hunters and Gatherers*, ed. R.B. Lee and D. Richard, Cambridge University Press, London: pp. 465-72.

Bose, B.K. 1990. *The Onge.* Seagull Publication, Kolkata.

Bose, S. 1964. 'Economy of the Onges of Little Andaman', *Man in India*, 44(4): 298-310.

Botanical Survey of India. 2002. 'Report on Plant Resources the Jarawa Territory', unpublished, Port Blair.

Brookfield, H.C. 1975. *Interdependent Development.* Methuen, London.

Brothers, T.S. 1993. 'Fragmentation and Edge Effects in Central Indiana Old-growth Forests', *Natural Areas Journal*, 13(4): 268-75.

Buckley, W. 1969. *Sociology and Modern System Theory.* Prentice Hall, New Jersey.

Castri, F. di. 1981. 'Ecology—The Genesis of Science of Man and Nature', *UNESCO Courier*, April, pp. 6-11

Census of India. 1931. *The Andaman and Nicobar Islands; General Report*, pt. I & II, vol. II, Central Publication, Calcutta.

——. 1961. *Andaman and Nicobar Islands; General* Report. Pt. I, vol. XVII, Delhi, Government of India.

——. 1981a. *The Andaman and Nicobar Islands Census of India.* Series 24, pt. IIA and IIB, Directorate Census Operations, Port Blair.

——. 1991. *General Population Table and Primary Census Abstract: Andaman Nicobar Islands.* Pt. II, A, Series 27, Directorate of Census Operation, A & N Islands, Port Blair.

——. 2001a. *Andaman and Nicobar Population Totals.* Series 36, Paper 2, Directorate of Census Operation, A & N Islands, Port Blair.

——. 2001b. *Primary Census Abstract: Andaman and Nicobar Island* (CD).

Chakraborty, D.K. 1990. *The Great Andamanese.* Seagull Books on behalf of the Anthropological Survey of India, Kolkata.

Chakraborty, S. and A. Dinda, 2002. 'The Jarawa and their Neighbour: The post-Independence Scenario', in *Jarawa Contact: Ours with Them and Theirs with Us*, ed. K. Mukhopadhyay. R.K. Bhattacharya, and B.N. Sarkar, The Anthropological Survey of India, Kolkata, pp. 43-57.

Champion, H.G. 1936. *Indian Forest Records* (New Series), vol. 1, Delhi, p. 31.

Champion, H.G. and S.K. Seth, 1968. *A Revised Survey of the Forest Types of India*. Govt. of India Publication, Delhi.

Chapman, G.P. 1970. 'Perception and Regulation: A Case Study of Farmers in Bihar', *Trans. Inst. Br. Geog.*, 62: 71-94.

Chorley, R.J. 1971. 'The Role and Relation of Physical Geography', *Progress in Geography*, vol. 3, ed. C. Board, C. et al., Methun, London.

——. 1973. 'Geography as Human Ecology, in *Direction in Geography*, R.J. Chorley, Methun, London, pp. 153-70.

Chorley, R.J. and P. Hagget, (eds.). 1971. *Models in Geography*. Methuen, London.

Cipriani, Lidio. 1966. *Andaman Islanders*. Wiedenfeld and Nicolson, London.

Cooper, J.M. 1946. 'The Patagonian and Pampean Hunters', in *Handbook of South American Indians*, J.H. Steward, (ed.), vol. I, Bureau of American Ethnology Bulletin 143, Smithsonian Institution, Washington, DC, pp. 127-68.

——. 1990. 'Archaeological Evidence for Resource Exploitation in the Andaman Island', *Man and Environment*, 15: 73-81.

——. 1992. 'Relevance of Forager/Collector Model to Islands Communities in the Bay of Bengal. *Man and Environment*, 17: 111-22.

——. 1994. 'Abandoned Onge Encampment and their Relevance in Understanding the Archaeological record in the Andaman Islands', in *Living Traditions: Studies in the Ethnoarchaeology of South Asia*, ed. B. Allchin, Oxford-IBH, New Delhi.

Damas, D. 1969. 'Characteristics of Central Eskimo Band Structure', in *Contribution to Anthropology: Band Societies*, ed. D. Damas, National Museum of Canada Bulletin 228.

——. 1984. *Handbook of North American Indians: Arctic*. vol.V, Smithsonian Institution, Washington. DC.

Danda, A.K. 1993. 'Indigenous Small Populations of Andaman and Nicobar Islands', in *Andaman and Nicobar Islanders: Studies on Small Populations*, ed. A. Basu, J. Sarkar and A.K. Danda, 10 Anthropological Society Occasional Papers, Indian Anthropological Society, Kolkata, pp. 85-100.

Davidson-Hunt, I.J., and F. Berkes, 2003. 'Nature and Society through the Lens of Resilience: Towards a Human-in-Ecosystem Perspective', in *Navigating Social-Ecological System: Building Resilience for Complexity and Change*, ed. F. Berks, J. Colding and C. Folke, Cambridge University Press, London, pp. 53-82.

D'Azevedo, W. (ed.) 1986. *Handbook of North American Indians: Great Basin.* vol. XI, Smithsonian Institution, Washington DC.

Deloria, V., Jr. 1995. *Red Earth, White Lies: Native American and Myth of Scientific Fact.* Scribner, New York.

Department of Environment and Forest. 1998. *Forest Statistics.* Vansadan, Port-Blair.

——. 2002. 'Records on Forest Resources', unpublished, Vansadan, Port Blair.

Department of Police. 1997. 'Records of Jarawa Attack', unpublished, Port Blair.

Deur, D. 2000. 'A Domesticated Landscape: Native American Plant Cultivation on the North-west Coast of North America'. Ph.D. dissertation, Department of Geography and Anthropology, Victoria, BC.

Directorate of Economics and Statistics. 2002. *Basic Statistics,* 2001-2002, Andaman and Nicobar Administration, Port Blair.

——. 2003. *Basic Statistics, 2002-2003.* Andaman and Nicobar Administration, Port Blair.

——. 2007. *Basic Statistics 2006-2007.* Andaman and Nicobar Administration, Port Blair.

Directorate of Health Services. 2002. 'Medical Report on Jarawa', unpublished, Port Blair.

Directorate of Health Services and Indian Institute of Public Hygiene and Health. 2002. 'Health Report on the Jarawa', unpublished, Port Blair.

Dunn, F.L. 1975. *Rainforest Collectors and Traders: A Study of Resource Utilization in Modern and Ancient Malaya.* Monograph 5 of the Malaysian Branch of the Royal Asiatic Society, Kuala Lumpur.

Dutta, P.C. 1974. *The Great Andamanese, Past and Present.* Anthropological Survey of India, Kolkata.

Edwards, W.H. 1987. *Traditional Aboriginal Society.* Macmillan, Melbourne.

Endicott, K. and P. Bellwood, 1991. 'The Possibility of Independent Foraging in the Rain Forest of Peninsular Malaysia. *Human Ecology,* 19 (2): 151-85.

Farb, P. and G. Armelago, 1980. *Consuming Passions: The Anthropology of Eating.* Houghton Miffin Company, Boston.

Fosberg, F.R. 1963. 'The Island Ecosystem', in *Man's Place in the Island Ecosystem,* ed. F.R. Fosberg, Bishop Museum Press, Honolulu, pp. 1-6.

Gardner, P.M. 1993. 'Dimensions of Subsistence Foraging in South India', *Ethnology,* 32: 109-44.

Gazette Notification. 2004. *Policy on the Jarawa.* Andaman and Nicobar Administration, Port Blair.

——. 2007. *Buffer Zone Notification.* Andaman and Nicobar Administration, Port Blair.

Gunderson, L.H., C.S. Holling, and S. Light, (eds.) 1995. *Barriers and Bridges to the Renewal of Ecosystems and Institutions.* Columbia University Press, New York.

Gowdy (ed.). 1998. *Limited Wants, Unlimited Means: A Reader on Hunter-Gatherer Economics and the Environment.* Washington, DC, Island Press.

Haeckel, E. 1866. *Generelle Morphologie der Organismen*, 2 vols. Georg. Remer, Berlin.

Harris, M. 1968. *The Rise of Anthropological Theory: A History of Theories of Culture.* Thomas Y. Crowell, New York.

——. 1985. *Good to Eat: Riddles of Culture.* Simon and Schuster, New York.

Hart, T.B., and J.A. Hart, 1986. 'The Ecological Basis of Hunter-Gatherer Subsistence in African Rain Forests'. *Human Ecology*, 14: 29-55.

Hawkes, K., K. Hill and J. O'Connell, 1982. 'Why Hunter Gather: Optimal Foraging and the Ache of Eastern Paraguay'. *American Ethnologist*, 9: 379-98.

Headland, T.N. 1986. 'Why Foragers do not Become Farmers: A Historical Study of a Changing Ecosystem and its Effect on a Negroito Hunter Gatherer Group in the Philippines' unpublished Ph.D. dissertation, University of Hawaii, Honolulu.

——. 1987. 'The Wild Yam Question: How Well Could Independent Hunter Gatherers Live in a Tropical Rain Forest Ecosystem?' *Human Ecology*, 15: 463-91.

Heizer, R. (ed.). 1978. *Handbook of the North American Indians*, vol. VIII, Washington, DC: Smithsonian Institution, California.

Helfer, J.W., and K.K. Millheil, 1859. *Geogr Fe Gesell Schaft.* Germany.

Helm, J. (ed.) 1981. *Handbook of North American Indians: Subarctic*, vol. VI, Smithsonian Institution, Washington, DC.

Hill, K. and A.M. Hurtado, 1989. 'Hunter-Gatherers of the New World', *American Scientist*, 77(5): 437-43.

Hoffman, C. 1986. *The Punan: Hunters and Gatherers of Borneo.* UMI Research Press, Ann Arbor.

Holland, T.H. 1904. *Ancient Kitchen Middens in the Andamans.* Records of the Geological Survey of India, 31: 45, pp. 107-8.

Holling, C.S. 1973. 'Resilience and Stability of Ecological System', *Annual Review of Ecology and Systematics*, 4: 1-23.

Howlett, D.R. 1973. 'Terminal Development: From Tribalism to Peasantry', in *The Pacific in Transition*, ed. H.C. Brookfield, Methun, London, pp. 249-74.

Husain, Z. 2002. *Geoecology of Kameng Himalaya.* Regency Publ., New Delhi.

Hutchinson, H.N., J.W. Gregory and R. Lydekkar (rpt.) 1985. *The Living Races of Mankind.* Mittal Publication, Delhi.

Imperial Gazetteer of India. 1909. *Andaman and Nicobar Islands, Provincial Series*. Superintendent of Govt. Printing, Calcutta.

India Meteorology Department. 1993. 'Weather Records', unpublished, Port Blair.

Indian Institute of Remote Sensing. 2003. *Biodiversity Characterisation at Landscape Level in Andaman and Nicobar Islands Using Satellite Remote Sensing and Geographic Information System*. Dehradun.

Justin, A. 2016. 'The Sentenelese of Andaman & Nicobar Islands', in *The Particularly Vulnerable Tribal Groups in India: Previlages and Predicaments*, ed. K.K. Misra, Manohar, Delhi, pp. 659-79.

Kaplan, H. and K. Hill, 1992. 'The Evolutionary Ecology of Food Acquisition, in *Evolutionary Ecology and Human Behaviour*, ed. E.A. Smith and B. Winterhalder, Aldine de Gruyter, New York.

Keene, A.S. 1981. *Prehistoric Foraging in a Temperate Forest: A Linear Programming Model*. Academic Press, New York.

Kelly, R.L. 1995. *The Foraging Spectrum: Diversity in Hunter Gatherer Lifeways*. Smithsonian Institution Press, Washington, DC.

Kent, S. 1993. 'Sharing in an Egalitarian Kalahari Community', *Man*, 28: 479-514.

Klein, R.G. 1973. *Ice-age Hunters of the Ukraine*. University of Chicago Press, Chicago.

Kumar, U. 2002. 'Marginalization of the Onges of the Little Andaman', *The Journal of the Anthropological Survey of India* (Special Issue, Marginal Communities), vol. 51(1), pp. 25-137.

Kumar, U. and S. Biswas, 2002. 'The Jarawa and their habitat: A Man-Nature Relationship', in *Jarawa Contact : Ours with Them and Theirs with Us*, K. Mukhopadhyay, R.K. Bhattacharya and B.N. Sarkar, The Anthropological Survey of India, Kolkata, pp. 58-71.

Kumar. U and R. Haider, 2007. 'Impact of Tsunami at the Onge Settlement at Dugong Creek, Little Andaman', in *Tsunami in South Asia: Studies of Impact on Communities of Andaman and Nicobar Islands*, Anthropological Survey of India, Allied Publishers, New Delhi, pp. 103-19.

Lal, P. 1976. *Andaman Islands: A Regional Geography*. Anthropological Survey of India, Kolkata.

Lee, R.B. 1968. 'What Hunter Do for a Living, or, How to Make Out on Scarce Resources', in *Man the Hunter*, ed. R.B. Lee and I. DeVore, Aldine, Chicago.

——. 1969. !'Kung Bushman Subsistence: An Input-Output Analysis', in *Ecological Essay*, ed. D. Mamas, Proceeding of the Conference on Cultural Ecology, Bulletin 230, National Museum of Canada, Ottawa, pp. 73-94.

——. 1979. *The !Kung San: Men, Women and Work in a Foraging Societies.* Cambridge University Press, Cambridge.

——. 1982. 'Politics, Sexual and Non-sexual, in an Egalitarian Society', in *Politics and History in Band Societies,* ed. E. Leacock and R.B. Lee, Cambridge University Press, Cambridge, pp. 37-59.

——. 1984. *The Dobe? Kung: Forager in a Changing World.* Holt, Rinchart and Winston, New York.

——. 1988. 'Reflections on Primitive Communism', in *Hunter and Gatherers: History, Evolution and Social Changes,* T. Ingold, D. Riches and J. Woodburn, Berg., London.

Lee, R.B., and R. Daly, 1999. 'Foragers and Others', in *The Cambridge Encyclopedia of Hunter Gatherers,* R.B. Lee and R. Daly, Cambridge University Press, London.

Lee, R.B. and I. De Vore (eds.) 1968. *Man the Hunter.* Aldine, Chicago.

Levi-Strauss, C. 1949. *Les Structures Elementaires de la Parente.* Presses Universitaires de France, Paris.

Majumdar, R.C. 1975. *Penal Settlement in Andamans.* Gazetteers Unit, Department of Culture, Government of India, Delhi.

Man, E.H. 1883 (rpt.) 1975. *The Aboriginal Inhabitants of the Andaman Islands.* Sanskaran Prakashan, Delhi.

Margalef, R. 1968. *Perspective in Ecological Theory.* University of Chicago Press, Chicago.

Marshall, L. 1968. 'The Medicinal Dance of the !Kung Bushmen', *Africa,* 39: 347-81.

——. 1976. *The !Kung of Nyae Nyae.* Harvard University Press, Cambridge.

Mathur, L.P. 1968. *History of the Andaman and Nicobar Islands (1756-1966).* Sterling Publishers, Delhi.

McArthur, M. 1977. 'Nutritional Research in Melanesia: A Second Look at the Tsembaga', in *Subsistence and Survival: Rural Ecology in the Pacific,* ed. T.P. Bayliss-Smith and Richarged G. Feachem, Academic Press, London and New York, pp. 91-128.

McCay, B. 2000. 'Edges, Fields and Regions' (Presidential Address, pt. II, IASCP 2000 Conference, Bloomington, Indiana). *The Common Property Resource Digest,* 54: 6-8.

Mckenzie, R.D. 1926. 'The Scope of Human Ecology'. *Publication of the American Sociological Society,* 20: 141-54.

Meek, R.L. 1976. *Social Science and the Ignoble Savage.* Cambridge University Press, Cambridge.

Meiners, P. and T.A. Pickett-Steward, 1999. 'Change in Community and Population Resources Across a Forest Field Gradient', *Ecography,* 22(5): 261-7.

Morren, G.E.B. 1977. 'From Hunting to Herding: Pigs and Control of Energy in Montane New Guinea', in *Subsistence and Survival: Rural Ecology in the Pacific*, ed. T.P. Bayliss-Smith and Richard G. Feachem, Academic Press, London and New York, pp. 273-315.

Mukerji, R.K. 1926. *Regional Sociology*. Madras.

——. 1938. *Regional Balance of Man*. University of Madras, Madras.

Mukhopadhyay, K. 2002. 'A Brief History of Relationship between the Jarawa and Others', in *Jarawa Contact: Ours with Them and Theirs with Us*, ed. K. Mukhopadhyay, R.K. Bhattacharya and B.N. Sarkar, The Anthropological Survey of India, Kolkata, pp. 25-42.

Mukhopadhyay, K., R.K. Bhattacharya and B.N. Sarkar (eds.). 2002. *Jarawa Contact: Ours with Them and Theirs with Us*. The Anthropological Survey of India, Kolkata.

Muller-Dombois, D. and K. Bridge 1981. 'Spatial Distribution of Island Biota', in *Island Ecosystem*, ed. D. Muller-Dombois, K.W. Bridge and H.L. Carson, Academic Press. New York, pp. 35-76.

Murty, M.L.K. 1985. 'The Use of Plant Foods by Some Hunter Gatherer Communities in Andhra Pradesh', in *Recent Advances in Indo-Pacific Prehistory*, ed. V.N. Misra and P. Bellwood, Oxford-IBH, New Delhi.

Ndagala, D.K. 1988. 'Free or Doomed? Images of the Hadzabe Hunters and Gatherers', in *Hunters and Gatherers, History: Evolution and Social Change*, ed. T. Ingold, D. Riches and J. Woodburn, (eds.), vol. I, Berg., Oxford, pp. 65-72.

O'Connell, J. and K. Hawkes, 1981. 'Alywara Plant Use and Optimal Foraging Theory', in *Hunter Gatherers Foraging Strategies: Ethnographic and Archaeological Analyses*, ed. B. Winterhalder and E.A. Smith, University of Chicago Press, Chicago.

——. 1984. 'Food Choice and Foraging Sites among the Alywara', *Journal of Anthropological Research*, 40: 504-35.

Odum, E.P. 1971. *Fundamentals of Ecology*, 3rd edn. Saunders, Philadelphia.

Oldham, R. D. 1885. *Records of Geological Survey of India*. Part II, Calcutta.

Oliver, W.L.R. 1984. 'Introduced and Feral Pig', in *Feral Mammals and Potential*, Proceedings of Workshop on Feral Mammals at the 3rd International Theoretical Congress, Helsinki, 1982, IUCN, Gland.

Palanichamy, M.G., et al. 2006. 'Comment on "Reconstrucing the Origin of Andaman Islanders"'. *Science*, 311 470.

Pandit, T.N. 1974. 'Jarawa: Story of a Century of Mutual Hostility', *Daily Telegrams*, 16 and 18 March, Port Blair.

——. 1976. 'The Ethnic Situation in the Bay Islands', *Yojana*, 20.

——. 1989. 'Tribal Policy in the Andaman and Nicobar Islands. The Impact of Nehru's Philosophy', in *Jawaharlal Nehru, Tribes and Tribal Policy*, ed. K.S. Singh, pp. 83-92.

——. 1990. *The Sentinelese.* Seagull Books on behalf of the Anthropological Survey of India, Kolkata.

Pandit, T.N. and M. Chattopadhyay, 1993. 'Meeting the Sentinelese: The Least Known of the Andaman Hunter Gatherers', in *Andaman and Nicobar Islanders: Studies on Small Populations*, ed. A. Basu, J. Sarkar and A.K. Danda, 10 Anthropological Society Occasional Papers, Indian Anthropological Society, Kolkata, pp. 169-78.

Pandya, V. 1993. *Above the Forest: A Study of Andamanese Ethnoanemology, Cosmology and the Power of Ritual.* Oxford University Press, Delhi.

Park, R.E. 1936. 'Human Ecology'. *The American Journal of Sociology*, XLII: 1-15.

Park, R.E., and E.W. Burgess, 1921. *Introduction to the Science of Sociology.* University of Chicago Press, Chicago.

Peacock, S. and N.J. Turner, 2000. 'Just Like a Garden: Traditional Plant Resource Management and Biodiversity Conservation on the British Columbia Plateau', in *Biodiversity and Native North America*, ed. P.E. Minnis and W.J. Elisens, University of Oklahoma Press, Norman, pp. 133-79.

Portman, M.V., 1899 (rpt. 1990). *A History of Our Relation with the Andamanese*, vols. I & II, Asian Educational Services, New Delhi and Madras.

Quinn, J.A. 1939. 'The Nature of Human Ecology: Re-examination and Redefinition', *Social Forces*, XVIII: 161-8.

Radcliffe-Brown, A.R. (1922). *The Andaman Islanders.* Cambridge University Press, Cambridge.

——. 1930-1. 'The Social Organization of Australian Tribes', *Oceania* 1: 34-63, 322-41, 426-56.

Rappaport, R.A. 1967. 'Ritual Regulations of Environmental: Relations among a New Guinea People', *Ethnology*, 6: 17-30.

——. 1968. *Pigs for the Ancestors: Rituals in the Ecology of a New Guinea People.* Yale University Press, New Haven.

——. 1971a. 'The Flow of Energy in an Agricultural Society', in *Energy and Power*, by W.H. Freeman, Scientific American Publication, San Francisco, pp. 69-82.

——. 1971b. 'Nature, Culture and Ecological Anthropology', in *Man, Culture and Society*, ed. H.L. Shapiro, Oxford University Press, London, pp. 237-67.

Riches, D. 1982. *Northern Nomadic Hunter Gatherer: A Humanistic Approach.* Academic Press, London, pp. 214-16.

Rizvi, S.N.H. 1990. *The Shompen.* Seagull Books on behalf of the Anthropological Survey of India, Kolkata.

Sahlins, M. 1972. *Stone Age Economics.* Tavistock, London.

——. 1976. *Culture and Practical Reason.* University of Chicago Press, Chicago.

Sargent, F. 1974. 'Nature and Scope of human ecology', in *Human Ecology*, ed. F. Sargent, Amsterdam, North Holland, pp. 1-25.

Sarkar, B.N. 1985. 'The Jarawa of Andaman Islands: An Anthropometric Study'. *Human Science,* 34: 186-94.

——. 1987. 'Dermatoglyphic Study of the Jarawa: A Negrito Tribe of Andaman Islands'. *Human Science,* 36: 346-58.

Sarkar, B.N. and R. Sahani, 2002. 'A Demographic and Health Profile of the Jarawas of Andaman Islands', in *Jarawa Contact: Ours with Them and Theirs with Us,* ed. K. Mukhopadhyay, R.K. Bhattacharya and B.N. Sarkar, The Anthropological Survey of India, Kolkata, pp. 132-47.

Sarkar, J. 1987. 'Befriending the Jarawa: A Challenging Task', *Human Science,* 36: 1-12.

——. 1990. *The Jarawa.* Seagull Books on Behalf of the Anthropological Survey of India, Kolkata.

——. 1993. 'Endangered Tribe and their Development in Andaman and Nicobar Islands', in *Andaman and Nicobar Islanders: Studies on Small Populations,* ed. A. Basu, J. Sarkar and A.K. Danda, 10 Anthropological Society Occasional Papers, Indian Anthropological Society, Kolkata, pp. 1-46.

——. 1996. 'Tribal Development Administration for the Small Population: The Andaman and Nicobar Situation', *Journal of Indian Anthropological Society,* 31: 57-61.

Sasikumar, M. 2018. 'The Sentenelese of the North Sentinel Island: Concerns and Perception', *Journal of the Anthroplogical Survey of India,* 67(1): 37-44.

Saxena, K.B. 2003. *Report of the Expert Committee of the Jarawa of Andaman Islands,* Andaman and Nicobar Administration, Port Blair.

Sekhsaria, P. and V. Pandya, 2010. *The Jarawa Tribal Reserve Dossier: Cultural & Biological Diversities in the Andaman Islands.* UNESCO, Paris.

Sen, P.K. 1962. *Land and People of the Andaman Islands.* The Post Graduate Book Mart, Calcutta.

Simmon, I.G. 1966. 'Ecology and Land-use', *Transaction Institute of British Geographer,* 38: 59-72.

Singh, S. 2017. *Report of the Committee on Land Matters in Andaman and Nocobar Islands.* Ministry of Home Affairs, Govt. of India.

Sinha, D.P. 1958. 'Cultural Ecology of the Birhor: A Methodological Illustration, *Journal of Social Research,* 1: 86-96.

Smith, E.A. 1983. 'Anthropological Application of Optimal Foraging Theory: A Critical Review', *Current Anthropology*, 24(5): 625-49.

——. 1991. *Inujjuamiut Foraging Strategies: Evolutionary Ecology of an Arctic Hunting Economy.* Adline de Gruyter, New York.

Sollas W. 1911. *Ancient Hunters and Their Modern Representatives.* Macmillan, London.

Sreenathan, M. 2001. *The Jarawa: Language and Culture.* Anthropological Survey of India, Calcutta.

Stearman, A.M. 1991. 'Making a Living in the Tropical Forest: Yuqui Foraging in the Bolivian Amazon', *Human Ecology*, 19(2): 245-60.

Stephens, D.W. and J.R. Krebs, 1986. *Foraging Theory.* Princeton University Press, Princeton, New Jersey.

Steward, J.H. 1936. 'The Economic and Social Basis of Primitive Bands', in *Essays in Anthropology in Honour of Alfred Louis Kroeber*, ed. R.H. Lowie, University of California Press, Berkeley, pp. 31-50.

——. 1938. *Basin-Plateau Aboriginal Socio-political Groups.* Bureau of American Bulletin 120, Smithsonian Institution, Washington, DC.

——. 1955. *Theory of Cultural Change: The Methodology of Multilinear Evolution.* University of Illinois Press, Urbana.

Stringer, C.B. and J. Galway-Witham. 2017. 'Palaeoanthropology: On the Origin of Our Species', *Nature*, 546: 212-14.

Stoddart, D.R. 1965. 'Geography and the Ecological Approach', *Geography*, 50: 242-51.

Sturtevant, W. (ed.) 1978. *Handbook of the North American Indians*, 20 vols., Smithsonian Institution, Washington, DC.

Suttles, W. (ed.) 1990. *Handbook of the North American Indians: Northwest Coast*, vol. VII, Smithsonian Institution, Washington, DC.

Terborgh, J. 1986. 'Keystone Plant Resources in the Tropical Forests', in *Conservation Biology: The Science of Scarcity and Diversity*, ed. M.E. Soule, Sinauer, Sunderland.

Thangaraj, K. et al. 2005. 'Reconstructing the Origin of Andaman Islanders', *Science* 308-996.

Tikader, B.K., A. Daniel and N.V. Subbarao, 1986. *Sea Shore Animal of Andaman and Nicobar Islands.* Zoological Survey of India, Kolkata.

Tipper, G.H. 1904-5. 'The Geology of the Andaman Islands with Reference to the Nicobars', *Memoirs of the Geological Survey of India*, Calcutta, vol. 35(4): 4-15.

Transley, A.G. 1935. 'The Use and Abuse of Vegetational Concepts and Terms'. *Ecology*, 16: 203-12.

Trigger, Bruce (ed.) 1978. *Handbook of the North American Indians: Northeast*, vol. XV, Smithsonian Institution, Washington, DC.

Turnbull, C.M. 1968. 'The Importance of Flux in Two Hunting Societies', in *Man the Hunter*, ed. R.B. Lee, and I. DeVore, Aldine, Chicago, pp. 132-7.

Turner, N.J., I.J. Davidson-Hunt and M. O'Flaherty, 2003. 'Living on the Edges: Ecological and Cultural Edges as Source of Diversity for Social-Ecological Resilience', *Human Ecology*, 31(3): 439-64.

Villoro, L. 1982. *Creer, Saber, Conocer.* Siglo XXI, Mexico.

Waddell, E.W. 1974. *Frost over Niugini.* New Guinea 8, 39-49.

Wadia, D.N. 1975. *Geology of India.* Tata McGraw Hill, New Delhi.

Wagner, R. 1977. 'Scientific and Indigenous Papuan Conceptualisation of the Innate: A Semiotic Critique of the Ecological Perspective', in *Subsistence and Survival; Rural Ecology in the Pacific*, ed. T.P. Bayliss-Smith and Richarged G. Feachem, Academic Press, London and New York, pp. 385-410.

Watanbe, H. 1973. *The Ainu Ecosystem.* University of Washington Press, Seattle.

Watt, K.E.W. 1968. *Ecology and Resource Management.* McGraw-Hill, New York.

Whitaker, R. 1988. *Endangered Andaman.* Environmental Service Group, WWF-India and MAB-India, Department of Environment, Government of India.

Winterhalder, B. 1981. 'Optimum Foraging Structures and Hunter Gatherers Research in Anthropology', in *Hunter Gatherer Foraging Strategies*, ed. B. Winterhalder and E.A. Smith, University of Chicago Press, Chicago.

——. 1983a. 'Opportunity-cost Foraging Models for Stationary and Mobile Predators', *American Naturalists*, 122 (1): 73-84.

——. 1983b. 'The Boreal Forest, Cree-Ojibwa Foraging and Adaptive Management', in *Resource and Dynamics of the Boreal Zone*, ed. R.W. Wein, R.R. Riewe and I.R. Methven, Proceeding of a Conference held at Thunder Bay, Ontario, August 1982, Association of Canadian Universities for Northern Studies, Ottawa, pp. 331-45.

——. 1986. 'Optimal Foraging: Simulation Studies of Diet Choice in a Stochastic Environment, *Journal of Ethnobiology*, 6: 205-23.

——. 1988. 'The Population Ecology of Hunter Gatherers in a Stochastic Environment', *Journal of Anthropological Archaeology*, 5: 369-92.

——. 1990. 'Open Field, Common Pot: Harvest Variability and Risk Avoidance in Agricultural Societies, in *Risk and Uncertainty in Tribal and Peasant Economies*, ed. E. Cashdan, West View Press, Boulder.

——. 1993. 'Work, Resource and their Population', *Man*, 28: 321-40.

Woodburn, J.C. 1988. 'African Hunter Gatherer Social Organization: Is it Best Understood as a Product of Encapsulation?' in *Hunters and*

Gatherers: History, Evolution and Social Change, ed. T. Ingold, D. Riches and J. Woodburn, (eds.), vol. I, Berg, Oxford, pp. 31-64.

Yellen, J.E. 1971. *Archaeological Approaches to the Presents: Models for Reconstructing the Past.* Academic Press, New York.

——, 1977. 'Long-term Hunter Gatherer Adaptation to Desert Environments: A Biogeographical Perspectives', *World Archaeology*, 8: 262-74.

——, 1986. 'Optimization and Risk in Human Foraging Strategies', *Journal of Human Evolution*, 15: 733-50.

Zeleznik, W.S. and I.M. Bennet, 1991. 'Assumption Validity in Human Optimal Foraging: The Hunters of Venezuela as a Test Case', *Human Ecology*, 19(4): 499-508.

Zimmermann, E.W. 1951. *World Resources and Industries.* Harper & Row, New York.

Zoological Survey of India. 2002. 'Report on Animal Resources of the Jarawa Territory', unpublished, Port Blair.

Index